The History
of
Lady Sophia Sternheim

SUNY Series, Women Writers in Translation
Marilyn Gaddis Rose, editor

The History
of
Lady Sophia Sternheim

Extracted by a Woman Friend of the Same
from Original Documents and Other Reliable Sources

Published in the Years 1771 and 1772
by
C. M. Wieland

by
Sophie von LaRoche

Translated from the German
and with a Critical Introduction by

Christa Baguss Britt

With a Foreword by Katherine Goodman

State University of New York Press

Published by
State University of New York Press, Albany

© 1991 State University of New York

All rights reserved

Printed in the United States of America

For information, address State University of New York Press,
State University Plaza, Albany, N.Y., 12246

Production by Marilyn P. Semerad
Marketing by Theresa A. Swierzowski

Library of Congress Cataloging-in-Publication Data

La Roche, Sophie von, 1731–1807.
    [Geschichte des Fräuleins von Sternheim. English]
    The history of Lady Sophia Sternheim : extracted by a woman friend
of the same : from original documents and other reliable sources /
by Sophie von LaRoche ; translated from the German with a critical
introduction by Christa Baguss Britt ; with a foreword by Katherine
Goodman ; published in the years 1771 and 1772 by C.M. Wieland.
        p.   cm. — (SUNY series, women writers in translation)
    Translation of: Geschichte des Fräuleins von Sternheim.
    Includes bibliographical references.
    ISBN 0–7914–0532–X (cloth). — ISBN 0–7914–0533–8 (pbk.)
    I. Title. II. Series.
PT2390.L6G43   1991
833'.6—dc20   90–41002
                                                                    CIP

10 9 8 7 6 5 4 3 2 1

To My Mother
Anne Baguss

CONTENTS

FOREWORD

The birth of the women's novel in Germany in 1771 was something of a miracle. It required nothing less than the midwifery of one of Germany's foremost authors, Christoph Martin Wieland. Had fortune not seen to it that he stood ready to intervene with the publisher as well as the readers, Sophie von LaRoche's *The History of Sophia von Sternheim* might well have been stillborn.

That this novel was even conceived was at least as much of a miracle. In the German states in the mid-eighteenth century, the literacy rate for the entire population (23 million) is estimated at about 20 percent. Assuming that no more than half as many women read as men, a generous estimate for female literacy is probably 10 percent, or about 1 million women. Just by virtue of being able to read, Sophie von LaRoche was one in ten. But even if women read, they did not necessarily write, at least not for publication and not if they had pretensions of respectability. Indeed, LaRoche's confidence in meeting public approval was so low that *Sophia von Sternheim* was first published anonymously. What marvels intervened to produce this novel!

The strange truth of the matter is that, in a real sense, women's very lack of education provided their entree into the literary world in Germany. The route by which this occurred is somewhat circuitous. Aristocrats at the hundreds of German courts represented all that the fragmented bourgeois class sought to avoid: mannered court life; friendship for gain; contorted, servile language—in short, hypocritical rather than heartfelt relations. (In part these views are reflected in *Sophia von Sternheim*.) By midcentury the increasingly class-conscious bourgeoisie began to esteem its women for their role in countering court culture. Many hailed women as the creators of family and social life founded on genuine sentiment. Precisely women's lack of training in sophisticated life-styles, their position as outsiders, was presented as their virtue.

This attitude extended to writing. For instance, manuals on letter writing suggested that men emulate women's epistolary style, no matter the misspellings, mispunctuation, or faulty grammar. Women wrote from the heart, and their lack of form was a sure sign of their spontaneous and natural emotion. So women in Germany were encouraged to write letters, and ultimately it was through these that they first entered the literary marketplace (Becker-Cantarino 1987). Letter writing trained them for epistolary fiction. Before Sophie von LaRoche wrote *The History of Sophia von Sternheim,* she had practiced her writing skills on real letters with edifying intent (Wiede-Behrendt 1987). When she set about educating a "paper girl", as she once referred to her heroine, she did so not as Rousseau had his "paper boy," Emile, with an extended discourse on education. Rather, she wrote an epistolary novel. Through these fictitious letters Sophie von LaRoche became the popular "teacher of Germany's daughters" (Milch 1935).

In a way, both the novel's popularity and its pedagogical effect can be associated with its epistolary narrative. For instance, its popularity was surely related to the readers' identification with sentiments expressed by various characters. The expression of sentiment was something new and irresistible in fiction; and the epistolary form is often credited with its plausible introduction. Sentimental novels like LaRoche's therefore triumphed in this form. The pedagogical potential of the form is less commonly emphasized. However, if it is done well, this narrative technique not only exercises sentiments, it also requires a more reflective style of reading. The alternation of limited narrative perspectives constantly challenges the reader to weigh various positions and form her own judgment. The shortcomings of all characters can be instructive, and the reader can grow in experience with the heroine. Sophie von LaRoche exploits this multiperspectival narration to moral advantage, especially in the first half of the novel. Active reasoning on the part of the reader was surely part of LaRoche's pedagogical plan, for she wrote explicitly for women and in hopes of encouraging their enlightenment.

Unfortunately, the very popularity of sentimental novels was a cause of concern for many critics in the mid- to late-eighteenth century. They feared such works corrupted the morals of young women. These women had been devouring the stories of domestic and familial turmoil so voraciously that one might think the plots expressed something of their own real lives. As critics strove to turn the novel into an acceptable moral form, the epistolary novel's sentimentality and limited perspective came under attack. In Germany the form was doomed. Three years after the appearance of *The History of Sophia von Sternheim,* Friedrich von Blanckenburg's influential treatise on the novel appeared. He wanted to raise the novel "to a very pleasant and very edifying means of passing time . . . not something for idle women, but rather for the thinking mind." He complained that contemporary novels lacked an all-encompassing, objective perspective that could assign meaning to the trivial events narrated in them. Because the epistolary form was narrated by persons in the midst of action, he argued, it could not plausibly develop such a broad and objective narrative perspective. Apparently one could no longer trust that the reasoning faculties of individual readers would derive the correct understanding. In the end, of course, Blanckenburg and those who agreed with him won out; and, although no one could halt the flood of domestic novels that began appearing by the end of the eighteenth century, canonical fiction not only moved away from women's themes, it also moved away from forms in which women had some expertise.

For a time, however, *Sophia von Sternheim* enjoyed enormous and rapturous success, even with the critics. It had not mattered that Wieland had not been able to correct all of LaRoche's awkward German. One critic, presumably Goethe, proclaimed it could not be criticized: it was not a book, but a human soul.

And Sophia von Sternheim's soul is very much the issue in this novel. Ruth Perry has written of the British epistolary novels of virtue besieged, that not only was the woman's virginity at stake, but the very core of her being. Here Sternheim's virginity becomes an issue, but in this "anti-Pamela" it is positioned thematically only to emphasize the more important virtue of philanthropy, "active virtue." Unlike scores of other heroines of the period, Sophia von Sternheim's choices are not virginity, harlotry, or death. The salvation of Sophia's soul does not lie in any passive state of being; it lies in action, in "doing." Moreover, women's philanthropic actions, lauded in other novels when they are found in the domestic sphere, are admired in *Sophia von Sternheim* even when they are found beyond the threshold of the home. Indeed, in the scenes with the Widow C., LaRoche makes a point of demonstrating that the exercise of this virtue does not depend on a woman relinquishing her independence in marriage. The moral to be derived is that a woman's virtue is not tied to her family status or even to what others may do to her; her psychic salvation resides in her own hands and in public activity.

There is a slightly religious undertone to Sophia von Sternheim's moral education, as though a pietist confession were not far from LaRoche's mind. As Job might relate the tests to which his faith was put, so Sophia tells us those to which her faith in the curative power of philanthropy was put. In its encounter with the world her soul builds its own inner strength. The fine points of the art of philanthropy are probably points on which most of us are not conversant in these times, but it is these that Sophia must acquire in the education of her soul. Between the first and second halves she learns to practice the secular virtue of generosity by relying on her own resources, rather than those of others. In the end her efforts are sanctified, and her friends make a pilgrimage to the stations of her sufferings and victories.

At the conclusion of the novel another character heralds Sophia as a "female genius." In the 1770s *genius* was a word not usually associated with women. Writers of the young *Sturm und Drang* movement, for instance, clearly referred to men when they used the term. For them it implied the natural right to freedom in thinking and acting. (Any women who may have felt inclined to claim the same right for themselves in these literary works were generally portrayed as demonic.) What a difference when Sophie von LaRoche gives us a "female genius" who asserts her independence by using her learning and skills for the benefit of strangers! This is particularly clear when LaRoche's novel is contrasted with another best seller of the 1770s, Goethe's *The Sufferings of Young Werther* (1774). Goethe's likely literary debt to *Sophia von Sternheim* has often been noted, and the two works compared. Both sentimental, epistolary novels incorporated fragments of observed and experienced reality. The criticism of court life in Germany is similar (hypocrisy, mannered friendships, selfishness); and so, too, is the preference for rural settings and natural relationships. But because of the similarities, the differences are all the more striking. Goethe's young *Sturm und Drang* genius can see only his own misery, whereas Sternheim is ever alert to the needs of those around her. She knows she is not alone in this world, and this awareness saves her from Werther's despair and suicide.

Sophie von LaRoche, the "foremother of the women's novel in Germany" (Scherer 1886), was born in 1730. That made her forty-five years older than Jane Austen; thirty-four years older than Ann Radcliffe; twenty-two years older than Fanny Burney; and thirty-six years older than Madame de Stael. These facts are not meant to establish her antiquity or priority, for there were earlier women writers in England, France, and Germany. Rather they are meant to place her historically and remind us in general that we are dealing with the earliest forms of the women's novel in modern Europe. They tell us that the tone and form of *Sophia von Sternheim* may seem antiquated even to avid readers of those other early women authors. It is the moral tone of Richardson and Rousseau. But that should not interfere with a modern appreciation of the marvelous character, the "female genius," Sophia von Sternheim.

KATHERINE R. GOODMAN

CRITICAL INTRODUCTION
and
TEXTUAL HISTORY

INTRODUCTION

Sophie von LaRoche is generally credited with being the first female German novelist and author of the first German women's novel. *Die Geschichte des Fräuleins von Sternheim* is the first German *Bildungsroman* (a novel tracing the cultural formative process of a young person)[1] with a female protagonist, the first full-fledged epistolary novel in German, and the first German sentimental novel.

The production of *Sternheim* was supervised by her friend Christoph Martin Wieland who persuaded his own publisher to bring out the work. It saw three printings in its first year and eight by 1783; and it was quickly translated into Dutch and French. Two English translations were also made (1776). These facts attest to its extraordinary popularity. Another indication is the wide notice it received in contemporary newspapers and journals, but most indicative of the sensation *Sternheim* created are the letters exchanged among members of the German literary establishment. A few of the comments and criticisms are given below in translation.

The *Erfurtische gelehrte Zeitung,* the first to review the work, accords it "deserved admiration" and marvels that this "lady of rank who through many years' reading has gathered much knowledge of place, men, and the times, has yet preserved the sensibility of her warm heart and lost nothing of her enthusiasm for virtue and morality."[2] Another reviewer in the *Allgemeine Deutsche Bibliothek* praises the "healthy morality" everywhere in evidence, but finds the character of Sophia Sternheim somewhat exaggerated and her love of virtue "bordering on the enthusiastic." He is, therefore, glad that the author has made her of English ancestry, since "striking behavior, necessary for moral heroism, seems to be a prerogative of the English."[3] Yet another critic recognizes "Weiland's [sic] usual delicacy, subtlety, his lively imagination, and metaphysics of the heart" in the work. He calls Derby a "well-drawn Lovelace."[4]

Some negative reviews from lesser journals, such as the *Braunschweigische Zeitung,* judge the work to be artistically mediocre,[5] and the *Auserlesene Bibliothek* castigates the author for her egalitarian tendencies, since "not everyone can eat meat every day, nor have clean clothes. There must be the rich and the poor."[6] Most famous, because it has been attributed to Goethe,[7] is an appraisal in the *Frankfurter gelehrte Anzeigen*. The reviewer deplores the misdirected critiques of the worldly wise, the aesthete, the critic, and pious zealot, in that "these gentlemen are in error when they believe they judge a book—it is a human soul!"[8] LaRoche had almost immediately become synonymous with her heroine, and the reviewer here pays tribute to her sensibility rather than her craftsmanship.

Members of the literary and social coterie, most of them ten to fifteen years younger than LaRoche, were much more enthusiastic than the press. Johann Gottfried Herder, friend and early mentor of Goethe, later court chaplain at Weimar,[9] went so far as to quote *Sternheim* from the pulpit. In a letter to Merck[10] he calls the various scenes with Derby, Seymour, and Rich "masterly, as is the voice of death from the lead mountains which moves me more than Job's. This excellent woman [LaRoche] has the strangest effect on me. Her favorite thoughts, little remarks, views of life . . . in all these she is unique and means far more to me than Clarissa with all her contrived situations and tears."[11] Other contemporaries, including the brilliant Julie Bondeli,[12] compared *Sternheim* with *Clarissa* and found the German work superior. When Herder's fiancée Caroline Flachsland read the first volume of *Sternheim,* she wrote of the heroine, "My complete ideal of a woman! I spent delicious, wonderful hours reading it. Oh, how far am I still removed from my ideal!"[13] Jakob Michael Reinhold Lenz,[14] twenty years LaRoche's junior, was her greatest admirer. He called her "sacred Sternheim" and "an angel, come down from heaven . . . to make mankind fall in love with virtue." He detests Wieland's footnotes, calling them "those stupid notes that always interrupted my feelings at the best places, just as if someone had poured cold water over me."[15] Believing that Wieland had exploited LaRoche and purposely pretended authorship, Lenz wrote a dramatic skit entitled *Pandaemonium germanicum,* in which Goethe confronts Wieland and shames him because of this supposed fraud, whereupon all characters prostrate themselves before the character of LaRoche, "Plato's virtue in human form."[16] In all these evaluations the work was praised because it engaged the *feelings* of its readers and expressed their *ideals;* intellectual appeal or superior craftsmanship are seldom mentioned. Here was indeed a "human soul" speaking to an audience weary of the polished and cerebral prose of the enlightened age.

In the period of transition from the Age of Enlightenment to the Romantic Age, when in Germany rationalism gave way to English empiricism and Rousseau's cult of nature and the individual, Sophie von LaRoche, to her own surprise, found herself popularizing the new ideals and concerns that had circulated for some time among the intellectual avant-garde and now were becoming common property. Her family background, education, and temperament had fitted her to appeal to both the older rationalist establishmentarians and the young enthusiasts of *Empfindsamkeit* (sensibility). The following text is a short biographical sketch of Sophie LaRoche and her sociocultural context, various aspects of which will be discussed in greater depth later on.

Marie Sophie Gutermann[17] was the daughter of a cultured, widely traveled Protestant physician and scholar. The Gutermanns had been ennobled in the seventeenth century, but had maintained the life-style of the well-to-do bourgeois. Girls received no formal schooling at the time; and like other young ladies of her class, Sophie was educated at home by her rationalist, strictly pietist father.[18] The teachings of pietism were to be of lasting influence on her life and works. Her earliest memories are of being carried into her father's library and shown his books; and at scholarly gatherings in her father's house, she later acted as page, bringing the books the gentlemen requested. As the first of thirteen children, she perhaps received more attention than her siblings; in any case, it is said that she read fluently at age three, and when she was five had completely read through her first book, the Bible. She studied French, history, geography, drawing, painting, embroidery, music, dance, and the management of a household. Her mother instilled in Sophie her life-long love of nature and the country life.

She matured early, and at age twelve was engaged to the Italian Bianconi, physician to the bishop of Augsburg. He taught her Italian, art history, and mathematics, all in French, since he spoke no German. After her mother's death in 1748, her father terminated the engagement because the Catholic Bianconi would not agree to bring up their children as Protestants. Bianconi had begged his young fiancée to elope with him, but she submitted to her father's authority and refused.[19]

She was subsequently sent to stay with the Wielands, distant relatives, where the young Christoph Martin Wieland fell in love with her as a romantic figure surrounded by an aura of tragic love. Together Sophie and Christoph read Richardson, Young, Sterne, Geßner, and Klopstock; and their discussions became an important formative element in her intellectual development. Sophie and Christoph became engaged, but because of general opposition from the two families their engagement was dissolved three years later. However, LaRoche and Wieland remained friends and influenced each other's literary careers. As late as 1805, Wieland wrote her, "Nichts ist wohl gewisser, als daß ich, wofern uns das Schicksal nicht im Jahre 1750 zusammmengebracht hätte, kein Dichter geworden wäre"[20] ("Nothing can be more certain than that I would not have become a poet if fate had not brought us together in 1750").

Bowing once again to her father's will, she married Georg Michael Frank von LaRoche, the recently ennobled natural son of Count Stadion. LaRoche was a counselor at the court of the Elector of Mainz and the closest advisor of Count Stadion, a minister in the elector's cabinet. After a period of adjustment, Sophie adapted herself to the French rationalism characteristic of her new environment. Count Stadion and Georg Michael LaRoche were freethinkers and skeptics. They admired Voltaire and the other French encyclopedists headed by Diderot and d'Alembert and including Rousseau, Montesquieu, Dumarchais, Holbach, and Grimm.[21] Sophie's task was to be the brilliant hostess at the count's dinners, always witty, entertaining, and ready without apparent effort to inject new intellectual topics into a flagging conversation. This task required constant reading on her part; and since she was also responsible for conducting the count's voluminous correspondence with foreign intellectuals, she had very little time left to devote to her children or private pursuits. Like her heroine, Sophie had been forced to give up her tranquil and romantic country life and become an elegant court lady. Her duties did not appreciably change even after Stadion's retirement, since the couple accompanied him to his retirement seat. There, her contact with Wieland once again increased. He was a frequent guest and continued in his role as her mentor, while she was his "muse." Whereas thus far French and English literature had chiefly influenced Sophie, Wieland now directed her attention to German literary works, and she was witness and confidante as he worked on his *Don Sylvio, Agathon,* and the *Humorous Tales.*

After Count Stadion's death in 1768, the LaRoches' circumstances were much reduced, and they lived in a small provincial town where Sophie no longer had any social obligations. She even had to forego the company of her two surviving daughters, Maximiliane and Luise, who were being educated elsewhere. She confided her melancholy and boredom to her friend Brechter, the Protestant preacher whose portrait as Emilia's husband we find in *Sternheim* (p. 178).[22] Brechter advised her to put on paper her feelings of loneliness and her thoughts on education, philanthropy, and other matters that she had discussed with him, in order to exercise her mind and fill the lonely hours occasioned by her daughters' absence. Sophie agreed and in her late thirties began to work on her first novel. In a preface to a later work she tells us that she wanted at least to educate a "papiernes Mädchen" ("paper girl"; i.e., her heroine), since she did not have her own two anymore, "und da half mir meine Einbildungskraft aus der Verlegenheit und schuf den Plan zu Sophiens Geschichte"[23] ("and now my imagination came to my aid and created the plan for Sophia's story").

Although it was avowedly written for personal consolation and with didactic intent, because of Sophie LaRoche's eclectic *Bildung* (cultural formative process) it is not surprising that her novel would have broad appeal. She has been aptly characterized as a "novelist between reason and emotion,"[24] and as such she was uniquely appealing to an equally ambivalent age. In her fifties she accounts for this duality as stemming from her parental role models: "My father was a very learned but very hard man, my mother a sensitive, gentle woman. He inclined my head towards knowledge, she my heart towards goodness."[25] Her mother's influence must have been the stronger one, because elsewhere Sophie says of herself, "Ich bin mehr Herz als Kopf"[26] ("I am more heart than head"). Nevertheless, although highly emotional, she bowed to her father's will and gave up Bianconi, who had offered to abduct her. Later, letting her head govern her heart, she in turn forced her daughters into marriages of convenience.

In *Sternheim,* and perhaps even more in *Rosalie's Letters,*[27] her social conscience and compassion cause her to point out social injustices, but as a member of the establishment, cool calculation keeps her from advocating anything but token reforms. She saw not legislation but noblesse oblige of the wealthy as the means to improving the lot of the poor and exploited classes.

Even her writing style shows these dual characteristics. As Ingrid Wiede-Behrendt points out, LaRoche wavers between pragmatic and stylized writing,[28] and Burghard Dedner's close analysis of the text shows her "representation [wavering] between contrasting and harmonizing techniques."[29]

Somewhat ambivalent also was her relationship with Wieland. During and after their youthful, highly romantic, even "seraphic" relationship, Wieland imbued her with his feminist ideals. In theory at least, he felt that women were dehumanized and oppressed by men, owing to male superior strength, and he believed that contrary to popular and "scientific" belief of his day, they were not inferior to men in reason and "even surpassed them in delicacy of feeling, refinement of taste, and beauty of *Weltanschauung.*"[30] At a time when only the daughters of professors and *Privatgelehrten* (independently wealthy, nonteaching scholars) had access to books other than Bible, hymnal, and almanac, Wieland advocated education for all women.

In his novel *Agathon,* Wieland's views on women's rights are perhaps most clearly enunciated. The heroine Aspasia complains that men have assumed power without title, made an unfair division between the rights of the sexes, and excluded women from all important deliberations. They have written the laws to serve themselves and allow them to rob the female sex of all rights inherent in rational, free-born beings.[31] In his famous periodical, *Der Teutsche Merkur,* he calls women *"Genossen der Nationalverbindung, als Glieder des politischen Körpers"*[32] ("comrades in the national union, as members of the body politic"). When we consider that in Germany witches were burned at the stake as late as 1775,[33] one year before *Agathon* was written, we see how remarkably avant-garde Wieland's views were.

A number of respected scholars have recently claimed that despite the lofty ideals Wieland espoused in his writings, his actions as LaRoche's editor show him to have been a hypocrite, incorrigibly convinced of male superiority, and that his criticisms of her manuscript were dictated by jealousy, niggardly pedantry, and even the desire to diminish the literary merits of her work. Barbara Becker-Cantarino, for example, tries to show "how he relegates Sophie to the female reading public and its world, [how he] simultaneously fosters and confines to the feminine sphere the form of literary expression [employed] by LaRoche and other women writers of the time" [my trans.].[34] As proof of that assessment, Becker-Cantarino shows that Wieland repeatedly stressed "the usefulness of the work for the female sex" ("Muse," p. 577), rather than its "general validity and universal efficacy" [my trans.] (587), the two criteria considered by the Weimar literary establishment to be crucial attributes of great literature. Becker-Cantarino hints at the possibility that this typecasting of LaRoche, the author, may have prematurely capped her artistic development, causing her to resign herself to addressing most of her later works to "Germany's daughters" (588).

This is perhaps too severe a view. Fear and jealousy felt by established writers toward new and promising ones—even of the same sex—are a well-known phenomenon in literary circles past and present. Further, LaRoche was not so much in awe of her editor that she slavishly believed or obeyed him. (An example of her independent spirit is her refusal to change the novel's name.) It seems unlikely that Wieland's somewhat condescending remarks could have stunted her genius. Any repressive effects they might have had in the short "editorial period" were surely offset after publication by the almost maniacal adulation LaRoche and her novel received and the ridicule heaped on Wieland and his editorial efforts by Herder, Flachsland, Lenz, Goethe, and the literary coterie in general.

As for Wieland's frequent references to the work as being of great value to young women, leaving the question of genuine conviction on his part aside, surely this was merely smart marketing strategy, rather than a sinister attempt at narrowly categorizing LaRoche's entire future literary output. She herself had, after all, stated that she wished to "educate a 'paper girl.' " Specific admonitions in such a work would, therefore, be addressed to young female rather than male readers. To recommend the work to young men for its practical applicability would have been like recommending Machiavelli's *Prince* to young ladies for their instruction. Sophie seems to have freely aspired to the role of teacher to "Germany's daughters," rather than having been forced into it by external influences. Moreover, she appears to have been content with that role. There is no evidence anywhere in her writings that she saw herself as a frustrated artist whose mission was "art for art's sake." Perhaps we should give Wieland a little more credit for his efforts on her behalf. It seems rather doubtful that without his help—condescending and pedantic though it may have been—*Sternheim* would have seen publication. Without that help, her contribution to literary history and the female canon might well be lost to us.

Sternheim clearly reflects LaRoche's conviction that, besides possessing a virtuous soul and a philanthropic heart, the ideal woman must be educated. Again and again, we hear the heroine proclaiming the benefits of education in general and her own in particular. Transplanted to the court, she takes her books with her and is angry at her aunt for removing them (S. 88). In the "Wieland letter" (S. 115–119), she has a long discussion with Mr. —, who tells her that women have "indeed equal claim with men to all virtues and to all such knowledge that fosters their exercise, enlightens the mind, or improves the feelings and moral conduct, but that in exercising that claim, the differences of the sexes must always be observed" (S. 115–116). Many examples in the work show clearly that LaRoche wholeheartedly shared the view held by her male contemporaries that by nature and divine providence each sex has been assigned a certain role in the social as well as in the biological sphere; and that, although women should be educated, their education must necessarily vary to some extent from that of men. Although, as we have seen, LaRoche was a true pioneer with many literary "firsts" to her credit, it would be inaccurate to imbue her with insights and convictions that lay outside her cultural and temporal horizon.

After Wieland, the second most important philosophical influence reflected in *Sternheim* is that of Jean-Jacques Rousseau. His seminal ideas on the political structure of society, expounded in *Du Contrat Social* (1762), and partly discussed by him in an earlier (1755) article in the *Encyclopédie;* his beliefs concerning the right way to educate children, described in *Émile* (1762); and his concept of the superiority of nature over civilization, demonstrated in the epistolary novel *La Nouvelle Héloïse* (1761), are all echoed in LaRoche's work.

Several tableaulike scenes in *Sternheim* show the great chasm between the aristocracy and the common people, the hopeless toil of the peasants that was slavery in all but name, and the complete absence of education for the lower classes. These conditions are openly criticized by the heroine (S. 86, S. 90, S. 92, S. 198). On her "deathbed" in the lead miner's hut, confronted with the cringing cowardice of her hosts, Sophia is moved to exclaim, "How deplorable an effect of poverty it is that the oppressed seldom have the heart to oppose the violence done them by the vicious rich!" (S. 225).

Clearly, LaRoche agreed with Rousseau's ideas on social justice, and she tried to give voice to them in *Sternheim*. However, as she was a member of the conservative establishment that she presumably did not wish to offend, she compromised in regard to the practical application of those ideas. Her heroine wishes to alleviate the condition of the poor without disturbing the existing social order. In devising a plan for improving the lot of Councillor T.'s family, she admonishes Mrs. T. to teach her children "the order which God has established among men through differences among estates" and to guide them "into a reverent satisfaction with their Creator, who has appointed them to a certain estate through the parents he gave them" (S. 136–137). Similarly, when Sophia awaits Derby, she speaks to her landlady's nieces about "the duties of the station in which God had placed them and also of those pertaining to mine. Thus I brought them to consider themselves fortunate to be chambermaids rather than ladies" (S. 166). La-Roche dares to become controversial only in the early part of the work when she shows Colonel Sternheim "distributing the acreage more equitably by means of which each of his subordinates received exactly as much as he can cultivate" (S. 67).

Rousseau's ideas on nature and pedagogy were somewhat less controversial, and LaRoche generally agreed with most of his premises. If Rousseau and his followers thought that wisdom and happiness was to be found by going "back to nature," then that was merely a matter of *chacun a son goût* and did not threaten the established order. Accordingly, LaRoche gives Rousseau's views on nature full play. All the reprehensible characters and all the evils that befall the heroine originate at the court of D. as the center of "civilization," where an unfeeling and lascivious prince is surrounded by scheming, greedy courtiers and their shallow and vain ladies. They live in a "moral desert" (S. 104) where religion and virtue receive a "show of respect" (S. 105), where the "deafening clamor of noisy diversions" makes it impossible for Sophia "to find one quiet moment in order to collect her thoughts" (S. 97–98). The young are assailed by rampant prurience on every side. Sophia asks, "How shall the young man escape who enters . . . [the theater] with a sensitive heart and is there besieged by nature and art at once?" (S. 98). LaRoche implies an inevitable outcome: those young men will turn into full-fledged roués and seducers like Derby, who thinks Sophia fusses unduly at being raped, a "liberty which, after all, means so little in our circumstances" (S. 170). In contrast, nature, exemplified by the country and rustic life, is the source of true happiness, brought about by wholesome and virtuous pursuits enhanced by fine vistas, fresh air, and sunshine. Such a place is Sophia's home, Sternheim. [Literally, "star home," it is not only a star's distance removed from the evils of the court, but is also the lodestar in all her wanderings.] From the moment she leaves it, through all the vagaries of her fortunes until she marries Seymour and becomes mistress of an equally fine country seat, she plans and pleads to return to her country home.

Rousseau's theories on education are only minimally reflected in *Sternheim*. Sophia and her children receive their early education in the country; Sophia makes repeated statements that humankind's inborn self-love should be utilized in education, changing it in the process into love of neighbor (S. 165, S. 218, S. 221, and elsewhere); and she voices the belief that nature is the best teacher—though LaRoche seems to place almost equal value on book learning. We read further that nature teaches us the different attributes and roles of the sexes (S. 116). LaRoche stops short, however, of Rousseau's rather primitive dictum in *Émile ou l'éducation* (1762), "La femme est faite spécialement pour plaire à l'homme"[35] ("Woman was made especially to please man"). Of all her womanly skills, Rousseau's Sophie in *Emile* likes lace making best, because among all needle crafts it is the one that is done in the most charming body posture and shows the hands in the most graceful and light motion.[36] In sharp contrast, LaRoche's heroine shuns all posturing and subtle or overt seduction.

Two of Sophia Sternheim's pedagogic pronouncements seem interestingly advanced for the time. She tells Mrs. C., "Never raise your hand menacingly, but only in a friendly gesture!" (S. 197); and she advises her to allow young ladies to read novels, "especially since you will not be able to prevent it" (S. 198).

Many direct parallels exist also between *Sternheim* and *Héloïse*. The scene where Julie persuades her friend to marry St. Preux and says that a man of noble character and good education, even if he comes from a bourgeois family, is a fitting match for a baroness[37] corresponds to the scene in *Sternheim* where Baron P. asks his mother to approve the match between Colonel S. and the first Sophia (S. 59–61). Later, Baron P. describes their life in admiring terms (S. 67–68), similar to those St. Preux uses to describe the Wolmars' idyll at Clarens.[38] Like St. Preux, Rich lives in his beloved's house for the purpose of educating her son; and like the Wolmars, the Seymours join in their tenants' festivities, adding to the peasants' enjoyment. Both houses are simply furnished; and nature, not art, is the dominant force in their lives.

If Sophie von LaRoche is interesting as an author reflecting these diverse influences in her first work, she is perhaps even more so because of her close relationship with the young Goethe during his sentimental period. Wilhelm Spickernagel has made a thorough study of LaRoche's influence on Goethe as he was writing *Die Leiden des jungen Werthers*.[39] He tells us that Johann Heinrich Merck first introduced Goethe to LaRoche in 1772. One year after the publication of *Sternheim*, she was at the height of her fame; and because her husband had again obtained an important position, she kept a brilliant literary salon frequented by many famous writers. Here, as the focal point in a circle of *schöne Seelen* (beautiful souls), Sophie

made an "indelible impression on . . . [Goethe's] heart"[40] because he
shared with her a passion for *Empfindsamkeit* and sentimental writing.
Goethe and LaRoche, who was eighteen years older than he, enjoyed a
typical *empfindsame* friendship and, characteristically, Goethe fell in love
with Sophie's sixteen-year-old daughter Maximiliane. Later in 1772, Carl
Wilhelm Jerusalem, a young diplomat, shot himself because of his hopeless
love for a married woman. At Sophie's suggestion, Goethe collected the
details of the sensational story which became the basis for his *Werther* plot.
What finally caused him to begin writing *Werther* were heated arguments
with the merchant Peter Brentano, who had in 1774 married the much
younger Maximiliane von LaRoche, a match arranged by her mother against
the girl's wishes. Curiously, Goethe bore Sophie no ill will. Instead, at this
time, while he was writing *Werther*, their friendship was especially close.
He begged her to read and comment on his manuscript and to give him
"ein Wort vom Herzen. Sie werden sehen wie sie [sic] meinem Rad Schwung
geben, wenn Sie meinen Werther lesen"[41] ("a word from your heart. You
will see how you give my wheel momentum when you read my Werther").
Spickernagel points out many correspondences between *Werther* and *Sternheim* and refutes the French critic Pierre Leroux's claim in the preface of
his 1872 *Werther* translation, "Si l'on devait rattacher plus particulierement
Werther à quelques autres oeuvres antérieures, il est évident qu'il faudrait
nommer l'Héloïse de Rousseau et les six premiers livres des Confessions"[42]
("if one wanted very specifically to connect *Werther* with another, earlier
work, it is obvious, one must name Rousseau's *Héloïse* and the first six
books of the *Confessions*"). *Werther*, published three years after *Sternheim*,
shares with LaRoche's novel (but not with *Héloïse* or Richardson's works) a
hero who writes "from the soul." If it could be said that in *Sternheim* "a
human soul" speaks to us, this is even truer of *Werther*. The protagonist
confesses the innermost stirrings of his heart and soul immediately after a
significant incident, while his feelings are still at high tide. There are no
answering letters (the reader "answers" involuntarily in his mind). The protagonist's problems are centered in his psyche, as is the case in *Sternheim*.
Rosina clearly speaks for the author when she says that Sophia's journal "will
show how a violent affliction of the soul can distract a noble heart" (S. 216).
Werther suffers a similar trauma. We see a *schöne Seele* in mortal anguish.

Both *Sternheim* and *Werther* have an introductory report by an "editor," creating a frame around the events of the plot and heightening the
reader's sense of realism. In *Sternheim*, Rosina tells the story of Sophia's
parents and how she was sent to the court of D.; in *Werther*, the dead hero's
friend recommends "the little book" as consolation to those who feel as
Werther did. At the end of the book the same "editor" narrates very realistically how Werther was found after he had shot himself, how the neighbors reacted, and so on.

A major philosophical difference between the two works is, of course, that after he realizes his misfortune, Werther despairs and takes his life, whereas Sophia resolves to go forward and meet the challenges of a new and useful life.

Other scholarly studies dealing with the LaRoche-Goethe relationship also note the common characteristics of *Sternheim* and Goethe's *Werther* and point out LaRoche's influence on the conception and execution of the later work.[43] She is frequently referred to as a "pathfinder for Goethe"[44] and twice his precursor, with *Sternheim* of his *Werther,* and *Rosalie's Letters* of Goethe's *Wilhelm Meister.*[45] We read that "without books such as *Sternheim,* the German nation would not have been prepared for *Iphigenie.*"[46]

More recent critics also attest to Goethe's indebtedness, though sometimes indirectly. Siegfried Sudhof, for example, credits LaRoche with "anticipating the Werther-feeling,"[47] and Günter Giesenfeld notes the artistic and philosophical "proximity" of *Sternheim* to *Werther.*[48] An interesting sidelight of the newer studies is that in varying degree they tend to reflect the current, less unquestioningly reverential attitude toward Goethe the poet and the man; we catch a glimpse of his less admirable side. The aspiring poet had frequented Sophie LaRoche's literary salon, flattering her outrageously and seeking her influence and help at a time when her fame was, briefly, greater than his; the mature Goethe, revered as Germany's greatest poet and the ultimate authority in German letters, on occasion heaped scathing ridicule on his erstwhile friend and benefactress. The best known of his unkind remarks about her, made in a letter to Schiller, shows his contempt for her later literary efforts: "Sie gehört zu den nivellierenden Naturen, sie hebt das Gemeine herauf und zieht das Vorzügliche herunter und richtet das Ganze alsdann mit ihrer Sauce zu beliebigem Genuß an"[49] ("She is one of those whose nature it is to level everything; she elevates that which is common and drags down that which is excellent. Then she dresses the whole thing with her own sauce and serves it up for popular consumption").

It is not surprising that LaRoche's *Sternheim* enjoyed such great popularity. We have seen that certain elements in Sophie von LaRoche's life, prior to writing *Sternheim,* combined to make the philosophical content of her work appealing to enlightened thinkers like Wieland. But in *Sternheim* she also voices the ideas of Rousseau and the proponents of the new *Empfindsamkeit.* They no longer looked to France but to England for literary inspiration. It was the time of the great Shakespeare translations; Wieland, for example, translated twenty-two of Shakespeare's plays. The "moral weeklies," such as *Tatler* and *Spectator,* were being translated (LaRoche constantly referred to her annual edition of the latter), and Richardson's works in translation were greatly admired and frequently imitated.[50]

Until the publication of Richardson's *Pamela* in 1740, the (baroque) novel had been decried by theologians and pedagogues alike for fostering sloth, lustfulness, melancholia, restlessness, insomnia, loss of memory, and a host of other moral and physical ills. The habitual perusal by the young of such novels, it was feared, would create a generation of useless dreamers, full of false expectations and inferior moral fiber. By contrast, *Pamela,* so the arbiters of good taste and guardians of morals urged, had great didactic value. It was thought to present, in the convenient and popular form of the novel, exemplary characters and situations and to aid its readers in morally elevating themselves.

Pamela, Clarissa, and, to a lesser degree, *Sir Charles Grandison* were as enthusiastically received on the continent and as eagerly imitated—especially in France and Germany—as they had been in England. Richardson's followers, ranging from the most prominent to the most obscure writers, imitated not only his seemingly "perfect" protagonists; they also copied his epistolary technique and his recurring themes of trial by temptation and "virtue rewarded."

In France, his admirers included Diderot, Georges Sand, Balzac, Prevost, and de Musset, who judged *Clarissa* to be the foremost novel in the world. Prevost, who translated *Pamela,* left out anything that might bore or offend the French, thereby aiding the novel's favorable reception in France. Upon Richardson's death, Diderot composed an extravagantly laudatory and emotional eulogy in which he exclaimed, "O Richardson, Richardson, first of men in my eyes, you shall be my reading at all times!"[51] No wonder then that, like Rousseau's *Nouvelle Héloïse* and the works of many lesser French writers, Diderot's novel *La religieuse* also shows Richardson's pervasive influence.

Richardson's reception in Germany was equally enthusiastic. *Pamela*'s foremost advocate there was C. F. Gellert, a highly respected writer and popular professor of rhetoric at Leipzig University.[52] In his lectures, Gellert praised Richardson's "prosaic [read, "prose"] poems" and considered it his "duty to recommend them,"[53] while continuing to condemn novels in general. He translated *Pamela* and later *Grandison,* a task that gave him great emotional satisfaction and caused him to emulate the English writer in his own novel, *Das Leben der schwedischen Gräfin von G.* (The Life of the Swedish Countess of G.). Gellert's influence on German public opinion can hardly be overrated; as the *Frankfurter gelehrten Anzeigen* put it at the time, "With our public, to believe in Gellert, virtue, and religion is almost one and the same thing."[54] In a lengthy commemorative inscription over Richardson's portrait, Gellert concludes, "Immortal is Homer, but among Christians the British Richardson is more immortal still."[55] F. G. Klopstock was equally enthralled. He penned an ode on the death of Clarissa and is said to have sought employment in England in order to be near Richardson.[56] Reading *Pamela* was considered a better means to acquiring true virtue than "a hundred thousand books purporting to teach it."[57]

It is curious indeed that so many great writers, philosophers, and teachers, both in England and on the continent, seem to have genuinely believed in the moral purity and educational value of Richardson's novels, when in fact these works continued to depict the same prurient and titillating scenes, and in the same salacious detail, as the baroque novels. The only difference was that now the unchaste actions in those scenes were explicitly or implicitly condemned in the surrounding text. Some modern scholars have been more analytical in their assessments than Richardson's contemporaries. Clara L. Thomson sums up *Pamela*'s merit: "*Pamela*, a book . . . whose warped morality, glaring want of taste, and improbability of incident would seem sufficient to obscure all the merit that cannot be denied to it" because of the originality of the plan and subject matter and the believability of the heroine.[58] She speaks of Pamela's "vulgar, practical little soul" and calls her "virtuous, but . . . anything but pure-minded" and "her behavior . . . repulsive."[59] In her perceptive study on the German woman's novel at the close of the eighteenth century, Lydia Schieth feels that Richardson's "moral mantle serves merely to satisfy the conventions. That Richardson himself was convinced of the virtuous intent [of his characters] . . . does not change the fact of their subliminal erotic message."[60] In support of that observation she cites the bedroom scene in *Pamela* as an example. Pamela, half undressed, swoons at the sight of her invading employer. She later relates that when she came to, "he had his hand in my bosom." She reports that upon that awful discovery [without the slightest attempt to defend herself] she fell into another swoon which this time lasted three hours, and on "awakening, I found myself in my bed,"[61] etc., etc. Schieth also cites a rare contemporary dissenting opinion; it is voiced indirectly and by a woman. In Johanna Schopenhauer's *Die Tante* (*The Aunt,* 1870), the protagonist surely speaks for the author when, in a conversation with her nieces, she tries to justify her father's decision to let her read *Pamela* when she was twelve years old. She says that, "After all, even in England the more than suggestive [German: "zweideutige"] Pamela had been recommended from the pulpit to the people as a book of edification."[62]

Knowing how very carefully Richardson constructed his characters and plots, how much thought he gave to each detail, can we believe that he was not being consciously and calculatingly hypocritical? And if he was, where did the humble little printer get the keen insight to predict accurately that his cunning stratagem would "go over," resulting in phenomenal sales *and* universal approbation of his novels? We must turn to the Richardson scholars for a solution to this puzzle.

Approximately during the decade 1750–60, Wieland, too, had been one of Richardson's ardent admirers, but he later objected to him, not on moral grounds, but because Richardson's "perfect" characters, especially Grandison, could not be successfully dramatized.[63] While under Richardson's spell, he had written the tragedy *Clementina von Poretta*[64] in emulation of *Sir Charles Grandison*. The reviews had been devastating, and perhaps this fiasco had soured Wieland on Richardson; for when LaRoche sent him her first draft for *Sternheim*, he deplored "the tone of this 'Richardsoniad.' "[65] In a letter to her in 1770 he writes, "je n'aime pas les Clarisses, les Charles Grandison, les Henriettes Byron par la seule raison, qu'ils sont trop parfait pour moi"[66] ("I don't like the Clarissas, the Charles Grandisons, the Henrietta Byrons for the sole reason that they are too perfect for me").

In spite of Wieland's opinion, Sophie von LaRoche remained one of Richardson's faithful disciples. She and Wieland had read Richardson's works together after they first met in 1750, and the similarity between her own ill-starred engagement to Bianconi and the Grandison-Poretta subplot undoubtedly made *Grandison* particularly poignant for her. Again and again, LaRoche testifies to her admiration for Richardson. In her *Briefe an Lina (Letters to Lina)*,[67] for example, she says that in writing about the lives of characters like Grandison and Henrietta Byron, Richardson intended to instruct the reader by showing "daß wahrhaft edle, tugendvolle Menschen in allen Fällen nach den Vorschriften der Klugheit und Güte handeln können"[68] ("that truly noble, virtuous people can in all situations act according to the rules of prudence and goodness").

The extent to which the philosophical ideas LaRoche espouses in *Sternheim* were inspired by Wieland, Rousseau, and Richardson may be debatable, but there can be no doubt that for the epistolary form, the structure, the characterization, and major plot elements used in her work she looked to Samuel Richardson for inspiration.

Although the use of letters within works of fiction goes back in England at least as far as Nicholas Breton's *A Poste with a Packet of Mad Letters* (1602) and in Germany to J. Wickram's novels around 1550, Richardson's *Pamela* (1740) is the first genuine epistolary novel. The exclusive use of letters—sometimes with the addition of "journal entries" and an "editor"—arose naturally out of the eighteenth-century infatuation with letter writing. (Sophie LaRoche's private correspondence is said to have consisted of several thousand letters.[69]) To find the cause for this predilection, at least in Germany, a brief look at pietism is helpful.

Pietism, the German Protestant movement in opposition to the rigid and impersonal dogmatic approach of the orthodox Protestant church, flourished from circa 1670 to 1740. The pervasive and lasting influence of the pietist teachings LaRoche absorbed as a child on her life and works has already been mentioned. *Sternheim* provides strong evidence of how thoroughly she had embraced the tenets of pietism. Bernd Heidenreich has identified five major streams of pietist thought that run through LaRoche's novel: first, the repudiation of shallow amusements like dancing, gambling, and the theater; second, that it is virtuous to bear life's misfortunes with patience and humility; third, the imperative that everyone, no matter what his or her social class, is responsible for helping those less fortunate; fourth, a strong belief in the benefits of public education; and finally, the conviction that a truly Christian way of life and a "beautiful soul" can be achieved only through finding a personal, mystic relationship with God and basing one's actions on the revelations gained from that relationship.[70] As we have seen from numerous examples, *Sternheim*'s heroine not only affirms, but consistently enacts, all five of these principles throughout the novel.

In the course of the quest for a personal faith, the individual believer was encouraged to practice introspection and self-analysis, leading to recognition of one's shortcomings and insights concerning how to conquer them. One would thereby elevate one's soul to a more nearly "beautiful" state. This process of "breaking through" to God was, of course, a highly emotional individual experience that was eagerly communicated to fellow seekers. Rather than attend formal church services, the Pietists would meet in small groups, or conventicles, where they shared their emotions and revelations with one another.

We may say that *Empfindsamkeit* was the secularized manifestation of pietism, in which the need for self-analysis, the resulting heightened emotions, and the urge to share these with friends and confidants were transferred to the worldly sphere of life. When the intended recipients of such confidences were not close by, lengthy emotional letters were exchanged. But since these, too, were intended to be shared with others, a certain amount of sentimental posturing inevitably crept into these epistles. As correspondents sought to outdo one another in the intensity and beauty of their feelings, their effusions became increasingly sentimental, sometimes to the point of being maudlin or downright silly. Grown men thought nothing of "confessing" that they had shed "delicious tears" for hours on end upon reading or hearing about events that would seem fairly ordinary and insignificant to people of the preceding or following centuries. Well-to-do women in particular devoted themselves to the cult of friendship, the acquisition of a beautiful soul, and the passion for writing letters.

This epistolary passion was equally strong in England and France, and the brilliant letters of famous persons like Lady Mary Wortley Montagu, Voltaire, Walpole, Lord Chesterfield, and many others gave to letter writing the status of a fine art comparable to music and painting; a talent greatly envied by a multitude of bourgeois letter writers, who strove to emulate their betters. An earnest concern with style—as well as with properly emotional content—was everywhere in evidence, creating a sudden demand for manuals on the correct way to write various types of letters. Enterprising booksellers took steps to supply this new demand.

In 1739, two London booksellers asked Samuel Richardson, a printer by profession and known to be an accomplished letter writer, to prepare a series of model letters "for all occasions." He accepted the commission, stipulating only that the letters should also be morally instructive. *Letters Written to and for Particular Friends, on the Most Important Occasions* came out in 1741, but before they did, Richardson conceived and wrote *Pamela* (1740), based on his sample letters LCXXXVIII and LCXXXIX, "A father to a daughter in service, on hearing of her master's attempting her virtue" and "The Daughter's Answer." His epistolary technique caught on and was quickly imitated in France by Rousseau (*Nouvelle Héloïse,* 1759) and Choderlos de Laclos (*Les Liaisons Dangereuses,* 1782), to name just two of his most important followers. In England his imitators included Smollett (*Humphrey Clinker,* 1771) and Fanny Burney (*Evelina,* 1778). In Germany, where Gellert had published a letter-writing manual in 1751,[71] Musäus (*Grandison der Zweite,* 1760–62), Hermes (*Sophiens Reise,* 1769–73), LaRoche (*Sternheim,* 1771), Goethe (*Werther,* 1774), Tieck (*William Lovell,* 1795–96), and Hölderlin (*Hyperion,* 1797), among others, wrote epistolary novels based on Richardson's example.

Sophie von LaRoche did not express a theory about the epistolary technique, as Richardson did in the prefaces and postscripts of his works; but since she closely followed his example, we may assume that she shared his belief that the use of familiar letters creates greater intimacy, immediacy, and credibility than narrative writing.[72]

Richardson employs three basic letter types and so does LaRoche: the characteristic letter, which describes the writer's character; the dramatic letter, which reproduces dialogue; and the narrative letter, which relates events prior to the fictional present.[73] We find in *Sternheim,* as in *Clarissa,* that the heroines write most of their letters in a familiar, intimate tone, allowing the reader to identify with the person addressed. The letters are usually written immediately before or after significant events, giving the reader a sense of the present rather than the past. Richardson believed that such letters are also more likely to move the reader than a narration in which "the relator [is] perfectly at ease; and if himself unmoved by his own story, not likely greatly to affect the reader" (vol. I, p. xiv).[74] The qualities of intimacy and immediacy combine to heighten the verisimilitude of the characters and the action. Both writers intensify these realistic effects by auxiliary devices such as the interrupted letter and the postscript (although LaRoche uses the postscript in only 1 of the 54 letters in *Sternheim,* whereas Richardson uses it in 48 of the 537 letters in *Clarissa*). An additional device heightening intimacy and immediacy in *Sternheim,* which LaRoche may have adopted from *Pamela,* is the journal of the heroine in exile.

Two aspects of LaRoche's epistolary technique may make her work less realistic than *Clarissa.* They are her use of initials instead of ordinary given and family names[75] and her omission of complimentary closes and salutations. On the other hand, increasing her realism is her device of the editorial report and interpolation as a frame—albeit faultily executed as it remains open-ended; that is, there is no closing editorial comment. A radical departure from Richardson's technique is the complete absence of answering letters in *Sternheim.* This absence approximates the *Ich-Erzählung* (first-person narrative) and moves the action along at a lively pace, helping to keep the work to a reasonable length and making it perhaps more attractive to the modern reader.[76]

Richardson considered the appropriately placed catastrophe the most important structural element in a work of fiction.[77] Such a work should maintain an air of probability; the actions should be motivated by natural causes; and all elements of the narrative structure should arise naturally from the subject and illustrate the work's design. Accordingly, Richardson mentions in his letter to Solomon Lowe[78] that he has a design for constructing *Clarissa* and, as he puts it, a "no-plan."[79] In comparing the structure in *Clarissa* and *Sternheim,* one notices that Richardson preserves these principles and implements them with meticulous care. LaRoche does not state such principles, and if she was trying to emulate Richardson's, she succeeded only in part.

In *Clarissa* Richardson develops a central conflict: the heroine's parents are trying to coerce her into marrying Solmes, a man she detests. Out of this conflict, step by inexorable step, arises the catastrophe of her violation and death. As Ball points out, the framework of the novel consists of five major sections: the entrance of the main characters, the definition of the conflict, the crisis, the culmination, and the conclusion.[80]

The organization of *Sternheim* suggests LaRoche's attempts to imitate Richardson, but the work is constructed far less carefully. LaRoche ingeniously lets Rosina, the "editor," narrate the antecedents and introduce the characters. As in *Clarissa,* the heroine is in conflict with relatives who have power over her and are trying to force her into a hated union (here a dishonorable one.) The point of no return occurs as it does in *Clarissa,* when the heroine is abducted by the villain. Although Sophia goes with Derby of her own free will, he is in reality abducting her by trickery, as Lovelace does Clarissa.

The crisis consists of two parts: Sophia's rape and her discovery that her marriage was a hoax. Like Clarissa, she has a chance to right her social situation. If she can bring herself to prostitute her feelings, Derby will marry her, but like Clarissa, she has too much integrity for such a compromise. At this point LaRoche goes her own way with the structure and plot of *Sternheim*. For Sophia the violation of her body is not the end of all hope for future happiness. She attempts to put it out of her mind and, under an assumed name, make a new beginning. She resolves to live a life of service to her fellow human beings. After she has established a "seminary for domestics," the scene shifts to England, and a second conflict arises logically out of the first: Derby crosses her path; and fearing that she will denounce him to Lady Summers, he has her abducted, this time by force, to Scotland. She is again isolated from all help and expects to end her days miserably in the lead miner's hut. The second crisis comes when she is thrown into a crumbling tower and left for dead because she has refused Derby's attentions a second time. The culmination occurs as Rich and Seymour stand at her "grave" and order the miner and his son to exhume her body. The miners confess their deception; they have helped Sophia escape and find refuge with Lady Douglas. The conclusion includes the reunion and subsequent marriage of Sophia and Seymour. LaRoche allows the twice-tried heroine to find a twofold reward: not only does she get a noble, wealthy, and adoring husband but also a permanent platonic lover in Lord Rich.

Among the many defects of this structure are the following: the narration of the first Sophia's courtship is much too detailed and prolonged (approximately 40 of the total of 279 pages), considering her relative unimportance. Later, when LaRoche has apparently decided that the daughter, not the mother, would be the heroine, the author devotes less than a complete sentence to the first Sophia's demise. Another structural weakness is the treatment of Lady P., who plays a fairly important part at the beginning but is dropped unceremoniously after Baron P.'s death, which is, incidentally, also given very short shrift. Surely it would have been structurally better to use Lady P. as the aunt in Florence who never materializes but is at least mentioned. The statistically absurd coincidences of Derby marrying the niece of Sophia's English hostess *and* of neighbor Rich being Seymour's brother must also be considered serious faults that strain the reader's capacity for suspending disbelief.

Given these structural weaknesses, one is astonished and gratified by the very skillful use LaRoche makes of the masked ball as a major structural and symbolic device[81] immediately before the "point of no return."

The masked figures in disguise who gaily deceive one another adumbrate Sophia's cruel deception soon to follow; Seymour who is blind to Sophia's virtue, wears the costume of a bat. Masquerades occur in *Pamela II* and *Grandison* (though not in *Clarissa*), and LaRoche may have taken this structural element from one or both of these works.

Richardson quite obviously gave considerable thought to creating the characters in his novels. In his prefaces, postscripts, and in many of his letters[82] we find statements pertaining to his theory of characterization. His most salient tenet is that even exemplary characters should not be either perfectly good or perfectly evil. In the Preface to *Clarissa* Richardson says that the heroine of that work "is proposed as an Exemplar to her Sex. Nor is it any objection to her being so, that she is not in all respects a perfect character" (vol. I, p. xiii). Elsewhere he is apprehensive, lest he "should draw [in Grandison] a *faultless monster.*"[83] There is no evidence that La-Roche shared Richardson's concern about creating characters that were too perfect to be credible. Richardson also believed that the principal characters should be developed through self-analysis or analysis by others and through the test of events.[84] He carefully implemented his theories in trying to develop *Clarissa*'s many characters, as when Miss Howe's description of Clarissa (vol. I, pp.2–4) reveals the heroine's character, and through self-analysis, as when Clarissa discovers the sin of pride in herself (vol. IV, pp. 209–10). He is successful with Lovelace, as well as with the secondary and minor characters. They are well-drawn and entirely believable.

LaRoche introduces her characters in the same way Richardson does. Others describe them; for example, Seymour describes Sophia to Dr. T. (S. 94–95). The characters engage in self-analysis and confide their findings to an intimate friend, as Sophia does when she writes to Emilia after talking to Mrs. C. And they are tested against adversity, as Sophia is in her exile.

To create a complex character like Lovelace (that is, one with good and bad qualities who could be reformed if the plot required it) was apparently beyond LaRoche's skill. Because her plot has a happy ending, she needed a hero and a villain. But even though she simplified her task by having two male protagonists, these characters leave much to be desired. Derby has neither the charm of Lovelace nor his believability. He is a deranged murderer who has young women abducted; and when they have succumbed to the rigors of their wilderness exile, they are buried in unmarked graves. On other occasions he is a drawing-room gallant who converses sensitively on Italian architecture. In Derby, LaRoche tried to create a character probably unlike anyone she had ever met, and she simply did not have the skill to make him believable. Seymour is even less well developed. He remains a somewhat bloodless, static character. LaRoche lets him weep an ocean and foam with rage, but he does not manage to engage the reader's sympathy.

LaRoche may have been well aware of her difficulties with characterization, as she abstained from using as many characters as Richardson. Apart from the main and secondary characters, only seven minor characters write letters in *Sternheim,* whereas Richardson uses about thirty such characters in *Clarissa.* Minor figures like Baron and Lady P., Mrs. C., Mrs. Hills, Lady Summers, and the Loebaus are well drawn and as realistic as those in *Clarissa.*

Sternheim's appeal to the reader rests on LaRoche's characterization of the heroine. The author has drawn an idealized portrait of a person she knew very well—LaRoche herself. When we first meet Sophia, she is governed by narrow self-love. She recognizes the wise use her parents made of that inborn quality to inspire her to excel in her educational pursuits. The author shows effectively how in a virtuous person the test of events can change self-love into love of humankind.

What makes Clarissa interesting and attests to Richardson's genius is her psychological complexity. She is possessed of great courage, integrity, and an iron will, but she is seemingly motivated entirely by self-love. Her "virtue" seems suspect for two reasons: she is rather contemptuous of some of the other characters, understands their faults so thoroughly, and comments upon them so pointedly, as to suggest that she has observed them in herself. Second, on a perhaps subconscious level, she is in league with her destroyer. With her languid resistance at the garden gate she lures him into abducting her. Later when she briefly leaves Lovelace, she could easily have walked into the office of a magistrate, as Sir Walter Scott has cruelly suggested.[85] Whatever Clarissa is, she is at the beginning of the story and still at the end; that is her tragedy, that is why she must die.

Sophia, on the other hand, develops into a better and wiser human being than she was before her misfortune. She learns at least three things: after she finds out at the court of D. that the wealthy and high born can be vicious and unscrupulous, she learns to discount outward appearances; she learns that personal misfortune cannot degrade us if we are not culpable; and she learns that even when we are in great distress of body and soul, the best medicine is to think of others and actively assist them as much as is in our power. In teaching others, Sophia makes use of her privileged education and the hard-earned wisdom her downfall has brought her. At the end she finds her true calling in caring for her family and the villagers.

Both Richardson and LaRoche reveal their didactic aims, but in different ways. In the Preface to *Clarissa,* Richardson lists four very specific goals:

To warn the inconsiderate and thoughtless of the one sex, against the base arts and designs of the specious Contrivers of the other—to caution Parents against the undue exercise of their natural authority over their Children in the great article of Marriage—To warn Children against preferring a Man of Pleasure to a Man of Probity, upon that dangerous but too commonly-received notion, *That a reformed Rake makes the best Husband*—But above all, to investigate the highest and most important Doctrines not only of Morality, but of Christianity, by showing them thrown into action in the conduct of the worthy characters; while the *unworthy,* who set those Doctrines at defiance, are condignly, and, as may be said, consequentially punished. (vol. I, p. xi)

LaRoche's didactic intent is enunciated in more general terms. Three statements at various places in *Sternheim* sum it up. Rosina speaks for the author when she says that Sophia's journal "will show how a violent affliction of the soul can distract a noble heart" (S. 216). In the second statement Sophia supplies the intended conclusion: after she has analyzed the causes of her misfortune she says, "Despite my sincere love of virtue, my obstinacy and imprudence have exposed me to sorrow and contempt. I have lost much and suffered greatly; but should I, for that reason, forget the happiness of my early years and regard with indifference the opportunities which still present themselves, exclusively devoting myself to the sensibilities of my self-love?" (S. 178) Sophia states another important goal when she tells Mrs. C. that, above all, the young must be taught "the meaning of the term *noble soul*" and the exercise of "the practical virtues" (S. 198).

The two authors' statements illustrate characteristic differences in their didactic methods. Richardson shows his readers examples of parental tyranny and filial rebelliousness aided by mistaken romantic notions. He intends the tragic results of such misguided behavior as we see in *Clarissa* to act as deterrents to young readers and warnings to their parents. The hoped-for effect is prevention of immoral or unchristian behavior and the suffering that is its inevitable consequence. LaRoche's didacticism does not specifically aim at prevention of reprehensible behavior or its dire consequences; she focuses her attention on the sufferer's rehabilitation. LaRoche's intention is to show how humiliation and sorrow are didactic tools that, used properly, help the sufferer to subjugate his self and develop greater love for his fellows. Although LaRoche does not specifically state that suffering is a necessary instrument of human perfection, she clearly shows that Sophia's character has been improved by it.

After identifying the several important common elements in *Clarissa* and *Sternheim* and noting and evaluating the differences between them, one comes to the conclusion that Richardson was a far greater artisan than La-Roche. The structure and plot in Richardson's work are carefully worked out; he has complete mastery of the many active characters; his epistolary technique cannot be faulted; his characters are well conceived and developed. The fact that Clarissa is unable to change and remains a tragic character indicates a certain ambivalence on Richardson's part toward the society he portrays realistically, but whose rigid standards he perhaps cannot wholly applaud. Richardson's ambivalence is a challenge to the discerning reader and as such constitutes an artistic refinement that LaRoche could not possibly emulate.

In *Sternheim* everything is much simpler. Sophia is a *schöne Seele* filled with passionate idealism. The heroine is fully realized. Whereas Clarissa is complex but unchanging, LaRoche's heroine is simpler but undergoes a transformation from being a selfish and self-righteous paragon of knowledge and virtue to becoming more loving, tolerant, and aware of her own fallibility. *Sternheim* has the distinction, therefore, of being a true *Bildungsroman,* the first one with a female hero. The minor characters are believable but Derby and Seymour lack credibility, owing to LaRoche's inability to create her characters without real-life models.

Although LaRoche is Richardson's inferior in all matters of craft, she shows flashes of creative ingenuity; her advanced characterization of the heroine, her innovations in the epistolary technique, and her individualistic structure add interest and compensate to some extent for her lack of technical brilliance. Her didactic intent, which embraces concerns common to all civilized humankind, gives her work and heroine a certain aura of greatness and establishes LaRoche as an independent artist, notwithstanding her obvious indebtedness to Richardson.

The textual history of *Geschichte des Fräuleins von Sternheim* is somewhat unusual, in that even the first edition (1771)[86] was not supervised by LaRoche, but by her friend Wieland. In the second half of the eighteenth century a stigma was attached to female authorship, especially of novels. It is safe to say that Sophie von LaRoche would have found it difficult to have her novel published if she had not had the help of a well-known writer like Wieland. To preserve feminine decorum, Wieland and LaRoche used the ruse of pretending unauthorized publication by another.[87] Wieland apologized elaborately for "die ganze Verräterei" ("the whole treason") in having her work published though she wrote it only for her own diversion. The author remained anonymous, although the initials by which Wieland addressed her were but a thin disguise; and as soon as a favorable reception was assured, LaRoche came forward.

While Wieland was guiding her manuscript to press, he frequently suggested improvements to her. They included, for example, changing the name *Sternheim* (a change to which she did not agree) because it was "trop resemblant à d'autre dans quelques romans allemands vulgaires"[88] ("too similar to those in other, common German novels"). He was concerned, however, mainly about her use of the German language.

In the second half of the eighteenth century, the German language was in a crucial period of its development. According to Kluge, "The third quarter of the eighteenth century [LaRoche worked on her manuscript from 1767 to 1770] was a time of the most turbulent language struggles surrounding the written language which was then still new."[89] Patriotic German intellectuals sought to establish a standardized literary language and end the dominance of French as the language preferred by the bourgeois and upper classes. The "classical" writers (Goethe, Schiller, Lessing, et al.), and especially the learned grammarians (Gottsched, Bodmer, Breitinger, Nast, Fulda, Adelung), were often at odds among themselves as to what constituted correct German usage. They were unanimous, however, in repudiating the use of French.

The new, standard German was based on the East-Central German idiom, the so-called chancellery language of upper Saxony; that is, the language used in and around Meißen, and Luther's German. (Because Luther had tried to make his Bible translation [1534] accessible to the greatest number of Germans, his language was itself a composite that included elements from various German dialects and had become somewhat archaic by LaRoche's time.) The speakers of provincial language variants such as the Swiss and Swabian dialects were stubbornly opposed to the emerging standard written German. In Bavaria and Swabia, strongholds of resistance, opposition finally weakened around 1770.[90] A major reason for the strong resistance in these two predominantly Catholic states was that most Bavarians and Swabians considered acceptance of Luther's language tantamount to aiding and abetting Protestantism.

Sophie von LaRoche came from this very region, the border area between Bavaria and Swabia. In addition, Sophie spoke far better French than German, since French was spoken almost exclusively in her patrician childhood home, in Count Stadion's household, and at the court of the Elector of Mainz. From a linguistic point of view, her first novel is, therefore, particularly interesting, as her unsure usage and inconsistencies mirror the state of the German language at that time. Two problems that she most anxiously tried to guard against were the encroachment of French words and the influence of French on her sentence structure; nor did she understand the system of standard German declensional endings. The most puzzling (and most fought over) of these was the "infamous" final *e* that was considered essential by the reformers, but regarded by the opposition as weak and effeminate. In his study on LaRoche's language, Carl Riemann writes that the *e* endings that she must have omitted—as her private letters consistently lack them—("die Reiß" [Reise], "die Leut," "seine Freund," etc.)—were with very few exceptions quietly inserted by the Leipzig printer.[91] That LaRoche managed to avoid all but a few French words (Actrice, coquettes, Bel-esprit, Meubles, fête) is surely owing to Wieland's continual exhortations—frequently in French!—to use only German in her manuscript and private correspondence. Her efforts to comply led to some fanciful "translations" (Badesaison to Wasserzeit, Fundament to Grundtheile, etc.). But more than these faults, Wieland deplored her often French sentence structure. He used her own sentences to demonstrate to her their incorrect structure, faulty punctuation, and inconsistent orthography; and he recommended that in reading German books she pay as much attention to the language as to the contents. The results of his advice and her efforts were mixed, as we have seen.

Riemann rightly concludes that in her first novel LaRoche did "not quite achieve the connection in every detail to the new literary German."[92] Because all her life German had been merely her "survival" language, to be used with shopkeepers and servants, her idiom had a rustic, vernacular quality. When the elevated characters in *Sternheim* speak in that "common" idiom, the result is often unintentionally humorous. Her intimate knowledge of Luther's Bible language caused numerous archaisms (Witwe as Wittib; Ahnung as Ahndung; dornig as dornicht). As for the grammar and orthography in *Sternheim,* it is obvious that if Wieland, his copyist, or the Leipzig printer corrected these, they were not very thorough or, in the case of the last two, themselves unsure. As Riemann notes, a comparison of LaRoche's handwritten letters and the printed novel is particularly interesting. The linguistic divergences between the two show "how far the development around 1770 was still removed from a general use of a standard German literary language."[93]

Once LaRoche turned over her manuscript to Wieland, she had no further part in its initial publication or the subsequent editions; Wieland was in charge. She merely ventured to express her horror at the many misprints in the first (A) edition.[94] In his scholarly introduction of the 1907 edition,[95] Kuno Ridderhoff tells us in his summary of the publication history[96] that in the subsequent eighteenth-century editions (B–H), most of the mistakes in (A) were corrected.

Apparently no new editions appeared in the nineteenth century. The twentieth century has seen four editions so far. The first (1907) was the one edited by Ridderhoff. It was the catalyst for renewed interest in German women authors. It inspired, for example, Christine Touaillon's thorough analysis of LaRoche as part of her study of the German *Frauenroman* (women's novel). The avid interest in women's literature was at least partly responsible for Fritz Brüggemann's 1938 edition, which is based on the first (A) of 1771, "mit Berücksichtigung der Verbesserungen, durch die technische Fehler der ersten Ausgabe in den nachfolgenden Ausgaben beseitigt worden sind"[97] ("taking into account the corrections by which technical errors of the first edition have been eliminated in the subsequent ones"). The rapid rise of feminism and women's studies in literature, as in other fields, resulted in two recent editions. The first (1976) was edited by Marlies Korfsmeyer and based on the original version (A). Günter Häntzschel contributed a thorough analysis of the work and its background in his *Nachwort* (epilogue).[98] The second and to date most recent edition (1983) is based on the third edition of the original issue (Ridderhoff's edition C).[99] It was edited by Barbara Becker-Cantarino who added copious notes, excerpts from contemporary documents, a short bibliography, and a concluding essay.

A close study of the variances among the four modern versions of the text revealed that the Korfsmeyer had the greatest number of mistakes. It reinstated grammatical errors and faulty usages of (A) that later editions had corrected, for example, "gemißhandelt" (p. 26) and "gemißbraucht" (p. 26), and inconsistencies, such as "das jüngere Fräulein" (p. 14) but "die ältere Fräulein" (p. 25). The chief merit of the edition by Becker-Cantarino lies in its accompanying scholarly apparatus. In the text itself the editor concentrated on improving the orthography, but she did not eliminate the grammatical inconsistencies or incorporate the relatively slight improvements of other eighteenth-century editions (Ridderhoff's D through H). The Ridderhoff edition had relatively few mistakes, but its spelling was, of course, rather antiquated, that is, closer to (A) than in the other three editions; and some grammatical errors remained, such as the occasional substitution of the accusative for the dative case. The Brüggemann edition, the cleanest of the four, or rather a 1964 facsimile reprint by the Wissenschaftliche Buchgesellschaft,[100] serves as the text for this translation.

In his introduction to the 1907 edition of *Sternheim*, Kuno Ridderhoff mentions two English translations of the work, both published in 1776.[101] No other English translations have preceded the present one. Of the 1776 publications one was done by Joseph Collyer[102] and survives in the United States in only a single copy in the rare books collection at Yale University; the other, by Edward Harwood,[103] is extant in two copies, at the University of Michigan at Ann Arbor, and the University of Illinois at Champaign-Urbana.

Collyer and Harwood had tried to cater to the English reading public's tastes and were not concerned primarily with being faithful to the original. Their productions were not intended to be scholarly but rather were calculated to take advantage of the work's immense popularity in Germany, France, and Holland. A veritable Sternheim cult had arisen among the young German intellectuals; and although the work went through eight editions by 1783,[104] copies were so scarce that they were passed from one friend to another, one reading by day and the other by night.

Neither Harwood nor Collyer translates Wieland's footnotes or epistolary introduction, although Collyer gives a partial summary of it. Perhaps neither of them carefully read the introduction, or they may have thought it a hoax. Their translations, as they say, are "from the German of Mr. Wieland," but Harwood misspells the name *Wieland* as *Weiland*. Collyer, in his introduction, corrects the misconception that Wieland is the author but in his translation was particularly guilty of omissions, leaving out more and more of the German text as he progressed. In addition, he summarized passages and added material as he saw fit. Besides omitting the lengthy (205 lines) and philosophical letter (S. 000), which is LaRoche's tribute to Wieland (see note 8 in Notes on the Translation), he omitted approximately 144 lines throughout the text. In brief, he left out anything "difficult" or possibly controversial, such as intellectual discussions on improving the lot of the poor, and especially any parts criticizing formal religion and its practices. Collyer may have felt that these passages would do nothing to popularize the book in England and might even get him unwanted notice from the authorities.

Surprisingly, the reverend Mr. Harwood, D.D., seems to have had no such qualms, as he did not leave out the passages critical of the established church. Though Harwood omitted less than Collyer did, he made very free with the original text, creating a smooth and pleasing English rendering, but in the process often changing the meaning considerably. In the manner of an Elizabethan gentleman, Harwood states in his Preface that after first enjoying the work in French translation, he obtained it in German and, having "for some weeks been employed in learning German . . . [the] following translation was some of the exercises I made for my own amusement and improvement during the long evenings in January and February."[105]

It is amusing to read the contemporary reviews of these translations; for example, a typically peevish one from the *London Review:* "There is considerable merit in this performance; a translation of which, by the late Mr. Collier, was, if we mistake not, published some Time ago. . . . We have not that version at hand to compare it with the present; it must have been but indifferent, however, if it made the present necessary." The reviewer adds as a parting shot, "We think it a pity also that the respectable and reverend Dr. Harwood should not be more characteristically employed

than in translating novels.''[106] Another reviewer congratulates Harwood on
''very properly making choice of an agreeable Novel for his Exercise book,
when he undertook the tedious task of learning German; and [he] is doubtless to be commended for having so happily provided for his own amusement and improvement during the long evenings in January and February:
but we are surprised to find that he has ventured to publish his
Exercises.''[107] After this lukewarm reception, it is doubtful that either of
these translations was subsequently reissued, and no evidence to that effect
is available.

The present translation of *Sternheim* was a formidable challenge, owing
to LaRoche's cumbersome syntax with its inversions, repetitions, exclamations, and asides, resulting from her imperfect command of German and
highly emotional style. This rendering follows the original text faithfully,
neither adding nor omitting any units of meaning. Occasionally LaRoche
made lexical choices that did not fit the context, but her meaning was usually clear. Appropriate substitutions were a relatively simple matter. These
changes are documented in the Notes on the Translation.

The translation modernizes the original diction by curbing empty prolixity and eliminating archaisms, while endeavoring to retain the period
feeling of the language and transmit the nuances of meaning as exactly as
possible.

NOTES ON THE INTRODUCTION

1. My translations of German or French quotations, titles, literary terms, etc., are given in parentheses.

2. Review of *Geschichte des Fräuleins von Sternheim, von einer Freundin derselben aus Originalpapieren und anderen zuverlässigen Quellen gezogen,* vol. 1, ed. C. M. Wieland, *Erfurtische gelehrte Zeitung,* 5 (1771), pp. 35–36.

3. Review of *Geschichte,* 2 vols., *Allgemeine Deutsche Bibliothek,* 16 (1772), 475.

4. Review of *Geschichte,* vol. 1, [ed.] by C. M. Wieland, *Göttingische Anzeigen von gelehrten Sachen* (3 Oct. 1771), p. 1023. (Lovelace is the villain in Samuel Richardson's *Clarissa Harlowe*).

5. Review of *Geschichte,* [ed.] by M. Wieland, *Braunschweigische Zeitung* 12 (1771), pp. 192–94.

6. Review of *Geschichte,* ed. C. M. Wieland, *Auserlesene Bibliothek der neuesten deutschen Litteratur,* vol. 1. (Lemgo: Meyer, 1772), p. 225.

7. For a thorough discussion of this attribution see Wilhelm Spickernagel, "Die *Geschichte des Fräuleins von Sternheim* von Sophie von LaRoche und Goethe's *Werther,*" Diss., Greifswald, 1911, p. 26–33.

8. Review of *Geschichte,* vol. 2, ed. C. M. Wieland, *Frankfurter gelehrte Anzeigen* (1772), p. 101.

9. Herder met Goethe in 1770. He introduced him to Shakespeare's works and to German folk lyrics. For a short biography of Herder, see "Herder," *Deutsches Dichterlexikon,* ed. Gero von Wilpert (Stuttgart: Kröner, 1963), p. 247.

10. Johann Heinrich Merck, critic for the *Frankfurter gelehrten Anzeigen* and contributor to Wieland's *Teutschem Merkur.* S.v. "Merck," *Dichterlexikon,* p. 403.

11. *Briefe an J. H. Merck von Goethe, Herder, Wieland und anderen bedeutenden Zeitgenossen,* ed. von K. Wagner (Darmstadt, 1835), p. 29.

12. Brilliant Swiss philosopher. Wieland became engaged to her during his stay in Bern in 1759. Later she became Rousseau's friend. For her relationship with Wieland, see Cornelius Sommer, *Christoph Martin Wieland* (Stuttgart: Metzler, 1971), pp. 22–23.

13. *Aus Herders Nachlaβ,* ed. Heinrich Duntzer and F. G. V. Herder, vol. 3, pp. 67–68. As quoted by Ridderhoff in *Geschichte des Fräuleins von Sternheim,* 2 vols., ed. Kuno Ridderhoff (1907; rpt. Nendeln, Liechtenstein: Kraus, 1968), p. xxxv.

14. Jakob Michael Reinhold Lenz, friend of Kant, Rousseau, Goethe, and Herder. Lenz and Klinger were the two greatest "Storm and Stress" dramatists. S.v. "Lenz," *Dichterlexikon*, p. 362.

15. Lenz to LaRoche, as quoted by Ridderhoff in *Geschichte*, pp. xxx–xxxi.

16. L. Assing, *Sophie von LaRoche, die Freundin Wielands* (Berlin, 1859), pp. 373–74.

17. For biographical information, also see Christine Touaillon, *Der deutsche Frauenroman des 18. Jahrhunderts* (1919; rpt. Bern: Peter Lang, 1979), pp. 73–92.

18. For a detailed examination of the state of women's education in Germany from 1500 to 1800, see Barbara Becker-Cantarino, *Der lange Weg zur Mündigkeit* (Stuttgart: Metzler, 1987), pp. 149–89.

19. Touaillon, p. 75.

20. *Wielands Briefe an Sophie von LaRoche*, ed. Franz Horn (Berlin, 1820), p. 332.

21. Jacob Ludwig Karl Grimm, founder of modern Germanistics, author of many standard works on historical and comparative linguistics. S.v. "Grimm," *Dichterlexikon*, p. 202.

22. Subsequent references to the text of my translation will be given in parentheses with an "S." preceding the page number. Among other persons represented in the work are Wieland (see note 8 of Notes on the Translation), Countess Stadion as the canoness at G. (S. 90), and Georg Michael von LaRoche, the author's husband, as the friend whose son Mr.—takes in (S. 141). (Characteristically, LaRoche here weaves a personal experience into her story: the LaRoches' oldest son had stayed with Wieland for a while to benefit from the latter's influence.)

23. Sophie von LaRoche, *Melusinens Sommerabende*, ed. C. M. Wieland (Halle, 1806), pp. xxiv–xxvii.

24. See Peter Petschauer, "Sophie von LaRoche, Novelist between Reason and Emotion," *Germanic Review*, 57 (1982): 70–77.

25. (My trans.). *Ich bin mehr Herz als Kopf*, ed. Michael Maurer (Munich: C. H. Beck, 1983), p. 301.

26. Maurer, p. 149.

27. See Burghard Dedner, "Sophie La Roche: *Die Geschichte des Fräuleins von Sternheim* und *Rosaliens Briefe*: Die Umdeutung der Tradition im Bereich 'realistischen' Erzählens," *Topos, Ideal und Realitätspostulat*, Studien zur Darstellung des Landlebens im Roman des 18. Jahrhunderts, vol. 16 (Tübingen: Niemeyer, 1969), pp. 54–87.

28. Ingrid Wiede-Behrendt, *Lehrerin des Schönen, Wahren, Guten* (Frankfurt am Main: Peter Lang, 1987), p. 25.

29. Dedner, pp. 56 f.

30. Touaillon, 193.

31. Christoph Martin Wieland, *Geschichte des Agathon*, 2 vols. (Leipzig, 1766), p. 162.

32. C. M. Wieland, editorial, *Der Neue Teutsche Merkur* (Feb. 1791), p. 201.

33. Gabriele Becker et al., *Aus der Zeit der Verzweiflung* (Frankfurt am Main: Suhrkamp, 1977), p. 319.

34. Barbara Becker-Cantarino, " 'Muse' and 'Kunstrichter': Sophie La Roche und Wieland,"*Modern Language Notes* 1 (1984): 572.

35. Jean-Jacques Rousseau, *Émile ou de l'éducation*, ed. M. Raup (Stuttgart: Reclam, 1978), p. 726.

36. Ibid., p. 791.

37. Rousseau, *La nouvelle Héloïse, ou Lettres des Deux Amans*, vol. 2 (Aux Deux-Ponts, 1782), p. 72.

38. Ibid., vol. 2, pp. 65–66.

39. See note 7.

40. *Briefe Goethes an Sophie von LaRoche und Bettina Brentano*, ed. G. V. Loeper (Berlin, 1879), p. 30.

41. Ibid., p. 33.

42. Spickernagel (note 7), p. 11.

43. See Erich Schmidt, *Richardson, Rousseau und Goethe* (Jena, 1875), p. 62.

44. Adalbert von Hanstein, *Die Frauen in der Geschichte des deutschen Geisteslebens*, vol. 2 (Leipzig, 1899), p. 154.

45. Werner Milch, *Sophie La Roche: Die Großmutter der Brentanos* (Frankfurt am Main: Societätsverlag, 1935), p. 183.

46. Wilhelm Scherer, "Sophie von LaRoche und ihre Enkelin," *Aufsätze über Goethe* (Berlin, 1886), p. 75.

47. Siegfried Sudhoff, "Sophie Laroche," *Deutsche Dichter des 18. Jahrhunderts: Ihr Leben und Werk*, ed. Bennno von Wiese (Berlin: n.p., 1977), p. 306.

48. Günter Giesenfeld, "Die Leiden des papiernen Mädchens," *Erfahrung und Ideologie: Studien zur massenhaft verbreiteten Literatur*, ed. Jürgen Schutte (Berlin: n.p., 1983), p. 15.

49. In a letter by Goethe to Schiller, dated 24 July 1799. In Emil Staiger, ed., *Der Briefwechsel zwischen Schiller und Goethe* (Frankfurt am Main: n.p., 1966), p. 784.

50. Alan Dugald McKillop, *Samuel Richardson, Printer and Novelist* (Chapel Hill: University of North Carolina Press, 1936), p. 250.

51. Denis Diderot, *Oeuvres completes*, ed. J. Assézat and M. Tourneux, vol. 5 (Paris, 1875), p. 215.

52. S.v. "Gellert," *Dichterlexikon*, p. 172.

53. Christian Fürchtegott Gellert, *Sämmtliche Schriften*, ed. J. L. Klee, vol. 6 (Leipzig, 1839), p. 257.

54. Cited in Lydia Schieth, *Die Entwicklung des deutschen Frauenromans im ausgehenden 18. Jahrhundert* (Frankfurt am Main: Peter Lang, 1987), p. 25.

55. Cited in Clara L. Thomson, *Samuel Richardson* (1900; Port Washington: Kennikat, 1970), p. 286.

56. Ibid., p. 285.

57. From a poem by Barthold Brockes, cited in L. M. Price, *Die Aufnahme englischer Literatur in Deutschland 1500–1960* (Munich: n.p., 1961), p. 169.

58. Thomson, p. 170.

59. Ibid., p. 156.

60. Schieth, p. 26.

61. Quoted in Schieth, p. 26. My retranslation from the German edition of *Pamela* may not be a verbatim reproduction of the original text.

62. Johanna Schopenhauer, *Die Tante, ein Roman* (Leipzig, 1870), p. 83.

63. Schmidt, p. 48.

64. Ibid., p. 61.

65. Ibid., p. 49.

66. Ibid.

67. First published in *Pomona für Teutschlands Töchter,* vol. 3 (1783–84), cited in Kuno Ridderhoff, "Sophie von LaRoche, die Schülerin Richardsons und Rousseaus," diss. (Göttingen: Einbeck, 1895), p. 8.

68. Ridderhoff, "Schülerin," p. 8.

69. Wiede-Behrendt, p. 86.

70. Bernd Heidenreich, *Sophie von LaRoche—eine Werkbiographie* (Frankfurt am Main: Peter Lang, 1986), p. 62.

71. Gellert, *Schriften,* vol. 6.

72. Donald L. Ball, *Samuel Richardson's Theory of Fiction* (The Hague: Mouton, 1971), p. 23.

73. The first two types are mentioned in the Preface to *Clarissa,* vol. 1, p. xiv. The third kind is referred to in Samuel Richardson, *The History of Sir Charles Grandison,* 3 vols., ed. Jocelyn Harris (London: Oxford University Press, 1972).

74. Samuel Richardson, *Clarissa, or, The History of a Young Lady,* "Shakespeare Head Edition," 8 vols. (1747–48; rpt. Oxford, 1930). All page references are to this edition.

75. Ian Watt in *The Rise of the Novel* (Berkeley: University of California Press, 1964), pp. 18–21, comments on Richardson's ingenious use of "subtly appropriate and suggestive, yet . . . ordinary, realistic" names to individualize his characters and make them more realistic. We recall, of course, one instance in which he uses an initial name: the well-known Mr. B. in *Pamela,* a character as abbreviated as his name, who represents an early stage in Richardson's progress toward his later mastery of character development and individualization.

76. Ridderhoff, p. 13. Both Ridderhoff and Christine Touaillon (p. 113) consider the omission of answering letters and the editorial frame a significant improvement over Richardson's technique.

77. Ball, p. 22.

78. John Carroll, *Selected Letters of Samuel Richardson* (Oxford: Clarendon Press, 1964), p. 123.

79. Ibid., p. 71.

80. Ball, p. 62.

81. Terry Castle, "The Carnivalization of Eighteenth-Century English Narrative," *Publications of the Modern Language Association of America* 99 (1984): 903–14. Castle points out that in eighteenth-century narrative the masquerade is almost always associated with "sexual impurity—and consequent danger to heroines." It is "a point for narrative transformation." He cites *Roxana, Tom*

Jones, Amelia, Pamela, vol. 2, *Grandison, Peregrine Pickle, Fanny Hill,* and Burney's *Cecilia,* among others, as novels in which masquerades are used in this way.

82. Ball, pp. 203–204, 221, 240–41, 244–45, 248–91.
83. *Clarissa,* vol. 1, p. xiii.
84. Ball, pp. 40–41.
85. Quoted by George Saintsbury, *Grandison,* p. xxiii.
86. Sophie von LaRoche, *Geschichte des Fräuleins von Sternheim,* 2 vols., ed. C. M. Wieland (Leipzig: Weidmanns Erben und Reich, 1771).
87. See Wieland's introduction.
88. Horn, p. 65.
89. Cited in Carl Riemann, "Die Sprache in Sophie von LaRoches Roman *Geschichte des Fräuleins von Sternheim:* Ein Beitrag zur Geschichte der Schriftsprache im 18. Jahrhundert," *Wissenschaftliche Zeitschrift der Friedrich—Schiller-Universität Jena* (Gesellschafts- und sprachwissenschaftliche Reihe) 8, no. 1 (1958–59): 179.
90. Riemann, p. 180.
91. Ibid.
92. Ibid., pp. 192–93.
93. Ibid., p. 193.
94. Ridderhoff, Introduction, *Geschichte,* p. xxxvi.
95. Ibid., pp. v–xxxix.
96. Ibid., pp. xxxvi–xxxix.
97. LaRoche, *Geschichte des Fräuleins von Sternheim,* ed. Fritz Brüggemann (Leipzig: Reclam, 1938).
98. LaRoche, *Geschichte des Fräuleins von Sternheim,* ed. Marlies Korfsmeyer (Munich: Winkler, 1976).
99. LaRoche, *Geschichte des Fräuleins von Sternheim,* ed. Barbara Becker-Cantarino (Stuttgart: Reclam, 1983).
100. LaRoche, *Geschichte des Fräuleins von Sternheim,* ed. Heinz Kindermann (1938; rpt. Darmstadt: Wissenschaftliche Buchgesellschaft, 1964).
101. Ridderhoff, Introduction, *Geschichte,* p. xxxiii.
102. LaRoche, *The History of Lady Sophia Sternheim,* 2 vols., trans. Joseph Collyer (London: T. Jones, 1776).
103. LaRoche, *Memoirs of Miss Sophy Sternheim,* 2 vols., trans. E. Harwood (London: T. Becket, 1776).
104. Günter Häntzschel, Afterword, *Geschichte des Fräuleins von Sternheim,* by Sophie von LaRoche, ed. Marlies Korfsmeyer (Munich: Winkler, 1976), pp. 307–308.
105. *Memoirs,* trans. Harwood, pp. iii–iv.
106. Review of *Memoirs of the Life of Miss Sophy Sternheim,* [ed.] by C. M. Weiland [sic], trans. Edward Harwood, *London Review* 4 (1776): 306.
107. Review of *Memoirs, Monthly Review,* 55 (1776): 319.

SELECTED BIBLIOGRAPHY

Assing, L. *Sophie von LaRoche, die Freundin Wielands.* Berlin: 1859.

Ball, Donald L. *Samuel Richardson's Theory of Fiction.* The Hague: Mouton, 1971.

Becker, Gabriele, et al. *Aus der Zeit der Verzweiflung.* Frankfurt am Main: Suhrkamp, 1977.

Becker-Cantarino, Barbara. *Der lange Weg zur Mündigkeit.* Stuttgart: Metzler, 1987.

————. " 'Muse' und 'Kunstrichter': Sophie von La Roche und Wieland." *Modern Language Notes* 99 (1984): 571–88.

Blackwell, Jeannine. "Bildungsroman mit Dame." Diss. University of Michigan, Ann Arbor 1982.

Carroll, John. *Selected Letters of Samuel Richardson.* Oxford: Clarendon Press, 1964.

Castle, Terry. "The Carnivalization of Eighteenth-Century English Narrative." *Publications of the Modern Language Association of America* 99 (1984): 903–14.

Collyer, Joseph, trans. *The History of Lady Sophia Sternheim,* 2 vols., by Sophie von LaRoche. London: T. Jones, 1776.

Dedner, Burghard. *Topos, Ideal und Realitätspostulat: Studien zur Darstellung des Landlebens im Roman des 18. Jahrhunderts.* Studien zur deutschen Literatur vol. 16. Tübingen: Max Niemeyer, 1969.

Diderot, Denis. *Oeuvres completes,* 20 vols., ed. J. Assézat and M. Tourneux. Paris: 1875–77.

Gellert, Christian Fürchtegott. *Sämmtliche Schriften,* 10 vols., ed. J. L. Klee. Leipzig: 1839.

Giesenfeld, Günter. "Die Leiden des papiernen Mädchens." *Erfahrung und Ideologie: Studien zur massenhaft verbreiteten Literatur,* ed. Jürgen Schutte. Berlin: 1983.

Hanstein, Adalbert von. *Die Frauen in der Geschichte des deutschen Geisteslebens des 18. und 19. Jahrhunderts.* 2 vols. Leipzig: 1899.

Harwood, Edward, trans. *Memoirs of Miss Sophy Sternheim*, 2 vols., [ed.] C. M. Wieland. London: T. Becket, 1776.

Heidenreich, Bernd. *Sophie von LaRoche—eine Werkbiographie*. Frankfurt am Main: Peter Lang, 1986.

Horn, Franz, ed. *Wielands Briefe an Sophie von LaRoche*. Berlin: 1820.

LaRoche, Sophie von. *Geschichte des Fräuleins von Sternheim, von einer Freundin derselben aus Originalpapieren und anderen zuverlässigen Quellen gezogen*, 2 vols., ed. C. M. Wieland. Leipzig: Weidmanns Erben und Reich, 1771.

————. *Geschichte des Fräuleins von Sternheim*, 2 vols., ed. *Kuno Ridderhoff*. *1907. Rpt. Nendeln, Liechtenstein: Kraus, 1968.*

————. *Geschichte des Fräuleins von Sternheim*, ed. Fritz Brüggemann. Leipzig: Reclam, 1938.

————. *Geschichte des Fräuleins von Sternheim*, ed. Heinz Kindermann. 1938. Rpt. Darmstadt: Wissenschaftliche Buchgesellschaft, 1964.

————. *Geschichte des Fräuleins von Sternheim*. ed. Marlies Korfsmeyer. Munich: Winkler, 1976.

————. *Geschichte des Fräuleins von Sternheim, ed. Barbara Becker-Cantarino. Stuttgart: Reclam, 1983.*

————. *Melusinens Sommerabende*, ed. C. M. Wieland. Halle: 1806.

Loeper, G. V., ed. *Briefe Goethes an Sophie von LaRoche und Bettina Brentano*. Berlin: 1879.

Maurer, Michael, ed. *Ich bin mehr Herz als Kopf: Sophie von La Roche, ein Lebensbild in Briefen*. Munich: C. H. Beck, 1983.

McKillop, Alan Dugald, *Samuel Richardson, Printer and Novelist*. Chapel Hill: University of North Carolina Press, 1936.

Milch, Werner. *Sophie La Roche: Die Großmutter der Brentanos*. Frankfurt am Main: Societätsverlag, 1935.

Petschauer, Peter. "Sophie von LaRoche, Novelist between Reason and Emotion." *Germanic Review*. 57 (1982): 70–77.

Price, L. M. *Die Aufnahme englischer Literatur in Deutschland 1500–1960*. Munich: 1961.

Review of *Geschicte des Fräuleins von Sternheim, von einer Freundin derselben aus Originalpapieren und anderen zuverlässigen Quellen gezogen*, 2 vols., by Sophie von LaRoche, ed. C. M. Wieland. *Allgemeine Deutsche Bibliothek* 16 (1772): 475.

Review of Vol. 1 of *Geschichte*, by Sophie von LaRoche, ed. C. M. Wieland. *Auserlesene Bibliothek der neuesten deutschen Litteratur*. Lemgo: Meyer, 1772.

Review of Vol. 1 of *Geschichte*, [ed.] by C. M. Wieland. *Braunschweigische Zeitung* 12 (1771): 192–94.

Review of Vol. 2 of *Geschichte*, by Sophie von LaRoche, ed. C. M. Wieland. *Frankfurter gelehrte Anzeigen* (1772): 101.

Review of Vol. 1 of *Geschichte*, [ed.] by C. M. Wieland. *Göttingische Anzeigen von gelehrten Sachen* (3 Oct. 1771): 1023.

Review of Edward Harwood, trans. of *Memoirs of the Life of Miss Sophy Sternheim*. [ed.] by C. M. Weiland [sic]. *London Review*, 4 (1776): 306.

Review of Edward Harwood, trans. of *Memoirs*. *Monthly Review*, 55 (1776): 319.

Ridderhoff, Kuno von. "Sophie von LaRoche, die Schülerin Richardsons und Rousseaus." Diss., Göttingen, 1895.

Richardson, Samuel. *Clarissa, or, The History of a Young Lady*, 8 vols. 1747–48: The Shakespeare Head Edition; rpt. Oxford: Blackwell, 1930.

―――. *The History of Sir Charles Grandison*, 3 vols., ed. Jocelyn Harris. London: Oxford University Press, 1972.

Riemann, Carl. "Die Sprache in Sophie von La Roches Roman *Geschichte des Fräuleins von Sternheim:* Ein Beitrag zur Geschichte der Schriftsprache im 18. Jahrhundert." *Wissenschaftliche Zeitschrift der Friedrich-Schiller-Universität Jena (Gesellschafts- und sprachwissenschaftliche Reihe)* 8, no. 1 (1958–59): 179–93.

Rousseau, Jean-Jacques. *Émile, ou de l'éducation*. 1762, ed. M. Raup. Stuttgart: Reclam, 1978.

―――. *La Nouvelle Héloïse, ou Lettres des Deux Amans*. 2 vols. Aux Deux Ponts: 1782.

Scherer, Wilhelm. "Sophie von LaRoche und ihre Enkelin." *Aufsätze über Goethe*. Berlin: 1886.

Schieth, Lydia. *Die Entwicklung des deutschen Frauenromans im ausgehenden 18. Jahrhundert*. Frankfurt am Main: Peter Lang, 1987.

Schmidt, Erich. *Richardson, Rousseau und Goethe*. Jena: 1875.

Sommer, Cornelius. *Christoph Martin Wieland*. Stuttgart: Metzler, 1971.

Spickernagel, Wilhelm. "Die *Geschichte des Fräuleins von Sternheim* von Sophie von LaRoche und Goethes *Werther*." Diss., Greifswald, 1911.

Staiger, Emil, ed. *Der Briefwechsel zwischen Schiller und Goethe*. Frankfurt am Main: 1966.

Sudhoff, Siegfried. "Sophie Laroche." *Deutsche Dichter des 18. Jahrhunderts: Ihr Leben und Werk*, ed. Benno von Wiese. Berlin: Erich Schmidt, 1977.

Thomson, Clara L. *Samuel Richardson*. 1900. Port Washington: Kennikat, 1970.

Touaillon, Christine. *Der deutsche Frauenroman des 18. Jahrhunderts*. 1919. Rpt. Bern: Peter Lang, 1979.

Wagner, K., ed. *Briefe an J. H. Merck von Goethe, Herder, Wieland und anderen bedeutenden Zeitgenossen*. Darmstadt: 1835.

Watt, Ian. *The Rise of the Novel*. Berkeley: University of California Press, 1964.

Wiede-Behrendt, Ingrid. *Lehrerin des Schönen, Wahren, Guten: Literatur und Frauenbildung im ausgehenden 18. Jahrhundert am Beispiel Sophie von La Roche.* Frankfurt am Main: Peter Lang, 1987.

Wieland, Christoph Martin. *Geschichte des Agathon.* 2 vols. Leipzig: 1766.

————. Editorial. *Der Neue Teutsche Merkur* (Feb. 1791).

Wilpert, Gero von, ed. *Deutsches Dichterlexikon.* Stuttgart: Kröner, 1963.

APPENDIX:

Sophie von LaRoche's Works

1771   *Geschichte des Fräuleins von Sternheim (The History of Lady Sophia Sternheim)*, 2 vols.

1779–1781   *Rosaliens Briefe an ihre Freundin Mariane von ST.* (Rosalie's Letters to her Friend Marianne von S.)* LaRoche a contributor to J. G. Jacobi's periodical *Iris, Vierteljahresschrift für Frauenzimmer* (Iris, a Quarterly for Women).

1782–1784   *Moralische Erzählungen im Geschmack Marmontels* (Moral Tales à la Marmontel).

1783–1784   LaRoche's periodical *Pomona für Teutschland's Töchter* (Pomona for Germany's Daughters) is published.

1785–1787   *Briefe an Lina* (Letters to Lina), 3 vols.

1786   *Neuere Moralische Erzählungen* (Later Moral Tales).

1787   *Tagebuch einer Reise durch die Schweiz* (Diary of a Journey through Switzerland).

1788   *Tagebuch einer Reise durch Holland und England* (Diary of a Journey through Holland and England).

1788   *Moralische Erzählungen. Nachlese* (Moral Tales: Gleanings).

1789   *Geschichte von Miss Lony* (The History of Miss Lony).

1791   *Rosalie und Cleberg auf dem Lande* (Rosalie and Cleberg in the Country).

1791   *Briefe über Mannheim* (Letters about Mannheim).

1793   *Erinnerungen aus meiner dritten Schweizerreise* (Memories of My Third Journey to Switzerland).

---

*None of the translated titles are italicized except the first, because it has been published in English.

1795–1796	*Schönes Bild der Resignation* (A Fair Image of Resignation), 2 vols.
1798	*Erscheinungen am See Oneida* (Apparitions at Lake Oneida), 3 vols.
1799	*Mein Schreibetisch* (My Writing Desk), 2 vols.
1801–1802	*Fanny und Julie, oder die Freundinnen* (Fanny and Julie, or the Friends), 2 vols.
1803	*Liebe-Hütten* (Tabernacles of Love).
1805	*Herbsttage* (Autumn Days).
1806	*Melusinens Sommer-Abende* (Melusina's Summer Evenings), with a biographical sketch, edited by C. M. Wieland.
1807	*Erinnerungen aus meinem Leben* (Memories of My Life).

THE TRANSLATION
of
THE NOVEL

INTRODUCTION BY THE EDITOR-PUBLISHER
OF THE FIRST EDITION

To D. F. G. R. V.*

Do not be alarmed, my friend, to receive, instead of the manuscript of your "Sternheim," a printed copy, which reveals the whole treason that I have committed against you. The deed seems at first glance inexcusable. You entrust to me, in the name of our friendship, a work of your imagination and your heart, which was written down only for your own diversion. "I send it to you," you write me, "so that you can give me your opinion of my sensibility, of the point of view from which I have become accustomed to judge the affairs of human life, of the considerations that customarily arise in my soul when it is vividly moved, and so that you may rebuke me where you find me in error. You know what prompted me to devote the few idle hours that remained to me after the discharge of essential duties to this recreation of the spirit. You know that I have always cherished the ideas I sought to realize in the character and actions of Miss von Sternheim and her parents; and with what does one occupy one's mind more gladly than with that which one holds dear? There were hours when this occupation was a kind of necessity for my soul. Thus, before I knew it, this little work came into being, though I began and carried it on without knowing whether I would be able to complete it, and though I feel its imperfections as keenly as you do. But it is intended only for you and me—and if, as I hope, you approve of how this daughter of my mind thinks and acts, for our children. If through their acquaintance with her, they were strengthened in true, general, active goodness and honesty—how that would delight the heart of your friend!''

---

* Complete as follows: An D(ie) F(rau) G(eheime) R(aetin) V(on LaRoche). [To Lady (the wife of) Privy Counsellor Von LaRoche].

Thus you wrote when you entrusted your "Sternheim" to me—and now, my friend, let us see whether I have betrayed your trust, whether I have in truth committed a crime, when I succumbed to the desire to present to all the virtuous mothers and all the amiable young daughters of our nation, a work that seemed destined to advance wisdom and virtue—the sole great advantages of mankind, the sole wellspring of genuine felicity among your sex and even among mine.

I need not mention the far-reaching benefits produced by writings of the kind to which your "Sternheim" belongs when they are good. Everyone of discernment agrees on this point, and after all Richardson, Fielding, and so many others have said, it would be superfluous to add even one word confirming a truth no one doubts. It is equally certain that our nation has too few original works of this kind, which are at once entertaining and destined to propagate the love of virtue. Does not this twofold consideration suffice to vindicate me? You will agree, I hope, or at least forgive me more easily, when I tell you exactly how it occurred to me to turn you into an authoress.

I sat down to read your manuscript with all the familiar languor of the past several years. The singular quality you give your heroine's mother even on the first few pages was—given my particular taste—more likely to influence me against her than for her. But I read on, and all my cold-hearted philosophy, the blighted fruit of many years observing humanity and its infinite folly, could not prevail against the truth and beauty of your moral representations. My heart warmed; I loved Sternheim the father, his wife, his daughter, and even—his parson, one of the worthiest I have ever met. All those little dissonances which your Miss Sternheim's strange, almost enthusiastic, ardor makes in my mind dissolved in the most pleasant attunement of her principles, sentiments, and actions with the best feelings and the most lively convictions of my soul. If only—I thought in a hundred places—if only my daughters would learn to think and act like Sophie Sternheim! If only heaven would let me experience the bliss of seeing in my daughters this unvarnished sincerity of the soul, this ever constant goodness, this delicate sense of the true and the beautiful; and—springing from an inner source—this exercise of every virtue; this unfeigned piety which—instead of being a hindrance to the beauty and nobility of the soul—is, in hers, itself the most beautiful and best of all virtues; this tender, compassionate, charitable heart; this healthy, genuine judgment of human affairs and their worth; of happiness, good repute, and pleasure! In short, I wished to see all those attributes of heart and mind that I love in this beautiful and moral figure expressed in these amiable creatures who—even now in their childish years—represent the sweetest joy of my present and the best hope of my future days!

Thinking thus, my first inspiration was to make a beautiful copy of your manuscript and present it a few years hence to our little Sophie (for you are so kind as to call her yours, too).[1] And how it has pleased me to think of cultivating, by this means, in our children the feelings of our friendship of so many years, which has been well tried and always found pure!

I delighted myself for a time with these pictures when, quite naturally, this thought came to me: How many mothers and fathers residing now in the far reaches of the German provinces are at this moment making similar wishes on behalf of children just as promising and as tenderly loved! Would I not gladden them if I let them partake of a treasure that loses nothing in the sharing? Would not the good which can be effected through the virtuous example of the Sternheim family be spread thereby to many? Is it not our duty to do good within the greatest possible bounds? And how many of the noble-minded would by this means come to know the worth of my friend's mind and heart, and would bless her memory when you and I are no more! Tell me, my friend, how could I—having the heart you have known for so many years now and that you, notwithstanding all my changes within and without, have ever found true to itself—resist such ideas?

Thus I determined at once to make copies for all our friends of both sexes and for all those who would be our friends if they knew us. I thought so well of our contemporaries that I felt a need for a great many such copies; and thus I sent mine to my friend Reich,[2] leaving it to him to make as many as he deemed desirable.

But no! It did not happen so quickly. Despite the warmth of my heart, my head remained cool enough to consider everything capable of deterring me from my purpose. Never, to my knowledge, has the prejudice for those I love made me blind to their defects. You know this quality in me, and you are as incapable of expecting or even wishing to be flattered as I am unwilling to speak against my convictions. Your Sternheim, amiable though she is, has—when considered as a work of the mind, a literary composition, or even merely as German writing—certain faults that will not remain hidden from the hecklers. Yet it is not they whom I fear on your behalf, but the art critics on the one side and on the other the despicable, worldly connoisseurs. Shall I confess to you, my friend, that I am not entirely without anxiety when I consider that I have exposed your "Sternheim" to the judgment of so many persons of such diverse turns of mind?

But listen to what I said to myself in order to calm myself again: Regarding whatever may be censured in the form and style of the work—the art critics must deal only with me. You, my friend, never thought of writing for the world or of producing a work of art. Notwithstanding all your wide reading in the best authors of diverse languages whom one may read without being learned, it was always your wont to regard less the beauty of the form than the worth of the contents; and this conviction alone would ever have made you banish all thought of writing for the world. Thus it would have been my responsibility as the unauthorized publisher of your manuscript, to remedy the faults which I expect the critics will wish absent, even if they are not actually objectionable.

Yet when I speak of art critics, I think of men of refined taste and mature judgment; of judges who are not offended by small blemishes in a beautiful work, and who are too reasonable to demand in the fruit of mere nature, spontaneously brought forth, a perfection equal to that of the fruit cultivated by art and nurtured by labor (although in regard to taste, the latter must not infrequently yield to the former). Such connoisseurs will presumably be of the opinion, just as I am, that moral literature can dispense with an artful form, as its concern is for the representation of a certain instructive and interesting chief character, rather than for complications and developments, and its moral utility is altogether the chief purpose and the amusement of the reader only secondary. All the more so, if it has inner and original beauties for the mind and heart that compensate for the lack of an artfully constructed plan and, in general, of everything that goes by the name of authorial art. Unless I greatly delude myself, just such connoisseurs will notice in the manner in which *Sternheim* is written a certain originality of imagery and expression and such a felicitous rightness and energy of the latter—often precisely in those places where the language teacher would, perhaps, be least satisfied—as seems to compensate generously for the carelessness of the style, unusual expressions, and turns of speech, and, in general, the lack of a perfect smoothness and roundness. I would not have known how to remedy this deficiency without sacrificing what seemed to me an essential beauty of my friend's manner of writing.

They will observe that our Sternheim, notwithstanding the advantages of her education that shine forth at every opportunity, nevertheless owes her taste and her way of thinking, speaking, and acting more to nature and her own experiences and observations than to instruction and imitation; for this reason she often thinks and acts otherwise than most persons of her condition. One can see that this singularity of her character—and particularly the individual course of her fancy—must naturally also influence the manner in which she clothes her thoughts or expresses her feelings; and this is why she also invents—for a thought that she herself has come upon—at the same instant her own expression, whose power is commensurate with the liveliness and truth of the intuitions from which she develops her thoughts. Ought not the connoisseurs be willing to find, as I am, that just this complete individualization of the character of our heroine constitutes one of the special merits of this work? This quality art could achieve only in the smallest measure and surely never so felicitously as here, where nature was at work.

In short, I have so high an opinion of the refined sensibility of the art critics that I am confident they will find the faults I mention interwoven with so many and such excellent beauties that they would hold me blameworthy were I to invoke for my friend the privilege of those ladies who are not authors by profession.

And should we then fear the fashionable and pampered tastes of the worldly more than the art critics? Indeed, the singularity of our heroine, her enthusiasm for the morally beautiful, the ideas and moods peculiar to her, her somewhat stubborn predilection for the noble lords and all that resembles them and comes from their country, and—worse still—the constant contrast of her manner of feeling and perceiving, of judging and acting, to the tastes, customs, and habits of high society presage ill for her favorable acceptance by these latter persons. Nevertheless, I do not abandon all hope that (in the character of the lovable crank) she might—simply because she is a phenomenon—make considerable conquests. Indeed, despite all her moral peculiarity, which at times seems to border on exaggeration or what some will call pedantry, she is an amiable creature. If, on the one hand, her entire character with all its conceptions and principles can be viewed as dramatized satire of court life and high society; on the other, it is equally certain that one cannot judge more fairly and leniently the merits and faults of the persons who move in this shining circle than our heroine does. We see that she speaks of things she has observed at first hand and that the fault lies neither with her intellect nor her heart when she finds everything incomprehensible in this country where art has completely supplanted nature and is herself incomprehensible to all.

Forgive me, my friend, for belaboring a point on which you have cause to rest very easy. With some characters there is never a question but that they will please; and I would be extraordinarily mistaken if our heroine did not belong in this class. The naive beauty of her mind, the purity, the limitless goodness of her heart, the correctness of her taste, the verity of her judgments, the sagacity of her remarks, the liveliness of her imagination, and the harmony between her expressions and her own manner of feeling and perceiving, in short, all her talents and virtues are my guarantors that—all her little faults notwithstanding—she will please all those who are blessed with a sound head and feeling heart. And whom else should we wish to please?

But the dearest wish of our heroine is not grounded in vanity. She wishes to be useful; she wants to do good; and she *will* do good, and will thereby justify the step I have taken without the foreknowledge or permission of her amiable creator: to introduce her into the world.

I am, etc.

The Editor

PART ONE

You need not thank me, my dear friend, for copying so much for you. You know that I had the good fortune to be brought up with the excellent lady from whose biography I send you excerpts and copies of letters that my Lord Seymour gathered from his English friend and from my Emilia. Believe me, it is a heartfelt pleasure that I can occupy myself with something that renews in me the sacred memory of the virtue and goodness of a person who has brought honor to our sex and to mankind.

The father of my beloved Lady Sidney[3] was Colonel von Sternheim, only son of a professor at W., who provided him with the most careful education. Magnanimity, greatness of mind, and goodness of heart were the basic traits of his character. At the University of L., friendship united him with the somewhat younger Baron von P. so closely that he not only accompanied him on all his travels but for love of him also entered into military service with him. By associating with him and through his example, the formerly unruly mind of the baron became so pliant and well-meaning that his whole family was grateful to the young man who had led their beloved son to the paths of goodness.

An unforeseen event separated them: Upon the death of his elder brother, the baron had to leave military service and prepare to take over administration of the estates. Sternheim, deeply revered and loved by officers and common men, remained in the service and was given a colonel's commission and ennobled by the prince. "Your merit, not fortune, has elevated you," said the general, when in the name of the prince and in the presence of many persons he handed him the colonel's commission and the patent of nobility. According to general testimony, all his campaigns occasioned the full exercise of magnanimity, charity, and bravery.

Upon the declaration of peace, his first desire was to see the friend with whom he had continuously exchanged letters. His heart knew no other bond. He had already lost his father long before, and as the latter had himself been a stranger in W., his son was left with no close relatives. Colonel von Sternheim therefore traveled to P. to enjoy the quiet pleasures of friendship.

Baron P., his friend, had married an amiable lady and lived happily with his mother and two sisters on the beautiful estates his father had left him. The von P. family, one of the most respected in those parts, was often visited by the numerous members of the neighboring nobility. Baron P. alternately gave parties and small fêtes. The solitary days were spent in reading good books, proper management of the domain, and genteel and decent conduct of the household.

At times he held small concerts as well because the younger of the two young ladies played the piano, while the older played the lute and sang beautifully, accompanied by her brother and some of his men. The latter lady's state of mind disturbed this quiet scene. She was the only child of Baron P. and his first wife, a Lady Watson, whom he had married during an ambassadorial mission in England. In addition to all the gentle amiability of an Englishwoman, this young lady seemed to have inherited from her mother the melancholy which distinguishes that nation. A secret sorrow suffused her countenance. She loved solitude, which she put to use in diligently reading the best books, without, however, neglecting any opportunities of sequestering herself with the members of her family without outside company.

Her brother, the baron, who loved her tenderly, was troubled by the state of her health. He tried his best to divert her and discover the cause of her sadness. On several occasions he begged her to open her heart to her faithful, loving brother. She looked at him, thanked him for his solicitude, and with tear-filled eyes begged him to let her keep her secret and merely to love her. This disquieted him. He feared that some past error might be at the root of this sadness. He observed her closely at all times but discovered nothing that provided him with the slightest confirmation of his fear. She was always under his or her mother's eyes, talked with none of the household, and avoided every kind of conversation. Then, for a time, she forced herself to remain in society, and a quiet cheerfulness gave hope that the attack of melancholy had passed.

The family's joy over this recovery was increased by the unexpected arrival of Colonel von Sternheim, of whom the whole family had heard so much and whose excellence of mind and heart they had admired in his letters. He surprised them one evening in their garden. The baron's delight and the eager attention paid him by the others cannot be described. It did not take long before his nobility and kindness spread the same joy through the whole household. The colonel was presented as a special family friend to all the nobility of their acquaintance and was included in all their gatherings.

In the baron's house he gave an account of his life, recounting, with grace, without prolixity, and in that manly tone which characterizes the man of wisdom and the friend of mankind, the remarkable and useful things he had seen. For him, in turn, they painted the picture of country life, with now the baron speaking of the benefits that the master's constant presence confers on those who serve him, now the old lady of that part of the rural economy which concerns the family matriarch, now the two young ladies of the pleasant diversions that life in the country offers at each season of the year. After this description followed the question, "My friend, would you not wish to spend the remaining days of your life in the country?"

"Yes, my dear baron, but it would have to be on my own lands and in the neighborhood of yours."

"That is quite possible, for only a mile from here there is an agreeable estate to be purchased. I have permission to go there whenever I wish; tomorrow we shall inspect it."

On the following day, both gentlemen rode there, accompanied by the pastor of P., a very worthy man from whom the ladies obtained a description of the moving scene that took place between the two friends. The baron showed the colonel the entire estate and conducted him into the pleasantly situated house adjacent to the garden. Here they took their breakfast. The colonel expressed his satisfaction with all that he had seen and asked the baron whether it were true that one might purchase this estate.

"Yes, my friend; do you like it?"

"Entirely; it would separate me from nothing that I love."

"Oh, how happy I am, my dear friend," said the baron as he embraced him; "I bought this estate these three years ago in order to offer it to you. I restored the house and have often, in this very cabinet, prayed for your preservation. Now I shall have the guide of my youth for my life's witness."

The colonel was extraordinarily moved. He could not sufficiently express his gratitude and his delight in the noble heart of his friend. He assured him that he would spend the rest of his life in this house, but at the same time he demanded to know what the estate had cost. The baron was obliged to reveal it and also to prove it by means of the bills of sale. The revenue was higher than seemed indicated by the purchase price, but the baron insisted upon accepting no more than he had spent.

"My friend," he said, "for three years I have done nothing but apply all the revenues of the estate to its improvement and beautification. I delighted myself with the thought, 'you are working for the retirement days of the best of men; here you will see him and relive in his company the happy times of your youth; his counsel and his example will add to the satisfaction of your soul and to the betterment of your family,'—these thoughts were my reward."

When they came home, the baron presented the colonel to his mother and sister as a new neighbor. All rejoiced to know that they would permanently enjoy his pleasant company.

The colonel took up residence immediately upon assuming ownership of the small domain consisting of only two villages. He also gave a banquet for the close neighbors, and thereafter he immediately began to build, adding two beautiful wings to the sides of the house, planting avenues of trees and a pretty grove for recreation, all in the English taste. He pursued this work with the greatest zeal. Nevertheless, from time to to time his face was clouded. The baron observed this without, at first, showing that he did so, but in the following autumn he felt certain that the colonel's temper had altered and could then no longer remain silent. Sternheim came less frequently, talked less, and soon departed again. His servants regretted the strange melancholy afflicting their master.

The baron was the more troubled as his heart was also oppressed by the renewed sadness of his elder sister. He went to the colonel, found him alone and, engrossed in thought, embraced him with tender sadness, exclaiming, "Oh, my friend! How vain are even the noblest, the purest joys of our hearts! For long I lacked nothing but your presence; now that I see you, now that I hold you in my arms, I find you sad! Your heart, your confidence, are no longer mine. Have you perhaps yielded too much to the demands of friendship in making your home here? Dearest, best of friends, do not torture yourself! Your happiness is dearer to me than my own. I shall take back the estate; it will be precious to me because every part of it will renew for me your treasured memory and your image."

Here he paused; tears filled his eyes as they fastened on his friend's face. In it he saw mirrored a soul in the greatest agitation. The colonel stood up and embraced the baron, saying, "Noble P., never believe that my friendship, my trust toward you, are diminished; even less believe that I regret the decision to spend my days close to you. Oh, your nearness is dearer to me than you can imagine! I find that I must fight a passion which has attacked my heart for the first time. I had hoped to be sensible and magnanimous, but I have not yet become so to the extent which the state of my soul necessitates. But it is impossible for me to speak to you of that; my heart and solitude are the only confidants I can have."

The baron pressed him to his breast. "I know you to be truthful in all things," he said. "Thus I do not doubt your assurances of your undiminished friendship. But why do you come so rarely to see me? Why do you hurry away again so coldly?"

"Coldly, my friend! Coldly I hurry from your house? Oh P., if only you knew the burning longing that draws me to you, that keeps me for hours at my window, from which I see the dear house where all my desires, all my felicity dwell. Oh, P.!"

The baron became alarmed because the thought occurred to him that his friend might perhaps love his wife, and that he might be avoiding his house because he sought to gain control of himself. He determined to be watchful and more reserved.

The colonel sat quietly and the baron, too, sought to regain his composure. At last the latter began thus: "My friend, I hold your secret inviolable; I will not force it from your bosom; but you have given me cause to think that at least part of that secret concerns my house. May I not inquire after that part?"

"No, no! Ask me nothing and leave me to myself!"

The baron fell silent and departed, sad and pensive.

The following day, the colonel came, asked the baron's pardon for having let him return home so unfeelingly the previous day, and said that it had distressed him the whole evening. "Dear baron," he added, "honor and magnanimity tie my tongue. Do not doubt my heart and love me!"

He remained the whole day in P. Lady Sophia and Lady Charlotte were asked by their brother to do all they could to cheer his friend. But the colonel stayed for the most part near the old lady and the baron's wife. In the evening, Lady Charlotte played the lute, the baron and two of the servingmen accompanied her, and Lady Sophia was entreated so earnestly to sing that in the end she complied.

The colonel placed himself in a window where, with the curtain half drawn, he listened to the little family concert, and became so entranced that he failed to notice his friend's wife standing so close as to hear him say, "Oh, Sophia, why are you my friend's sister? Why do the advantages of your birth oppose the lofty, the tender inclination of my heart?"

The lady was dismayed. To avoid the embarrassment he would have felt had he thought she overheard him, she withdrew, happy to be able to allay the uneasiness that plagued her husband because of the colonel's melancholy. As soon as all had gone to bed, she spoke to him of her discovery. The baron now understood what the colonel had meant when he defended himself on account of the supposed coldness of which he had been accused.

"Would the colonel be as dear to you as a brother, as he is as my friend?" he asked his wife.

"Certainly my dearest! For should not the deserts of this upright man have as much value as the advantages of name and birth?"

"Worthy, noble half of my being," cried the baron; "then help me overcome the prejudices of my mother and Sophia."

"I fear their prejudices less than I fear a prior inclination which our dear Sophia may nurture in her heart. I do not know its object, but she loves and has loved for long already. Attempts at writing down her observations, laments against fate, against parting, which I have found in her escritoire, have convinced me of it. I have watched her, but have been able to discover nothing further."

"I shall speak with her," said the baron, "and see whether there may not be a chink through which her heart might be espied."

On the next morning, the baron went to see Lady Sophia, and after many kind inquiries about her health, he took her hands in his. "Dear, precious Sophia," said he, "you assure me of your well-being; why then this sorrowful face? Why the tone of grief? Why the fondness for solitude? Why do so many sighs escape this noble and kind heart? Oh, if you knew how much concern you have caused me during your long period of melancholy, you would not have closed your heart to me."

Here she was overwhelmed by her affection for him. She did not withdraw her hands; she pressed her brother's to her breast and laid her head on his shoulder. "Brother, you break my heart! I cannot bear the thought that I have caused you sorrow. I love you as my own life. I am happy. Bear with me and never talk to me of marriage."

"Why, my child? You would make a worthy man so happy!"

"And a worthy man would make me happy too; but I know—" Tears prevented her from saying more.

"Oh Sophia, do not obstruct the honest emotion of your soul. Pour out its sentiments into the faithful bosom of your brother. Child, I believe there is a man whom you love, with whom your heart has an alliance."

"No brother, my heart has no alliance—"

"Is this true, my Sophia?"

"Yes, my brother, yes. . . . " Here the baron folded her in his arms. "Oh, that you had the resolute, the beneficent soul of your mother!"

She was surprised. "Why, my brother? What do you mean? Have I done aught that is wrong?"

"Never my dear, never. But you could come to that if prejudice mattered more to you than virtue and reason."

"Brother, you confuse me. In what event would I renounce virtue and reason?"

"You must not take it thus. The case of which I am thinking is not contrary to virtue and reason, and yet they could both lose their claims with you."

"Brother, talk plainly; I am determined to answer according to my innermost sentiments."

"Sophia, the assurance that your heart is without alliance permits me to ask you what you would do if a man of wisdom and virtue were to love you and ask for your hand, but were not of ancient nobility."

At these last words she became frightened; she trembled and could not compose herself. The baron did not wish to torture her heart for long, but rather continued, "If this man were the friend to whom your brother owes the goodness and felicity of his heart—Sophia, what would you do?"

She did not speak but became thoughtful and by turns blushed and grew pale.

"I alarm you, my sister. The colonel loves you. This passion accounts for his sadness, for he is doubtful of being accepted. I confess to you freely that I wish I could recompense him, through you, for all the favors he has shown me. But if your heart is against it, then forget all I have said to you."

The young lady struggled to find courage but was silent a good while. Finally she asked the baron, "Brother, is it certain that the colonel loves me?" Then the baron told her all he had learned of the colonel's love through conversations with him and finally through the longings which his wife had overheard.

"My brother," said Sophia, "I am of a candid nature, and you so well deserve my entire trust that I shall not defer telling you that the colonel is the only man on earth whose wife I wish to become."

"The disparity of birth then is not objectionable to you?"

"Not at all; his noble heart, his learning, and his friendship for you make amends for his deficiency of birth."

"Noble-minded maiden! You gladden me by your decision, dearest Sophia. But why did you ask me to say nothing of marriage to you?"

"Because I feared you were talking of another," said she softly, while her burning face lay on her brother's shoulder.

He embraced her and kissed her hand. "This hand," he said, "will be a boon to my friend. From me he will receive it. But, my child, Mama and Charlotte will oppose you; will you remain steadfast?"

"Brother, you shall see that I have an English heart. But as I have answered all your questions, I must pose one, too: What did you think of my sadness, seeing that you asked me about it so often?"

"I thought there might be a secret love, and I feared its object because you were so secretive."

"Then my brother did not believe that the letters of his friend which he read to us, and all else which he told us of that excellent man, could make an impression on my heart?"

"Dear Sophia, was it then my friend's merit that troubled you so? Fortunate man, whom a noble maiden loves for his virtue! God bless my sister for her candor! Now I can cure my friend's heart of its consuming grief."

"Do all that can content him, only spare me in doing so; you know that a woman may not love unbidden."

"Calm yourself, my child; your honor is my own."

Here he left her and went to his wife, to inform her of the joyful discovery. Then he hastened to the colonel, whom he found sad and grave. Various attempts at conversation met but with brief response. A fatal restlessness was in all his gestures.

"Did I disturb you, colonel?" the baron asked in a voice that expressed the tenderest friendship of a young man toward his mentor, while he took the colonel's hand.

"Yes, dear baron, you have interrupted my decision to go away for a while."

"Travel? And—alone?"

"Dear P., I am in a frame of mind which makes my company unpleasant; I want to see what diversion may do."

"My dearest friend, may I not look into your heart? Can I do nothing for your peace of mind?"

"You have done enough for me. You are the joy of my life. What I lack now must be supplied by good sense and time."

"Sternheim, you spoke lately of a passion which you must overcome. I know you; your heart can nurture no indecent, no evil passion. It must be love that makes your days a torment."

"Never, P., never shall you know what causes my present grief."

"Worthy friend, I shall deceive you no longer. I know the object of your love. Your affection has found a witness; I am indeed fortunate: You love my Sophia." The baron put his arms around the colonel who was quite beside himself; he tried to disengage himself; he was uneasy.

"P., what are you saying? What are you asking me?"

"I want to know whether the hand of my sister is the felicity you desire."

"Impossible, for it would be a misfortune for you all."

"I have then your confession; but wherein lies the misfortune?"

"Yes, you have my confession. Your sister is the first woman toward whom my whole soul inclines, but I shall overcome that inclination. You shall not be accused of sacrificing to your friendship a proper respect for your forebears. Lady Sophia shall not on my account lose any claim to happiness and privilege. Swear to me that you will not say one word of this to her, or you see me today for the last time."

"You think nobly, my friend, but you must not become unjust. Your departure would sadden not only me, but Sophia and my wife. You shall be my brother!"

"P., you torture me more with this encouragement than does the impossibility which counters my wishes."

"Friend, you have the voluntary, tender consent of my sister. You have my wife's and my own best wishes. We have thought of all that you can think of. Shall I *beg* you to become the husband of Sophia von P.?"

"Oh God, how severely you judge my heart! You believe then that it is stubborn pride that makes me irresolute?"

"I shall not answer. Embrace me and call me brother. Tomorrow you shall be so. Sophia is yours. Do not look upon her as Lady P. but rather as an amiable and virtuous young woman whose possession will felicitate all your days to come and joyfully accept this boon from the hand of your faithful friend."

"Sophia mine? Mine in free affection? Enough! You bestow all; I can do nothing other than freely renounce all."

"Renounce? After being assured that you are loved?—Oh my sister, how badly have I served your excellent heart!"

"What are you saying, P.? And how can you tear my heart with such a reproach? If you are high-minded, shall I not be so, too? Shall I close my eyes to the disapproving looks of the neighboring nobility?"

"Yes, you shall—when your joy and happiness is in question."

"What then would you have me do?"

"Let me return home with the request that I speak with my mother of my wish, and come to us when I send you word."

The colonel could say no more. He embraced the baron, who returned home and went directly to his mother, who was attended by the two young ladies and his wife. He conducted the older young lady to her room because he wanted to give her the account of his visit in private, and asked her to leave him for a while with their lady mother and Charlotte. On rejoining them, he made a formal proposal on behalf of his friend. The old lady was taken aback; he observed it and said, "Dearest mother, all your concerns are well-founded. The noble class must be perpetuated through noble alliances. But Sternheim's virtues have been the foundation of all great families. People are not wrong in thinking that great attributes of the soul could be inherited by daughters and sons and that every father should, therefore, seek the daughter of a nobleman for a noble son. I, too, do not really wish to advocate that marriage outside one's condition become the custom; but here is a special case, a case which rarely occurs: Sternheim's merits, together with the character of a genuine colonel, a title which should itself be considered noble, justify the hope I have given him."

"In truth, my son, I have scruples. But the man has earned my entire esteem. I should like to see him happy."

"My wife, what say you?"

"That in the case of a man such as this one, a justifiable exception may be made. I shall gladly call him brother."

"Not I," said Lady Charlotte.

"Why not, my dear?"

"Because this fine match is being made at the expense of my happiness."

"How so, Charlotte?"

"Because who will seek out our house for a marriage if the elder daughter has been thus thrown away?"

"Thrown away? On a man of virtue and honor, on a friend of your brother's?"

"Perhaps you have another university friend of like virtue who will apply for me in order to reinforce his budding honor, and you will then once again have ready reasons for your consent."

"Charlotte, my daughter, what language!"

"I must use it because no one in the whole family thinks of me and our forefathers."

"I see, Charlotte; and when one thinks of one's ancestors, one may insult one's brother and a noble-minded gentleman?" said the young Baroness P.

"I have already heard the exception you make on behalf of the 'noble-minded gentleman.' Other families will also make exceptions if a son of theirs should want Charlotte for a wife."

"Charlotte, he who renounces you because of Sternheim is not worthy of your hand or of a connection with me. You see that I am proud of the 'wicked' younger sister, even though I 'throw away' the 'good' older one on a university friend."

"The younger sister must certainly be wicked if she does not want to be used to repay a debt."

"How unreasonably malicious my sister can be! You have nothing to fear from my proposals. I shall speak for no one but a Sternheim, and for him a character like yours is not sufficiently noble, even if you were a princess."

"Gracious Mama, do you hear how I am mistreated because of that miserable fellow?"

"You have abused your brother's patience. Can you not advance your objections more calmly?"

She was about to speak, but her brother interrupted her: "Charlotte, say no more; the expression 'miserable fellow' has cost you your brother! The affairs of my house no longer concern you. Your heart dishonors the forebears of whom you are so proud. Oh, how few would be the nobility if only those could call themselves noble who could prove their claims by possessing the virtues of the noble souls which the founders of their houses had."

"Dear son, do not become too zealous. It really would be unfortunate if our daughters were so easily inclined to marry below themselves."

"There is no danger of that. Rarely does there exist a Sophia who loves a man merely because of his good sense and magnanimity."

Lady Charlotte here withdrew.

"But did not you yourself once cite your beloved English, who are less forgiving of daughters who marry outside their condition than of sons, because a daughter must give up her name and bear that of her husband, consequently demeaning herself?"

"That is quite true, but in England my friend would have been exempted a thousand times from conforming to this principle, and the maiden who loved him would have been renowned as a high-minded young woman."

"I well see, my son, that this alliance is a closed question. But have you considered that people will say you are sacrificing your sister to an exaggerated friendship and that I am acting the stepmother in consenting?"

"Dear Mama, let it be so! Our motive will console us; and the happiness of my sister, together with the merits of my friend, will be so apparent that people will cease to condemn us."

Lady Sophia was then brought in by her brother. She prostrated herself before her mother. The good lady embraced her. "Dear daughter," said she, "your brother has assured me that this bond accords with your wishes; otherwise I should not have consented. It is true, the man lacks nothing but a gentle birth. But—God bless you both!"

In the meantime, the baron had left to find the colonel, who entered the room almost beside himself; but he went straight to the old lady, kissed her hands on bended knee, and said with manly grace, "Madam, ever believe that I look upon your consent as a condescending goodness; be assured also that I shall never prove unworthy of that goodness."

She was kind enough to say, "I am pleased, colonel, that your merits have found a reward in my house."

Then he kissed the hands of his friend's wife. "How much gratitude and reverence do I owe to the generous first advocate of my heart's desire!"

"Not at all, colonel. I am proud to have contributed to the felicity of your heart; your brotherly friendship shall be my reward."

He wanted to speak to his friend who, however, motioned him toward Lady Sophia. He knelt silently by her, and finally the noble man spoke: "Madam, my heart was created to reverence virtue. How was it possible to see an excellent soul like yours, attended by all external charms, without my feelings being enlivened into wishes? I would have smothered those wishes, but your brother's faithful friendship emboldened me to hope for your affection. You have not spurned me. May God reward your loving heart and let me never lose these virtues that have gained me your respect!"

Lady Sophia replied only with a bow and gave him her hand with a sign to rise. Thereupon the baron approached them and, holding both by the hand, led them to his mother.

"Gracious Mama," he said, "in me, nature has given you a son by whom you are entirely honored and loved; in my friend, fate has given you a second son who is deserving of all your esteem and kindness. You have often wished that our Sophia might be happy. Her union to this brilliant, worthy man will fulfill that maternal wish. Lay your hands on the hands of your children; I know that your maternal blessing is sacred and precious to their hearts."

The lady placed her hands on theirs and said, "My children, if God vouchsafe you as many blessings and pleasures as I shall ask of Him, you will lack nothing."

Now the baron embraced the colonel as his brother, and also the happy bride, whom he thanked tenderly for the sentiments she had shown to his friend. The colonel dined with them. Lady Charlotte did not come to the table. The wedding took place without ostentatious display.

Several days after the ceremony, a letter was written by

Lady Sternheim to Her Mother

Although the bad weather and a slight indisposition prevent me from attending my gracious Mama in person, I shall not deny my heart the great pleasure of conversing with you by letter.

The company of my dear husband and the consideration of the duties assigned to me within the circle of my new life truly compensate me for the loss of all other amusements and pleasures, but they also vividly renew all the noble sentiments my heart has ever nurtured. Among these belongs the grateful love which your goodness has deserved from me for these many years, during which I have found in your excellent soul all the faithful and tender care that I could have received from my real mother.

And yet I must confess that your gracious consent to my union with Sternheim is the greatest kindness you have shown me. This has secured my life's whole happiness, which I neither seek nor recognize elsewhere than in circumstances wherein one can live according to one's character and inclinations. Such was my wish, and Providence has granted it to me: a man whose mind and heart are worthy of my entire admiration; a moderate but independent fortune whose amount and income suffice to maintain our household in noble moderation, yet agreeably to our rank, and that further affords our hearts the joy of succoring many families of industrious peasants and of encouraging them with small gifts.

Permit me to recount to you a conversation I had with the dear man whose name I bear.

After my gracious Mama, my brother, sister, and my sister-in-law were gone, I realized, so to speak for the first time, the whole significance of my union. The change in my name indicated to me the change in my duties which I saw ranged before me. These reflections, which wholly occupied my mind, were, I think, made more vivid by external matters: a different home, the absence of all those with whom I had lived from my childhood, the first agitation at their departure, etc. All this gave me I know not what grave appearance, which my husband noticed. With an expression of gentle joy he came to me as I sat thoughtfully in my closet, stopped in the middle of the room, looked at me with tender solicitude, and said, 'You are thoughtful, dearest wife, may I disturb you?'

I could not answer, but gave him my hand. He kissed it; and after he had pulled up a chair close to me, he began: "I revere your whole family;

but I must say that I welcome this day, from whence I can dedicate all the sentiments of my heart solely to my wife. Give me your trust as you have given me your esteem, and believe that you will never be unhappy with the man whom you have so generously preferred to all others. Your father's house is not far from us, and here in this one your magnanimous heart will take pleasure in making me, our servants, and our tenants happy.

"I know that for many years you had charge of the economy of your mother's house. Let me ask you to keep that office and all that pertains to it in this house also. You will greatly oblige me by doing so, since I intend to employ all my leisure for the good of our little domain. I view that employment not only as the exercise of benevolence and justice, but I intend also to determine whether the circumstances of my dependants might be improved by a different distribution of the farms, by better management of the schools, tillage, and animal husbandry.

"I have acquired some knowledge of all these matters; for in the fortunate middle class of human society into which I was born, the enlargement of the mind and the exercise of most virtues are considered not only as duties but also as the basis for our prosperity. I shall always gratefully remember these advantages because it is to them that I owe the inestimable felicity of your love. Had I been born to the rank and fortune that I now possess, perhaps my eagerness to make a name for myself would not have been so great. But the most valuable gift which Providence bestowed on me in the past years of my life was the father it gave me, because in other circumstances I certainly would have lacked the faithful and wise guide that he was to me in my youth.

"Because of his prudence and his knowledge of my mind, and perhaps of the human heart generally, he concealed from me the greatest part of his wealth, first to prevent the negligence with which only sons of the rich apply themselves to learning, and further to avoid the temptations to which this kind of young person is exposed, and because he thought that, when once I had learned to employ well the powers of my soul for myself and others, in times to come I would also know how to make wise and noble use of these earthly goods.

"Therefore, my father sought to make me good and happy through virtue and knowledge before he gave me the means by which I could gain for myself and distribute to others all the varieties of material wealth and pleasure. The love and exercise of virtue, he said, bestow on their possessor a happiness that is independent of fate and men. At the same time through the example of his noble actions and through the instruction and delight that his counsel and companionship afford, he becomes a moral benefactor of his fellow men.

"Through such principles and an education founded upon them, he made me a worthy friend for your brother and, as I flatter myself, a worthy possessor of your heart. Half of my life is now over. Thank God it has been marked neither by extraordinary misfortunes nor by transgressions against my duties! The blessed moment when the kind and noble heart of Sophia P. was moved to favor me was the moment when the design for the true happiness of my remaining days was complete. Tender gratitude and reverence for you will be the constant inclination of my soul.''

Here he paused, kissed both my hands, and asked my pardon for talking so much.

I could do no less than assure him that I had listened with pleasure, and I asked him to continue because I believed he wished to say more to me.

"I do not want to tire you, dearest wife; but I wish you to see my whole heart. Since you seem to wish it, I shall touch on just a few more points.

"At each step of my studies and military service, I have made it a habit to inquire carefully into all the duties to myself, my superiors, and others that I was obligated to fulfill there. According to the understanding thus gained, I apportioned my attention and time. My ambition urged me to do promptly and thoroughly all that was required of me. When it was done, I also considered the diversions which were best suited to my disposition. I have applied similar reflections to my present circumstances, and now I find myself charged with four kinds of obligations.

"The first, to my amiable wife, is easy for me because my whole heart will always be ready to fulfill it. The second is to your family and the rest of the nobility, whom I will show through my actions—without flattery or servility—that I was not unworthy of the hand of Sophia P. and of being accepted into the baronial class. The third obligation is to the persons of the class from which I was raised. I will never give them cause to think that I have forgotten my origin. They shall see neither pride nor base humility in me. Fourth, there are the duties to my subordinates, for whose well-being I shall take care in all ways, so that the subjection into which fate has placed them is not only tolerable but pleasant to their hearts; and I shall strive to conduct myself in a way that they shall gladly accede to the distinction that temporal fortune has made between me and them.

"The worthy pastor in P. has undertaken to provide me with a young man to be curate of my parish, with whose help I would like to fulfill a desire I have long cherished for several changes in the usual way of instructing the people.

"I am thoroughly convinced of the worth and value of the great truths of our religion; but the fact that their recitation has little effect on the hearts of most listeners has made me doubt the method of instruction, rather than making me suspect that the human heart is so absolutely inclined to evil as some believe. How often, after hearing the sermon of a famous man, have

I compared the moral profit I derived from it and that which the common man might have gained, and found it in truth empty for the latter. Those parts that the preacher dedicated to the glory of learning or to the detailed but not too intelligible exposition of various speculative propositions were useless for the improvement of most persons, and certainly not from any lack of good will on their part. For if I, who from early youth had exercised the powers of my intellect and acquainted myself with abstract ideas, had trouble finding useful applications for those parts of the sermon, how then would the workman and his children fare with them? Because I am far removed from that ungracious sort of pride that has caused persons of fortune and rank to believe that the common man must neither be given enlightened concepts of religion nor must his understanding be broadened, it is my wish that my pastor, out of genuine kindness toward his neighbor and the recognition of the whole extent of his obligations, shall impart to the congregation entrusted to him that measure of understanding that they need for the joyful and eager discharge of their duties toward God, their superiors, their neighbors, and themselves.

"The humble man is born with the same desire for happiness and pleasure as the great man and like him is often led astray by that desire. Therefore, I also wish them imbued with proper concepts of happiness and pleasure. The way to their hearts, I believe, can best be found through observations about the physical world, which are most likely to move them, as every glance of their eyes, every step of their feet, lead them in that direction. Once their hearts are opened through recognizing the benevolent hand of their Creator and made content through historical comparisons of their homes and circumstances with those of other people who are, like them, children of God, then one can also show them the moral side of the world and the obligations that they must fulfill to achieve a tranquil life for themselves and their loved ones and to assure their eternal well-being.

"Should my pastor be satisfied merely with a show of good behavior during the final days of his parishioners, I shall be very dissatisfied with him. And if he intends to safeguard the improvement of their souls merely with so-called fire-and-brimstone sermons without opening and convincing their minds, he will not remain my pastor for long. If he directs his notice more to their diligence in church attendance than their actions in daily life, I shall not consider him to be a true friend of mankind nor a good shepherd.

"I shall take great care with the school to ensure that it is well-appointed and that the schoolmaster receives proper compensation as well as possesses the forbearance that the weakness of childhood necessitates.

"A twofold catechism shall be taught there, namely the one on the established duties of a Christian and with each article a clear, simple application to their daily lives; and in addition a 'catechism' of thorough knowl-

edge of farming and gardening, of animal husbandry, and the management
of woodlands and forests, and such things as the obligations of their calling
and of benevolence toward their offspring. In general, I wish to see my
dependants act kindly toward their neighbors before they lay claim to a reputation for piety.

"I shall leave to the official whom I found here his salary and the
management of the accounts. But to administer justice, to superintend compliance with the laws, and to supervise the police and the people's indus-
triousness, I shall use the valiant young man whose acquaintance I made in
P. I shall seek to obtain my subjects' trust in him and myself, in order to
learn their circumstances and manage all their affairs like a true father and
guardian. Good counsel, friendly admonition, and reprobation aimed at improvement not oppression shall be the means I employ; and the generous
hopes of my heart would be sadly betrayed if my careful exercise of the
master's duties and an equal effort by the pastor and officials, in addition to
the example of goodness and benevolence, did not have a beneficial effect
on my subordinates' hearts."

Here he ceased and asked my pardon for having spoken so much and
so long.

"You must be tired, dearest Sophia," said he, while putting his arm
around me.

What could I do in the fullness of my heart but embrace him with tears
of joy.

"Tired, my dearest husband? How could I be tired by the happy prospect of future days marked by your virtue and charity."

Dearest Mama, how blessed is my lot! God keep you long to witness it!

There was no one happier than Sternheim and his wife, whose very
footprints were revered by their subjects. Justice and beneficence were practiced in equal measure within the boundaries of their small domain. Agri-
cultural experiments were first conducted on the master's lands, then taught
to the people; and the first peasant to show himself willing to change was
given the means necessary to do so. Sternheim was well aware that without
such inducements the peasants would never undertake even the most useful
change if it called for the loss of money or land.

"What I gave them at first," he said, "will later be returned to me
through the increased tithe, and the experience will best convince the good
people that I meant them well."

Though it takes me yet farther from the main subject of my narrative,
I must give you news of the poorhouse at S. (to my mind a good institu-
tion), as an example of the universally useful and beneficent acts which the

worthy pair derived part of their felicity from planning and executing. I can do this no better than by sending you an extract from a letter by Baron P. to his mother:

How faithfully does my friend fulfill the promise which I made you of the happiness of our Sophia! How pleasant is one's entrance into this house, where the noblest simplicity and natural order give an air of grandeur to the whole establishment! The servants are intent upon the discharge of their duties with cheerful deference and industry; the master and mistress wear a blissful expression that springs from kindness and sagacity—both of them blessing me for my resolute intercession in favor of their union.

And how great a contrast there is between my brother's two small villages and all those larger and more populous ones that I saw on my return journey from the court! Through the cheerful and diligent industry of their inhabitants, they both resemble two well-organized beehives; and Sternheim is amply rewarded for his care in distributing the acreage more equitably, by means of which each of his subordinates received exactly as much as he can cultivate with his own strength and means. But the newly purchased seat of the Count of A., situated exactly between the two villages, is intended for the execution of a still more blessed inspiration.

It has been converted into a poorhouse for his subjects. On one side, downstairs, lives a valiant schoolmaster who has become too old to supervise effectively the instruction of the children and is now appointed to maintain good order and oversee the work. Upstairs is the apartment of the physician charged with caring for the sick of the poorhouse and the two villages. In the summertime, all must work, as their strength permits, in an adjacent seed nursery and the vegetable garden that belongs to it. The yield of both is intended for the poor. On rainy days and in winter, the women must spin flax, and suitable men, wool, both of which will be used for their own and other needy persons' linen and apparel. They will receive well-prepared, healthful food.

The master of the house will pray with them in the mornings and evenings. The women will work in one and the men in the other room, both of which will be heated by one stove. The meals will be taken in the women's room. It is the larger one, because they must set the table and do the sewing and laundering. That poor widow or elderly spinster who has the best reputation for industry and good conduct in the village shall be the first overseer and director, as the poor man of like reputation shall be among the men.

For their sleeping quarters, the upper story of the house has been divided by a solid wall into two parts, each of which has five rooms with two beds each and everything necessary for each person. On one side, towards the garden, are the men; on the other, towards the village, the women. There will be two persons to each room, so that if one should meet with a mishap, the other can render or seek aid. From the middle of the window a wooden partition will run from the ceiling to the floor, several feet beyond the length of the bedsteads, so that both can, in a manner, be private; and also, so that if one grows ill, the other may better preserve his portion of wholesome air. Two separate stairs will lead to the two parts, so that no impropriety may occur.

The workmen who must attend to the cultivation of the fields will also be set under the worthy master, and since it is intended that they shall receive better wages than elsewhere, the best and most knowledgeable workers in farming matters will be selected, with preference given to those of good reputation.

Modest alms shall be dispensed to the vagrant poor, wages for the employment offered them, and they shall be permitted to stop working an hour earlier than is customary, so that while it is still daylight they can reach the nearest village outside the domain—an hour and a quarter removed. At his own expense, Sternheim has built a road to it, straight as an arrow and with trees planted along its sides, as he has done also from one of his villages to the other. During the night, the appointed watchmen of the two localities must walk all the way to the poorhouse by turns and call out the hours.

My sister intends to establish a small foundling home for poor orphans nearby, to earn grace for the child she carries under her loving, benevolent heart. My thought, gracious Mama, is to create such an almshouse within my larger and more far-flung domains, and, if possible, to encourage several other noblemen to do likewise.

Vagrant or local beggers receive nothing from any of the farmers. As their means and free will dictate, the latter merely give alms to the house after each harvest, and in this manner all the poor are cared for humanely and without abuse of their benefactors. Drunkards, gamblers, profligates, and idlers are assessed a fine—partly in forced labor and partly in money—which is used for the benefit of the poorhouse. Next month, four men and five women will take up residence in the house. My sister goes there each day to make the final preparations.

In his Sunday sermon, the pastor will preach on the subject of true charity and the worthy poor, and will read to the whole congregation the particulars of the endowment and the duties of those who will be admitted there. Then he will call those who have been admitted by their names before the altar and will admonish them, particularly regarding the proper use of this benefit and regarding their conduct toward God and their neighbor in the final and quiet days of their lives. Likewise, he will admonish the physician, the master of the house, and the housekeeper as to their duties. I am certain we will all come from P. for this event.

The neighboring nobility respected and loved Colonel Sternheim so much that they asked him to be host to several young noblemen who had returned from their travels and were now to be married in order to carry on their line. It was desired, therefore, that they observe and learn the actual management of a nobleman's estates. Among them was the Young Count Loebau, who had the opportunity to meet Lady Charlotte P.—now at last contented—at the Sternheims' and to unite with her in marriage.

Sternheim accepted quite gladly the noble task of instructing these young gentlemen in the proper governance of one's dependents. His humanity lightened his labor with the thought that he was perhaps instilling into them the necessary compassion for the lowly and unfortunate, whose hard and toilsome lives are so often burdened and embittered by the harshness and pride of the great.

Convinced that example is more effective than lengthy conversations, he took the young men everywhere with him and conducted himself before them as the occasion demanded. He explained why he had ordered this, forbidden that, or had made this or that other decision; and, according to his knowledge of each one's estate, he added little applications for them individually.

They witnessed all his employments and shared in his amusements. During the latter, he often earnestly implored them never to seek amusement at the expense of their poor dependants, for which the hunt offered especially ample opportunity. He called it a decent diversion which, however, a benevolent and humane master should always seek to combine with his people's well-being.

He sought also to imbue them with the love of reading; and history in particular afforded him the opportunity to speak of the moral world, its evils and mutability, and to explain to them the duties of service at Court and in the wars, and to exercise their mind in reflection and judgment.

"The history of the moral world," said he, "fits us to associate with human beings—to improve them, support them, and be content with our lot; but the observation of the physical world makes us good creatures, according to the will of our Creator. By showing us our weakness, while on the other hand teaching us to admire His greatness, goodness, and wisdom, we learn to love and revere Him nobly. Furthermore, these observations console and divert us in the various troubles and vexations which—in the moral world—are often heaped more copiously on the heads of the great and wealthy than on the cottage of the peasant who is oppressed by few other cares than for his sustenance."

Thus he alternated between discourse and example. In his house they saw how happy is the union of a worthy man with a virtuous woman. They saw them show affectionate and gentle regard toward each other, and observed how the servants revered them and stood ready to lay down their lives for their gracious as well as grave master and mistress.

Sternheim was also pleased that all these young gentlemen became grateful and devoted friends who, in their letters to him, always sought his advice. The association with the admirable Baron P., who often gave little fêtes for them, had contributed much to their perfection.

His wife had presented him with a daughter, who grew up very prettily and—as Sternheim had the misfortune of losing her mother in childbed together with a newborn son—she was from her ninth year her father's consolation and his sole joy on earth. This was the more true after Baron P., whose health had been weakened through a fall from his horse, died a few months later without issue. In his last will he had not only provided well for his excellent wife, but had also, in accordance with the law of the land, named as his heirs the Countess of Loebau, his younger sister, and the young Sophia von Sternheim, the daughter of his elder sister. This seemed unjust to the count and countess but was valid nevertheless.

Almost completely bowed by grief over the untimely death of her son, the old Baroness of P. took up residence with Sternheim and undertook to supervise the young lady. The colonel comforted her soul through his respectful affection and the example he set in his patient submission to fate. The high-minded parson and his daughters were almost the only company in which they took pleasure.

Nevertheless, young Sophia enjoyed the most excellent education of her mind and heart. A daughter of the pastor who was of the same age was given her for a companion, partly to excite competition in their learning and partly to prevent the young lady from gathering only somber impressions in her early youth, which might easily have occurred in the company of her grandmother and father. For both of them often wept over their losses; and then Sternheim would lead the twelve-year-old lady to the picture of her mother and would speak of her virtue and goodness of heart with so much emotion that the young lady, kneeling by his side, sobbed and often wished to die in order to be with her mother. This made the colonel fear that her sensitive soul might develop an overly strong inclination toward melancholy tenderness and, through overirritability of the nerves, might become unable to bear pain and sorrow. Thus he sought to control himself and show his daughter how to bear the misfortunes which usually wound the best persons most deeply.

Because the young lady displayed a fine talent for learning, he cultivated it with the study of the several parts of philosophy, history, and languages, among which she learned English to perfection. In music she achieved perfection on the lute and in singing. Dancing—as much as a lady should know of it—was an art that rather received perfection from her than gave it to her, for as everyone said, the indescribable grace which the young lady showed in all her movements gave to her dancing that distinction which the highest degree of art could not otherwise have attained.

Besides these daily exercises, she learned with uncommon ease all womanly tasks; and from her sixteenth year she was given the management of the entire household, her mother's diaries and account books being given to her as models. An innate love of order and the active life, heightened by an enthusiastic devotion to the memory of her mother, whose likeness she wanted to re-create in herself, brought her to the utmost perfection in this endeavor as well. When anyone mentioned her industry and accomplishments, her modest reply was: "Willing faculties, good example, and loving guidance have made me as accomplished as a thousand others could be, too, if only all circumstances had united for their good as they did for mine." Incidentally, in her soul was a particular inclination toward everything English, and her one wish was that sometime her father might make a journey to England and present her to her grandmother's relations.

Thus Lady Sophia blossomed forth until after her nineteenth year, when she had the misfortune of losing her worthy father to a consuming illness. With a sorrowful heart he commended her to Count Loebau and the excellent pastor in S. as her guardians. He addressed the following letter to the pastor a few weeks before his demise:

Col. Sternheim to the Pastor at S.

Soon I shall be reunited with the best half of me. My house and my Sophia's fortunes are provided for; that was the last task left for me to do for her. Her good and fruitful education, the first and most important duty of a faithful father, I have—as I can testify—never neglected. Her soul's innate love of virtue makes me certain that you, as the paternal friend who will take my place, will not be exposed to the worries and annoyances that common-thinking girls cause their families. Despite all the tenderness that she has inherited from her mother, love in particular will gain little power over her unless destiny were to bring her a man who was as virtuous as she could imagine.*

I ask you, dear friend, to ensure that the dear girl's high-minded heart will not be conquered by _seeming_ virtue. She seizes on the good in her fellow man with such eagerness and glides over the defects with so much forbearance that I am concerned for her solely on that account. No human

---

*The course and the whole context of this narration affords us an interpretation of this expression. Without a doubt it is meant to express nothing other than a man resembling, even in the smallest details, the special ideal of virtue and moral perfection that had developed in her soul [Wieland].

soul will be made unhappy by her, for I know that she would sacrifice her own good a thousand times to that of her neighbor, before burdening others with even a minute's discomfort, even if she could purchase her whole life's happiness by doing so. But as she is all sensibility, many have the terrible power to wound her.

I have until now concealed my fears about Countess Loebau's character, but I tremble at the thought that my Sophia will be with her. The outward meekness and kindness of that woman do not reside in her heart; the charmingly engaging wit, the refined, obliging tone which the court gave her hide many moral faults. I never wanted to teach my daughter distrust of this lady because I thought it ignoble and, as long as I enjoyed good health, unnecessary. But if under the burden of age and sorrow my dear mother-in-law should succumb, too, then take my Sophia into your protection! God will help lighten this care for you, because I hope He will hear the last prayer of a father who implores no riches and greatness but virtue and wisdom for his child.

I can no longer anticipate or prevent anything. Thus I commend her to Divine Goodness and to the faithful hand of a tried friend. And yet I part more easily from the whole world than from the thoughts of my daughter. I remember a conversation between us about the power of the impressions we receive in our youth. I am certainly sensible of one of them, with all the force that circumstance adds to it. My father had deeply impressed upon me two things: namely, the certainty of retribution and the beneficence of our example. The arguments he employed in this were so sublime, his instruction so loving, that they were necessarily fixed in my sensitive soul.

Of the first I have long been convinced because he often told me that I would be punished or rewarded through my own children for the sorrow or delight I caused him. Thank God that my conduct toward my venerable father has earned me the blessing of an obedient, virtuous child which lets me, near my life's end, remember with pleasure that I too crowned my father's last days with the most perfect delight a father's heart can feel, namely to be able to say: "You have never grieved me through any act of disobedience; your love of virtue, your diligence in exercising your intellect and making it useful have filled my heart with joy whenever I looked on you. God bless you for that and reward your heart for the comfort the sight of you gives your father through the certainty that, in my son, I leave to my fellow men a worthy member of society."

I, too, feel this delight now, my friend, because I can give the same testimonial to my daughter in whom I have enjoyed yet another sad felicity. I say "sad felicity" because as the true likeness of my sainted wife, she renewed in me—each time I beheld her—the memory of my happiest days and the pain of her mother's loss. How often misery snatched me away from table or company when during the last two years, in which she had attained the full stature of her mother and wore the clothes that I preferred, I perceived in her the singular tone of voice, the gestures, and all the kindness and amiable cheerfulness of her mother!

May God grant that this example of Divine justice will be passed down by my daughter to her remotest descendants, for I have spoken of this as often to her as my father did to me.

With vivid sadness I recall the last hours of this noble man and his conversations during the days of his progressive illness. The dear young lady could weep but little as she knelt beside her father's bed, but an expression of deepest grief was in her face and attitude. With his eyes upon her—one of his hands in hers—there came a sigh from her father: "My Sophia!" Then the lady's arms stretched toward heaven without a sound, but an inconsolable, pleading soul was mirrored in all her features. Oh, how this sight of solemn grief, of filial love, of virtue, and of submission, rent all our hearts!

"Sophia, nature does us no injustice; sixty years is not too soon. Death is no evil for me; it unites my spirit with its loving Creator, and my heart with that of your worthy mother. Grant me this happiness at the expense of the pleasure that a prolongation of your father's life would have given you."

She overcame her sorrow; it was she, herself, who attended her father most carefully and calmly. He observed this example of self-command and begged her to console his last few days by demonstrating the fruit of his efforts for her in the composure of her soul. She did everything he asked.

"Best of fathers, you have taught me how to live, and now you are teaching me how to die. God make you my guardian spirit and the witness of all my actions and thoughts! I want to be worthy of you!"

When he had expired and his whole house was filled with his weeping subjects, and his death chamber with kneeling, sobbing house servants, the young lady by his bedside, kissing his hands, was speechless and—now kneeling, now rising up—wrung her hands. O my friend, how deeply the memory of this day engraved itself upon my heart! How much profit can a sensitive soul glean at the deathbed of a just man!

My father looked on silently; he was himself so deeply moved that he could not speak immediately. At last he took the lady by her hand and said, "May God bequeath you your father's virtue for which he is now gone to be rewarded. Preserve in these affected hearts" (here he pointed to us) "the blessed memory of your honorable parents by your efforts to walk in their footsteps!"

The old lady was present, too, and my father made her the pretext for getting the young lady out of the room, by asking her to conduct her grandmother to bed. When the young lady began to leave, all of us made way for her. She looked at us and tears rolled down her cheeks; then all pressed about and kissed her hands and clothing, and the motive was surely not to recommend themselves to the heiress but to prove their reverence for the mortal remains of that best of masters whom we saw living in her.

My father and the steward arranged the interment, and never had there been such a funeral. Col. von Sternheim had directed that it take place quietly in the night because he wanted to shield his Sophia from the torture of seeing him laid to rest. But the church was filled with people, all solemnly dressed, and the chancel was illuminated as the sad occasion demanded. All wanted to see their master, their benefactor, once more. Aged men and youths alike wept, blessed him, and kissed his hands and feet, the shroud, and the lid of the casket; and they prayed God that He would reward the daughter for all the good that the father had done them.

Long afterwards all was sadness at S., and Lady Sophia was so quiet, so serious, that my father was uneasy on her account, especially as the old lady—who had straightway said that this event had broken her heart—grew weaker from day to day. The young lady tended her with such love that she said, "Sophia, your heart possesses all your mother's meekness and kindness, and you have the mind of your father. Thus you are the most fortunate creature on earth, for Providence has united the virtues of your parents in you! You are now left on your own and you begin using your independence by exercising benevolence toward your grandmother; for to cheer old age and tend it lovingly is even a more benevolent deed than to give gold to the poor."

She also commended her most warmly to the Count and Countess of Loebau when they paid her a visit before her end. Both of them were, in appearance, very obliging and wanted to take her with them forthwith, but she asked to spend her year of mourning at our house.

During this time the close friendship developed that she ever after entertained toward my sister Emilia. She often went to church with her to visit the tombstone of her parents. There she knelt, prayed, and spoke of them. "I have no relatives, other than these remains," she said; "Countess Loebau is not related to me; her soul is foreign to me, quite foreign. I love her only because she is my late uncle's sister."

My father sought to represent this antipathy to her as an injustice, and was generally at pains to renew her education, and especially to develop her talent for music. He often told us that it was good and true that all the virtues were linked together and that, therefore, modesty, too, belonged with the rest. "What would have become of Lady Sophia Sternheim," he asked, "if she had been as fully aware of her virtues as she was possessed of them?"

The Sternheim steward, a worthy man, married my eldest sister at this time; and his brother, a parson who visited him, took my Emilia away with him. Our young lady began corresponding with her, and so I can let her speak for herself more often from now on.

First, however, I must paint you a picture of my young lady, but you must not expect a perfect beauty! She was somewhat taller than average, of superlative proportions, her face an oval with a soulful expression, beautiful brown eyes full of spirit and goodness, a beautiful mouth, and fine teeth. Her forehead was high and somewhat too large for perfect beauty, and yet one could not wish it to be different for her face. There was so much grace in all her features, so much that was noble in her deportment, that wherever she appeared she drew all glances to herself. Every kind of dress suited her well, and I heard my Lord Seymour say that in each fold there nestled its own particular grace.

The beauty of her light-brown hair, which reached to the ground, was unsurpassable. Her voice was captivating, her expressions refined without seeming artificial. In short, her mind and character gave her an inimitably noble and gently charming air. For, although she practiced the utmost modesty in selecting material for her clothing, yet she was always singled out, no matter how numerous was the throng of ladies.

Such she was when her aunt presented her at the court of D. I need mention only one among the preparations for this journey, to which my father helped persuade her. She had painted enameled likenesses of her father and mother, and fashioned them into bracelets which never left her wrists. She wanted to have these reset, and a goldsmith had to come, with whom she conferred in private.

The likenesses were returned set with gems, and two days before her departure, she took my Emilia with her to her parents' tomb, where she took solemn leave. She renewed her vows of virtue and finally loosened her bracelets, wherein she had had the likenesses set over a hollow space with secret clasps in the center. She opened them and filled the small spaces with earth which she gathered from the tomb. Tears rolled down her cheeks while she did so, and Emilia said, "Dear Lady, what are you about? Why this earth?"

"My Emilia," she answered, "I do only what was always regarded a virtue by the wisest and most noble persons: to honor the dust of the righteous; and I believe it was a sensitive heart, like mine, that in later times began the practice of venerating relics. This dust, my dear, which covered the sacred remains of my parents, is dearer to me than the whole world; and when I am far from here, it will be the most precious thing I possess."

My sister was uneasy about this and told us that a premonition of disaster came over her; she feared that she would never again see the young lady. My father quieted us, and yet he, too, became alarmed when he heard that the lady had gone from house to house in the villages that belonged to her, encouraging the people lovingly, giving them presents, and exhorting them to industry and righteousness.[4] She had increased the charitable allowances for widows, orphans, the aged, and the infirm. She had warmly admonished the schoolmaster, augmenting his stipend, and had instituted prizes for the children. She had presented my brother-in-law, the steward, with a snuff box and my sister with a ring as mementos of her, and had asked the former to show true kindness and justice to her dependants. On hearing this account we all wept. My father consoled us by saying that people of melancholy and affectionate disposition characteristically gave their actions a certain solemnity. He said he was pleased that she entered the great world with such strong impressions of what is truly noble and good—that world where, after all, many of these sensibilities would be weakened. Unnoticeably, through an admixture of thoughtlessness and brilliant gaiety around her and through her increased knowledge of the human heart, her soul's enthusiasm would there be moderated and kept within proper bound.

My Emilia received her friend's picture and a pretty little box which contained money for her dowry. The lady left her manservant behind because he was married and because the Count of Loebau had written that his people would wait on her.

A few days later, her uncle the count came to fetch her, and I accompanied her as she requested. Her farewell from my father was moving. You who knew him—that venerable man—know that he deserved universal respect and love. We traveled first to the Loebau estate, and from there with the countess to D., where the unfortunate period began in which you will see this most amiable young lady enmeshed in difficulties and circumstances which destroyed at once her beautiful plans of a happy life but which, through a test of her inner worth, made her story instructive for the best among our sex.

Instead of continuing my narration, I think it best to put before you a series of original letters, or copies that later came into the hands of my beloved young lady. From these you can form a better idea of the character of her mind and heart and of her stay at D. than from mere summaries.

Lady Sternheim to Emilia

I have been here four days now, my friend, and in truth—judging by all my sensations—I am in a completely new world. I expected the noise of carriages and people, but for the first few days it greatly offended my ears, so used to rustic peace. Even harder to bear for me was my aunt's sending for the court coiffeur to style my hair according to the fashion. She had the goodness to come herself to my chamber, where she loosed my hair and said to him, "Monsieur LeBeau, this head can reflect credit on your art. Use all your devices, but take care not to damage this beautiful hair with any hot iron."

I suffered my aunt's flattering remark gladly, but the coiffeur annoyed me with his adulation. My pride told me that the man should have attended me carefully and kept his admiration to himself. But the dressmaker and milliner were even more unbearable. You may ask my Rosina about their silly babble and about the somewhat mischievous remark that escaped me: that the vanity of the ladies in D. must be very voracious because they had accustomed their kind of people to supply it with such crude—and to me, tasteless—food. The praises of the simple locksmith which pleased the beautiful Lady Montbason so much more than that of the courtiers was of quite a different kind because it was marked by the genuine feeling that arose in him at the sight of this beautiful woman, when he (quite engrossed in his work) looked up by chance just as she drove by his workshop. But how significant is the applause of those who seek to profit by me? And because of the loathing I feel for general applause, how glad I am that I am distinguished by no special beauty.

This afternoon I saw several ladies and gallants to whom my aunt had made known her arrival by declining to visit them under the pretext of being very tired from the journey. The true reason, however, was only that the clothes for court and town, in which I am to make my appearance, are not yet ready. Perhaps you are taken aback by the word "appearance," but today it was used very appropriately indeed by one of the wits, although he was referring only to my dress and first journey to town.

You know, Emilia, that my dear Papa wanted to see me always in my Mama's dresses, and that I too liked to wear them best. They are all out of fashion here, and in obedience to my aunt (to whom I gladly cede this much dominion over my taste), I am permitted to wear none of them except the white taffeta which I had ordered toward the end of the mourning period. "End of the mourning period," Oh my Emilia! Do not take this literally; I have laid aside its outward trappings, but my heart still mourns and, I believe, is in league with the secret observer of all my actions (I mean my conscience). For when a mass of materials and finery was lately shown me—this one destined for the next gala, that for the approaching ball, and another for the assembly—then, when I looked at this or that one, my Mama's picture on the bracelet turned from the movement of my hands. While setting it right, I fastened my eyes on it and saw her refined image adorned only with the simplest headdress and costume. Then the thought overcame me, how little I shall soon resemble her in this matter. God forbid that this dissimilarity should ever extend to more than my dress, which I consider a sacrifice even the best and most sensible people must offer up to custom, circumstance, and their connection with others in this or that particular. This thought seemed to me to be a combined lesson administered by my sorrow and my conscience.

But I digress from my appearance at court. However, you, my paternal[5] friend, have asked that, as the occasion demands, I write down my experiences and my accompanying thoughts, and that is what I intend to do. I shall speak little of others if their doings do not especially concern me. Nothing that I observe in them now astonishes me, because I know the real world from the picture of it my Papa and my Grandmama have drawn for me.

I went then into my aunt's apartments, where several ladies and gallants were already present. I had on my white dress, which had been trimmed with blue Italian flowers. My hair was coiffed quite beautifully, according to the fashion in D. I do not know what my bearing or the color of my face were like, but I may have looked pale, because shortly after my aunt introduced me as her beloved niece, a young man—pleasingly formed by nature—drew near with an oddly vivacious manner and, bending chest and shoulders strangely toward my aunt but his head sideways toward me with a kind of frightened expression, exclaimed, "Most gracious countess, is she really your niece?"

"And why don't you accept my testimony?"

"The first sight of her figure, dress, and light, sylphlike walk, made me think she might be the apparition of an amiable spirit of the house."

"Poor F.," said one lady, "and you are perhaps afraid of spirits?"

"To the ugly ones," rejoined the witty gentleman, "I have a natural aversion, but with those that resemble Lady Sternheim, I trust myself to spend hours on end alone."

"Ah, and with this pretty conceit you would give my house the reputation of being haunted?"

"Certainly—to deter all other gallants from coming here; but then I would also try to conjure the charming spirit to let me carry her away."

"Good, Count F., good! That is prettily said," was chorused around the room by all.

"Well, my niece, would you let yourself be conjured?"

"I know very little of the spirit world," I answered, "but I believe that for every ghost a special incantation must be chosen, and the terror my appearance caused the count leads me to think that I am under the protection of a mightier spirit than the one that taught him to conjure."

"Excellent, excellent! Count F., how now?" cried Col. von Sch.

"I have guessed more, after all, than any of you," answered the count, "for, although the lady *is* no spirit, yet I see that she must *have* limitless spirit."

"That you might have guessed; and that was presumably also the reason why you felt such terror," said Lady C., maid-of-honor to the Princess of W., who had been very quiet until then.

"You always mistreat me, my ungracious Lady C., for you mean by that remark that the lesser spirit has begun to fear the greater."

Yes, thought I, there is in truth much that is serious in this jest. I really am a kind of ghost, not only in this house but also in town and at court. Ghosts come among people with a knowledge of them, as I did, and are surprised at nothing they may see or hear; but they make comparisons, as I do, between this world and the one whence they came, and they lament the carefree way men regard their future state. Men, in turn, notice that although ghosts have human form, yet because of their inner character they do not belong among humans.

Lady C. then engaged me in conversation at the end of which she showed me much esteem and expressed the wish to be often in my company. She is very amiable, somewhat taller than I, and of good stature, with graceful walk and motions of her head. She has a longish face, beautifully formed in all its parts, blonde hair and the most excellent countenance: engaging features which express gentleness (but sometimes her frank, quite kind eyes seemed fixed too long and too significantly on the eyes of the menfolk). Her mind is amiable, and all her expressions are distinguished by a well-meaning heart. Among all the company, I liked her best, and I shall accept her offer of friendship.

At last, Countess F. arrived, and my aunt wanted me to show her much respect because her husband could be useful to my uncle in his lawsuit. I did all I could, but yet I felt displeasure at the thought that the civility of the niece toward the wife of the minister should help support the uncle's claim. In his place, I would bring neither my own wife nor the minister's into these matters but rather settle a man's business with men. The minister, whom his wife governs, is not to my taste either; but all this is a matter of established custom, and the one does not complain nor the other marvel at it.

Lady C. and the Countess F. stayed to supper. The conversations were lively but so interwoven that I cannot give an excerpt. Lady F. flattered me at every opportunity, whether I was talking or eating. If she has in mind to ingratiate herself with me, she misses her mark. For I shall never love this woman if I follow the voice of my heart; neither do I believe myself duty bound to overcome my dislike of her, as I did with my aunt—although, even with her, the aversion sometimes revives. But Lady C. I shall love. She was in my room with me, and our talk was as friendly as if we had known each other many years. She spoke much of her princess and how that lady would love me, as I was quite in her taste. When I was obliged to let her hear my lute and voice, she gave me yet more assurances of this, and in general I received a great deal of praise. Truly, I think the tone and assurances of the people at court are so pleasing because of the tender care each takes of the other's self-love.

My aunt was pleased with me, so she said, for she had feared that I might appear too strange or rustic. She said Countess F. had praised me but had found me somewhat proud and prosaic. So I was. I cannot lightly give assurances of my friendship and esteem; I cannot deceive anyone and say what I do not feel. My Emilia, my heart does not beat for everyone; in this I shall always remain a ghost to the world. That is my true feeling, not merely a fleeting indignant thought. I judged fairly: I did not impute evil intentions to anyone. I said to myself, an education which instills false ideas, the example which nurtures them, the obligation to live like others do—these things have led these persons away from their own selves and from the natural, moral purpose for which we are here. I look upon them as people who have inherited a family weakness. I shall treat them lovingly but not familiarly, for I cannot deny the fear of being infected with their plague.

Pray then, my dear friend, that the health of my soul may endure, and continue to love me. All the best to our reverend Papa. How will he be able to part from his Emilia, who cares for him so lovingly? But how auspiciously you enter the wedded state, for you bring with you the faithful blessing of a worthy father and all the virtues of your sex. Give my respects to the man whom you have chosen, who will have you, with all your treasures, for his own.

Lady Sophia to Emilia

I am glad, my Emilia, that you will receive this letter while still in your father's house, because it will present to you a seeming confusion of ideas that our Papa can best put in order. I have been presented to the Princess of W. and the entire nobility, and I now know the court and the great world at first hand.

I have already told you that I know both from the picture of them that has been painted for me. Let me employ this simile yet further and say that nothing appeared strange to my eye. But imagine a person of attentiveness and sensibility, who has long been acquainted with a painting of rich and detailed composition. She has often examined it and thought about the plan, the proportions of the objects, and the shading of the colors. All is familiar to her, but suddenly—through a strange power—the static painting with all it contains is set in motion. Naturally, this person is amazed and her feelings are affected in diverse ways. This amazed person am I. It is not the objects, nor the colors—it is the movement, the strange movement, that I find curious.

Shall I tell you how I was received in the various places? Well, every-where well! Because for such events the court has a ready language which the witless speak as facilely as the most reasonable person.

The princess, a lady of almost fifty years, has a very refined mind. In her assurances and expressions there prevail a tone of kindness whose uni-versal obligingness seems to be a remnant from a time when she may have deemed the friendship of all sorts of persons necessary. For I regard that motive as positively the only one capable of producing this effect in a noble-hearted person. I find it impossible to suspect her of the base desire to ingratiate herself indiscriminately with everyone. She conversed with me at length and said many good things about my beloved Papa, whom she had first known when he was a captain and later as a colonel. She called me the worthy daughter of a righteous man and said she would send for me often. You will surely believe then, my Emilia, that I love this princess the more because she honors my father's memory.

I cannot draw several of the characters for you. Most of them resemble one another to the extent they can be observed in the antechamber of the princess or during ordinary visits.

Yesterday I was interrupted while writing because *"assemblée"* (as they call it) at the princess' had been announced. Thus I had to waste the time at the dressing table that my heart had dedicated to friendship. Believe me, my dear, Rosina is just as ill-suited to being a methodical lady's maid, as I am to prove myself the lady by lingering long at the dressing table and by indecisive, loathsome deliberations on the choice of dress and jewels. My aunt seeks to remedy these flaws in us, and every day I must suffer about me—besides the coiffeur—one of her maids. Both of them continue to try my patience in a very unpleasant way by their affected manner and numerous formalities. This time, however, I was well satisfied in the end because I was indeed pleasingly attired.

In the past, you have never known me to take pleasure in that, but you shall not long seek the cause for the change; I shall honestly name it, as it seems significant to me: I was glad that my appearance turned out well solely because I was to be seen by two Englishmen whose approval in all things I wished to gain. One of them was my Lord G., the English envoy, and the other his nephew Lord Seymour, an attaché to the embassy who wishes to fit himself for these duties under the guidance of his uncle and to become acquainted with the German courts.

The envoy honors his calling by his stature, his noble and intellectual physiognomy, and a certain ceremoniousness that complements his cour-tesy. I heard him universally praised. I saw the young Lord Seymour for half an hour while I was in conversation with Lady C., whom he treats with tender and respectful friendship. She presented me as her new but dearest friend, from whom she would be inseparable if she could control her own and my fate. My lord merely bowed, but his soul spoke so clearly in his features that one could read at once his respect for all that Lady C. said and also his approval of her friend.

If I were asked to represent, in one picture, high-mindedness and love of humanity combined with an enlightened mind, I would merely use the person and attributes of my Lord Seymour; and all those who have ever harbored even an inkling of these three attributes would see each of them portrayed quite clearly in his form and in his eyes. I pass over the mild, manly tone of his voice which seems created specifically for expressing the emotions of his noble soul, over the fire in his fine eyes, subdued by a touch of melancholy, the inimitably pleasing seemliness—combined with a certain grandeur—of all his movements, and that which distinguishes him from all men (I have seen a great number in the few weeks I have been here); namely—if it is fitting so to express myself—the virtuous glance of his eyes the only ones here which do not offend me and cause no adverse, antipathetic emotion in my soul.

Lady C.'s desire to have me always with her caused him to ask whether I did not intend to remain in D. My answer was that I believed not, because I merely awaited the return of my aunt, the Countess R., who was on a journey to Italy with her husband and with whom I would then go to their estates.

"It seems to me impossible," he said, "that a lively mind like yours could take pleasure in the unchanging scenes of country life."

"And to me it seems incredible that my Lord Seymour can seriously believe that a lively, that is to say, an active mind can ever suffer from a want of diversion in the country."

"I do not mean a total want, Madam, but the aversion and weariness that must necessarily follow when we see our observations continually restricted to the same scene."

"I confess, my lord, that since my stay in town, I have found when comparing the two ways of life, that in the country, people are just as preoccupied with varying their occupations and pleasures as they are here, but with this difference: in the labors and amusements of the country people there resides an inner peace that I have not observed here, and this peace seems to me to be something excellent."

"I, too, regard it so and believe at the same time (he said in the direction of Lady C.) that, judging by the resolute tone of your admirable friend, she will retain that peace, even if thousands here were to lose theirs over her."

Because he did not look at me when he said this and because the lady merely smiled, I, too, kept silent; for in the first place I felt confused at this courtesy of his, which I did not want to show, and further I did not want to keep him in conversation with me any longer, but rather defer to his older friend, especially as he had quite studiously turned to her.

I can hear you say, "Why 'older friend'? Were you then his friend, too, already? You, who had known him for only half an hour?"

Yes, my dear Emilia, I was his friend before I ever saw him. Before he returned with his uncle from a short journey during the absence of the prince, Lady C. had spoken to me of his excellent character, and what I write you of him is nothing but a description of all the nobility and goodness the lady had attributed to him and which I now saw expressed in his face. I was touched even more, Emilia, by the pensive sadness with which he seated himself at the window where the two of us were sitting in conversation on a little bench. I pointed her friend out to Lady C. and said softly, "Does this happen often?"

"Yes, this is what is called 'spleen.' "

She then asked me what pastimes I could, in all seriousness, find for myself in the country. I told her briefly but with a full heart of the blissful days of my education and of those I had spent in the house of my beloved foster father, and I assured her that her person and friendship had been the only pleasures I had enjoyed in D. She squeezed my hand tenderly and assured me of her satisfaction at this. I continued and said that I did not like the word "pastime." First, because not once in my life had time grown long to me ("that is, in the country!" I whispered in her ear), and further, because it seemed to me to be a sign of an unworthy impulse of the soul. "Our lives are so short," I continued; "we have so much to observe if we want to know our abode the earth, and so much to learn if we want to use all the powers of our minds (which have not been given to us without a purpose!); we can do so much good that it fills me with abhorrence to hear time spoken of as a thing of that men try to rid themselves."

"Your gravity astonishes me, my dear, and yet I listen to you with pleasure. You are, as the princess said, in truth an exceptional person."

Emilia, I do not know what I felt. I knew well that this strain of my thinking was not suited to this company, but I could not help myself. An uneasiness had come over me, a desire to be far away, an inner unrest; I even wanted to cry, without being able to define the reason.

My Lord G. softly approached his nephew, caught hold of his arm, and said, "Seymour, you are like the child sleeping securely on the rim of the well. Look about you" (while pointing to us two). "Am I not Fortune awakening you?"

"You are right, uncle. A delightful harmony that I heard, held me captive, and meanwhile I was conscious of no danger."

While he said this, his eyes were turned to me with the liveliest expression of tenderness, so that I lowered mine and turned my head away. My lord then said in English, "Seymour, take care; these nets are not for nothing so beautiful and so far-flung."

I saw him pointing to my head and curls and blushed violently. It annoyed me that he thought me coquettish, and I was also conscious of the displeasure that he must feel when he heard that I understood English. I was embarrassed; but to save him and me from yet more confusion, I said quite curtly, "My lord, I understand the English language."

He was taken aback but praised my frankness. Seymour grew pale, but at the same time he smiled and turned immediately to Lady C., saying, "Would you not like to learn English, too?"

"From whom?"

"From me, madam, and Lady Sternheim. My uncle would also help with the lessons, and you would soon be able to speak."

"Never as well as my friend does. She is born to it, being half an Englishwoman."

"How so?" asked my Lord G., turning to me.

"My grandmother was a Watson and the wife of Baron P. who was with the embassy in England."

"Lady C. asked him to speak English with me. He did, and I answered in such a way that he praised my pronunciation and said to Lady C. that she should learn from me and that I spoke very well. As he withdrew, my Lord Seymour urged the lady to take the trouble of at least learning to read English. She promised and added that she would come to see me on those days when she was not completely occupied with her duties at court.

"But then I shall contribute nothing," he said sadly.

"You shall hear once a week how much I have learned."

He replied only with a bow.

Here the princess requested my attendance and I had to follow her into her apartment.

"There you have my lute, dear Sternheim," she said, "all the world plays; let me hear your voice and playing skill while we are alone."

What could I do? I played and sang the first piece that came to hand. She embraced me. "Charming girl," she said, "how you with the many talents you have acquired in the country put to shame the ladies who have been reared at court." She led me by the hand back into the hall, and I had to remain by her side until the end of the *assemblée*, while she spoke to me of a hundred matters. Lord Seymour frequently looked at me and, dear Emilia, (read this to my dear foster father), his attention pleased me! Many eyes stared after me, but they were a burden to me because it always seemed to me that there was an expression in them that offended my principles.

Today we visited the Countess F., and I endeavored to be obliging. One can easily see that her husband is a favorite with the prince, for she spoke of almost nothing else but the favors they enjoyed. She also made much ado about her husband's devotion to a master who was worthy of every good fortune. This was followed by mighty praises of the prince: she extolled the beauty of his person, his sundry talents, his good taste in everything—especially fêtes—and the splendid generosity which showed his princely soul. (I thought that the lady had good cause to praise this last attribute so highly.)

Of his penchant for the fair sex she said, "We are all human; it is true that there have been excesses in this," but the misfortune was merely that the gentleman had not yet found an object for his affection which captivated his mind as well as his eyes. "Certainly," she said, "such a person would have done wonders for the country and the renown of its ruler."

My aunt agreed. I sat silently and found in this picture of a sovereign no trace of what my father's annotations in the volumes of history I had read had left in my memory. That was the more true when I judged this portrait against the basic traits of the German national character. I was glad that they did not request my thoughts on the matter; for when the countess led me to her chamber to show me his life-size likeness, I could justly say that in truth the figure was beautiful. It is my aunt's wish that my portrait be painted, too. I will allow it and will then send my Emilia a copy; I know she will thank me for it.

Please ask my foster father to express his thoughts on this letter to me.

Lady Sophia to Her Friend Emilia

The sum of what you read in my last letter was that my Lord Seymour has found his best friend in me—and my dear foster father prays for me, "because that is the only thing humanly possible anyone can do for me now!" Emilia, you love me, you know me—and yet you did not think of the pain which your father's thoughts (being so important to me) would give me!

I can see it all: the enthusiastic esteem that I evinced for the merits, the excellencies, of my Lord Seymour's character, make you apprehensive on my account. Be reassured, dear friends! The only interest I will ever have in my Lord Seymour is that which my affection for Lady C. gives me; for it is she whom he loves; it is she whom he will make happy! The part I have in this is merely the joy of a noble heart in the contentment of its friends and the contemplation of its fellow creatures' goodness.

This interest has one more value for me, my Emilia: because I know of the existence of a perfect, noble, good, wise, and kind man, the base man, mere wit, or the solely obliging man will never, never gain power over my heart; and this is a great advantage which I derive from being acquainted with my Lord Seymour.

I regret that the disability in your Papa's right arm does not permit him to write me himself, not because I am dissatisfied with your letters but because he would tell me more of his own thoughts about me than you can. I hope this misfortune will pass, and I beg him to do so then.

Yesterday we attended a grand banquet at Lord G.'s. Count F. joined us in the afternoon, and finally, though it was already late in the evening, the whole company went on to the prince's. The count is a pleasant man of much good sense. His wife presented him to me. "There, speak with my favorite yourself," she said, "and tell me if I am wrong to wish such a daughter for myself." He paid me many compliments but watched me all the while with an attention that seemed strange to me and almost made me lose all my composure.

My Lord Seymour had been given his place at the table between Lady C. and myself and had conversed almost exclusively with us. Over coffee he attended us with the most charming gallantry and wrote English verses on cards, asking me to translate them for the lady. When Countess F. brought her husband to me,[6] the other two withdrew and conversed at length by another window. The count passed from me to Lord G. and, in leaving, took Lord Seymour by the arm with him to the former. Lady C. and I went to view the chamber, which was decorated with paintings and engravings, until we were called to play cards.

In the meantime, Count F. and Lord G. spoke with me of my father, whom F. had known very well, and of my grandmother Watson, whom he had seen immediately upon her arrival in Germany and to whom he claimed I bore a striking resemblance.

My Lord S. was with Lady C.; he looked grave and thoughtful, and it seemed to me as if his eyes were several times fastened on me and the two gentlemen with a kind of painful expression. Just then the patter of many feet in the street made everyone run to the windows. I went to the one where my Lord Seymour and Lady C. were standing. The noise came from a crowd of people who were returning from having watched the prince's short but very prettily arranged pleasure jaunt on the water, which they had gone in droves to observe. I noticed very many of them of poor figure and dress, and us, by contrast, in the greatest possible magnificence, with a quantity of gold scattered on the gaming tables. When Lady C. spoke of a similar fête, calculating its cost and also mentioning the innumerable throng of the people who had come running there from every place, I was moved to say, "Oh, how much against my nature are these amusements!"

"Why that? When once you have seen them, you will think quite differently." (My Lord Seymour was silent and cold the whole time).

"No, my dear C., I shall *not* think differently when I have seen the splendor of the fête, the court, and the squandered money on the gaming tables—right beside the multitude of the miserable, whose hunger and want show in their emaciated faces and ragged clothes. That contrast will fill my soul with anguish! I shall hate my own prosperous appearance and that of others; the prince and his court will appear to me an inhuman company who find pleasure in the immeasurable gulf between them and those observing their wantonness.''

"Dear, dear child, what a passionate lecture you are delivering!'' said the lady, "Do not speak so strongly.''

"Dear C., my heart was in turmoil. Yesterday Countess F. praised the prince's generosity so highly and today I see so many who are unfortunate.''

The lady took hold of my hands: "Hush, hush!''

My Lord Seymour had looked at me with a grave, unwavering glance and raised his hand toward me, saying, "Noble, worthy heart! Lady C., love your friend, she deserves it; but,'' he added for my benefit, "you must not judge the prince. The great lords are seldom told of the true conditions of their subjects.''

"I believe it,'' I countered, "but, my lord, did the people not stand on the bank where the boat passed? Has the prince no eyes that, unaided by others' instruction, could show him a thousand objects for his compassion? Why did he not feel anything then?''

"Dear lady, how beautiful your passion is! But show it only at Lady C.'s.''

Here my Lord G. called his nephew,[7] and shortly thereafter we went home.

Today a strange scene took place between my aunt and me. As soon as I was dressed, she came to my room where I was already seated at my books.

"I am jealous of your books,'' she said; "you arise early and dress immediately. Thus you could easily come to see me. You know how much I like to talk with you. Your uncle is always vexed by his gloomy legal proceedings, and I—poor woman—must once again think of yet another lying-in; while you, unkind girl, spend the whole morning with your dry moralists. Make me a present of that time, and give me your serious authors as a pledge.''

"My aunt, I shall gladly attend you, but I cannot knowingly have my best friends parted from me.''

"Come with me in any case; we shall at least quarrel in my chamber.''

She sat down at her dressing table, and I was diverted for a quarter hour by her two agreeable boys who were permitted to see their mother at this time of day. But as soon as they were gone, I felt quite foolish sitting there, observing the extraordinary trouble she took over her finery and listening to court tales (which I dislike) of ambition and love intrigues, of censure, of satires, and to inflated projects for raising the edifice of my uncle's good fortune.

"Please be very obliging toward Countess F.," she added; "you can do your uncle great service and secure considerable good fortune for yourself."

"I cannot see that and do not wish it, dear aunt; but whatever I can do for you shall be done."

"Dearest Sophia, you are a most charming girl, but the old parson has imbued you with a great many pedantic notions that annoy me. Let me lead you away from them a little."

"I am certain, madam, that court life is unsuited to my character; my taste and my inclinations run counter to it in all particulars, and I confess to you, gracious aunt, that I shall depart more gladly than I came here."

"But you don't know the court yet. When the prince comes we all revive. Then I want to hear your opinion. And be prepared: you will not go to the country before next spring."

"Oh yes, my gracious aunt; in the *autumn* I shall go to Countess R.'s—as soon as she returns."

"And my lying-in? I am to have it alone, without you?"

She looked at me tenderly when she said this and gave me her hand. I kissed it and assured her that I should stay with her when that time came.

Before dinner I went to my room, where I found my bookshelves empty. "What is this, Rosina?"

The count, she said, had come and ordered everything to be removed. It was the countess' joke, he had said.

A rude joke, which will not serve her, for I shall write the more. I shall not buy new books, in order not to make her angry at my obstinacy. Oh, if only my Aunt R. would come soon. To her, Emilia, to her I shall go gladly. She is affectionate and calm, and looks for and finds in the beauties of nature, in the sciences, and in good deeds, that measure of contentment for which they search here, where they cannot find it; and in thus searching they fritter their lives away.

My Lady C. has begun her English lessons. I think she will soon learn it. She knows many expressions already—all of them tender—in which I recognize the teacher. She was dining with us, when I jokingly accused my aunt of purloining my books. Lady C. took her part: "That is well contrived," she said; "we shall see what the mind of our Sternheim does when she lives among us without guide, without expositor."

I laughed with them and said, "I shall rely on the worthy scholar who once remarked, 'The feelings of women are often more accurate than the thoughts of men.' "*

---

*An observation to which the editor, from much experience of his own and of others, heartily subscribes [Wieland].

After that I received permission to work. I said it would be intolerable to me always to be a spectator at the dressing table, to play at cards every afternoon, or to be idle; and that a beautiful tapestry was just begun by the ladies, to which I should apply myself assiduously.

Tomorrow the prince arrives and the whole court with him. The foreign ministers arrived this evening. My Lord G. visited us, although it was late, and brought with him, besides my Lord Seymour, another Englishman called Lord Derby. He introduced him as a cousin who (through his and Lord Seymour's reports) had conceived a great desire to see me, particularly because I was half a country-woman of his. Lord Derby immediately addressed me in English. He is a distinguished gentleman of uncommonly great intellect and pleasant manner. These gentlemen were asked to supper. They accepted gladly, and my aunt suggested we should eat in the garden, since there would be moonlight and the evening was beautiful.

The little pavilion was quickly illuminated, and as she went out through the door with my Lord G., my aunt said tenderly, "Sophia, my dear, your lute in the moonlight would earn you our gratitude."

I ordered it brought to me. Lord Derby gave me his hand—Seymour was already ahead with Lady C. The little pavilion was at the end of the garden, near the river, so that we had a long walk. My Lord Derby entertained me in a very respectful tone with the many flattering things he had heard of me. My uncle joined us, and when we had gone just a few steps beyond half the distance, he nudged me with his arm and said, "Just look, how the prosaic Seymour can so tenderly kiss a lady's hands by moonlight!"

Dear Emilia, I looked up and it seemed to me that I felt a shiver. It may have been the cool evening air as we were very close to the water; but because I suspected another possible cause for this shiver (as I felt it only at that moment), I thought I should mention it to you.

The minister's nephew, young Count F., also joined us, and since he had met the servant who carried the lute and asked whose it was, he took it and strummed on it in front of the pavilion until my uncle looked outside and brought him in.

After supper was over, I had to play and sing. I was not lively, and, more from instinct than choice, I sang a song expressing longing for rustic freedom and peace. I myself felt that my tone was too pathetic, and my aunt promptly called out, "Child, you make us all sad. Why do you want to show us how gladly you would leave us? Sing something else."

I obliged quietly, choosing a gardener's aria from an opera, which was received with much applause. My Lord G. asked whether I could not sing something in English. I said, "No," but that if I heard something, it would not be difficult for me. Derby sang at once. His voice is beautiful but too impetuous. I accompanied him and sang along with him, too. For this they praised my musical ear.

Countess F. expressed her affection for me, but Lord Seymour said nothing. He frequently went into the garden alone and returned looking highly agitated, but he spoke only to Lady C. who also looked pensive. G. looked at me significantly, but there was pleasure in his face. Lord Derby's restless, fiery hawk's eyes were fastened on me. My uncle and aunt showered me with caresses.

At eleven o'clock we went to bed, and, once in my room, I wrote this letter. Good night, dear Emilia! Ask our reverend father to pray for me. I find consolation and joy in that thought.

I wish that my aunt would always make little journeys. I would attend her with so much more pleasure than I can here, in the perpetual round of our court and town visits. My uncle seeks to win over his half-sister in the convent at G. for the benefit of his children because she has come into a rich inheritance. For this purpose my aunt and her two sons journeyed to see her. She took me with her and by doing so provided me with a favorite pleasure: to look at changing scenes of nature and art in all their variety. Even had it been nothing more than a view of the rising and setting sun, I would have loved this escape from D., but I saw more: the road we traveled showed me much of our German countryside, sometimes consisting of a rough, niggardly piece of land that was patiently cultivated by its suffering, emaciated inhabitants with their bare hands.

Tender compassion, ardent wishes, and blessings filled my heart when I saw their hard labor and the sad yet composed glances with which they regarded the progress of our two chaises. I was much moved by the deference with which they greeted us as the favorites of providence, and I tried to give them a moment's happiness by responding with signs of my compassion, and although they did not beg, I tossed several coins to those standing closest to the road, especially to those poor women who had, here and there, a small child sitting on the ground near them while they worked. I thought to myself that my aunt was making a journey for the advantage of her sons, and that these women performed a lowly labor for the good of their loved ones. I wanted to let these mothers, too, benefit from an unexpected gift. The mounted servant later told us of these poor people's joy and of the thanks they called out after us.

Fertile fields, rich pastures, and the great barns of the farmers in other parts demonstrated the good fortune of their favorable location, and I hoped that they might put their blessings to good use. I felt glad, as we always do when we first behold the marks of good fortune. Then, after contemplating them for some time, there regrettably springs up in us, little by little, the thought of comparing them with our own less prosperous circumstances, admitting bitter dissatisfaction into our souls.

On the way, we called at the castle of the Count of W., the description of which I cannot possibly omit. It is built on the summit of a mountain and looks out, as far as a fourteen hours' journey, over the most beautiful valley adorned with fields, meadows, and scattered farmsteads. it is traversed by a stream teeming with fish, and enclosed by wooded knolls. Extensive gardens and rambling walks are laid out in the refined taste of the former owner, where I saw his favorite maxim, always to combine the pleasant with the useful, beautifully executed.

All this and the fine gentleman's farm, the choice library, the collection of physical instruments, the fine household appointments that are equally far removed from luxury and scantiness, the appointment of a physician for the entire domain, the lifelong maintenance which all the house servants enjoy, the employment of skilled and righteous men as officers of the estate, and a host of wise regulations for the benefit of the tenants—all these are living monuments to the late owner's taste, insight, and noble mind. He had spent his last few years at this pleasant country seat, after occupying for many years and with great renown the highest office at a great court. His heirs seem to have inherited his kindness and affability as well as his estates, which is why they attract all the best people of the surrounding countryside.

During the six days we spent there, an idea occurred to me through the card games, upon which I would like Mr. B. to comment: many strangers had arrived, for whose entertainment card tables were set up. Among some twenty persons, most were certainly of very diverse intellect and character. This was most evident at the dinner table and during the walks, where each one talked of some event according to his ruling concepts and inclinations, and in so doing frequently violated finer perceptions of virtue and the obligations of philanthropy. But when they were playing cards, all were of one mind in that they submitted to the game's established rules without the least objection. None became indignant upon being told that the rules had here and there been disobeyed; they admitted it and sought improvement from someone experienced in the game.

I admire and love the invention of card playing, for I regard it as a magic bond through which persons of different nationalities who are unable to converse with one another and those of quite opposite character can, in the space of but a few minutes, be sociably joined for hours on end, whereas without this expedient it would have been well-nigh impossible to propose a generally pleasing entertainment.

But I could not refrain from musing on the following observation: why a person would learn many kinds of card games and very carefully seek to

avoid all infractions against their rules, so that all distractions that might
occur in the room were powerless to cause that person to forget to disregard
the laws of the game; yet, only a quarter hour before, nothing could restrain
that person, when occasion offered, from making jokes and remarks
that offended all the rules of virtue and propriety. One of the people, famous for being an accomplished player, who indeed played with an ever
composed and friendly expression had, sometimes before when the question
of rulers and subjects was discussed, spoken of the latter as "dogs" and
advised a young gallant about to take up the management of his estates to
use the most severe and hard-hearted measures to keep the peasants in fear
and subservience and exact fully the taxes every year, so that he could indulge in all the expenditures proper to his class. Why, asked my heart, why
is it easier for people to submit to the arbitrary laws of men than to the
simple, beneficent rules which the eternal Lawgiver has instituted for the
good of our fellow man? Why can we not correct offenses against these
laws?

I did not want to tell my aunt of this chance thought, for she already
reproaches me because of my strict and precisely drawn moral ideas, which
she says cause me to see all the pleasures of life as tainted. I do not know
why I am always thus accused. I can be cheerful; I love company, music,
dance, and pleasantries—but I cannot see philanthropy and propriety
abused without showing my displeasure! Moreover, it is impossible for me
to find pleasure in mindless and unfeeling conversations or to listen for
days on end to talk about worthless trifles.

Oh, if I could find in each great gathering and among the friends of
our house at D. one person like the canoness at G.! People would no longer
find the tenor of my head and heart morose. This noble-minded lady made
my acquaintance at G. Her first feeling toward me was esteem; her wish
was to show me (though a stranger) more than formal courtesy. I had the
good fortune to please her and thus gained the advantage of full acquaintance with her amiable mind and heart. I have never encountered the faculties of the former and the sensibilities of the latter so equally refined,
noble, and strong, as in this lady! Her intellect and the pleasant temper
which characterizes her wit make her the most agreeable companion I have
ever seen. [And I almost believe that one of our poets thought of her when
he said of an amiable Greek lady:

> Even had her cheeks no roses,
> Her wit would make her lov'd!
> Her charming wit
> Whose power made it fit

To sting or to caress.
Yet smiling when it stung,
T'was never venomous!]*

She has the rare gift of finding uncontrived expressions for all she says and writes. All her thoughts are like beautiful images which the graces have clothed in a light and naturally flowing garment. Whether she is serious, cheerful, or moved by friendship—in each mood the justness of her thinking and the natural unvarnished beauty of her soul are engaging; and to complete the amiability of her character, she has a heart filled with feeling and sensibility for all that is good and beautiful, a heart made to be happy and to make others happy through friendship.

For the sake of this lady alone I wished for the first time to have noble forebears of ancient lineage, so that I might claim a place in her convent and spend all the days of my life with her. At her side, the hardships of the prebend would be very easy to bear for me. You can see that it was painful for me to leave this amiable countess again (although she is kind enough to compensate me by means of our correspondence for the loss of her charming companionship). You shall see some of her letters and then judge whether I have said too much of the charms of her mind.

Her friend, the Countess G., is extremely modest, but as she will never see this letter, I will say here that her influence has been mainly responsible for my wish to spend, if possible, my whole life in this felicitous retreat from the world. Hidden merit—the more engaging because it does not wish to shine—a refined mind adorned by wide reading and knowledge, together with unalloyed sincerity and goodness of heart make this lady worthy of the esteem and friendship of every noble soul. Even the veil which her almost excessively great, though unaffected, modesty draws over her excellencies heightens their value in my eyes. She seldom lays this veil aside except in the chamber of the Countess S., whose approbation makes her indifferent toward all other praise. Similarly, she deems her rare skill at the piano, which would serve to make a hundred others proud, of some value only as a pleasure to her friend.

Among the other worthy ladies of the convent, I must not forget to mention the Countess T. W., who marks all her days with the exercise of the practical virtues and who uses her special accomplishments instructing poor girls in all manner of ingenious skills becoming to their sex. But I

---

*To hold the excellent authoress responsible for only what is truly of her making, the editor confesses that as he has the good fortune to know personally the lady whose faithful likeness is here sketched, the lines enclosed in [ ] were inserted by himself [Wieland].

must especially remember the princess who is the head of the convent with the most affectionate reverence. She inspires that reverence in all around her by her great amiability, an ever constant serenity of soul, and the gracious dignity with which these attributes are expressed in her entire person. If I were capable of coveting anything, it would be the good fortune of spending my days under the guidance of the seasoned virtue and sagacity of so worthy and maternal a governess.

Regarding the main purpose of my aunt's journey, I shall be content to report to you that it was fully accomplished. We are now once again in D., and you must lay the blame for having been without news of me for so long on the great number of visits that we have been obliged to make and receive.

Lord Seymour to Dr. T.

Dear friend, I have often heard you say that the observations you made on your journeys through Germany about the basic character of that nation made you wish to unite, on the one hand, the profundity of our philosophers with the methodical discourse of the Germans and, on the other, the cold and phlegmatic temper of their other intellects with the fiery imagination of ours. For a long time you also tried to engender in me such a mixture, so that my vehement emotions might be moderated; for you said that this was the only obstacle that prevented me from reaching perfection in the sciences (though I loved them). You treated me gently and kindly because you thought to make my mind pliant through the sensibility of my heart.

I don't know, dear friend, how far you have succeeded. You have taught me to know and love the truly good and beautiful, and I have always wished to die rather than to do something ignoble or wicked; and yet I doubt whether you would approve of how impatiently I bear my uncle's authority over me. A threefold burden seems to restrict my soul in all its endeavors: my lord as uncle, as a rich man whose heir I am to be and as the minister to whom I am subordinate in my position as counselor to the embassy. But, don't be afraid that I shall forget myself or offend his lordship. No, I have that much power over my emotions; they show themselves only by a deadly melancholy which I try in vain to suppress.

Why do I thus beat about the bush, telling you at the end of my letter what I wanted to say when I began: that I have seen the beautiful and auspicious combination of the two national characters in a certain young lady. Her maternal grandmother was a daughter of old Sir Watson, and her father was a most meritorious man, whose memory still flourishes.

This young lady is a friend of Lady C.'s, of whom I have written you already, but Lady Sophia Sternheim (that is her name) has been here for only a few weeks and for the first time at that. Until now she has always lived in the country. Don't expect me to extol her beauty, but believe me when I say that in her person are united all the graces of which the figure and movements of a woman are capable: a charming seriousness in her face, a noble, well-bred courtesy in her expressions, the utmost tenderness toward her friend, a kindness worthy of reverent admiration, and the most delicate sensibility of soul. Is not this the greatness of the English inheritance from her grandmother?*

She has a mind adorned with learning and proper concepts and without the slightest prejudice, the courage of a man in averring and defending her principles, and many talents combined with the most engaging modesty. All these she received from the worthy man who had the good fortune to be her father.

From this description, my friend, you will be able to judge the impression which she made on me. Never, never has my heart been filled with so many and such happy feelings of love!

But what will you say to this: they have destined this noble, charming girl to become a mistress of the prince, and my lord has forbidden me to show her my affection because, even as it is, Count F. fears she may prove difficult. Yet he claims that is why she was brought to the court. I showed my uncle my contempt for Count Loebau's idea; I wanted to apprise the young lady of his loathsome intent and begged my lord on my knees to permit me by marrying her to preserve her virtue, honor, and condition. He asked me to hear him out calmly and told me that he himself admired the lady and was convinced that she would overthrow the whole shameful plan; and he gave me assurance that if she acted as befitted her upright character, he would take pleasure in crowning her virtue. "But as long as the entire court looks upon her as an intended concubine," he said, "I shall do nothing. You shall not take a wife of dubious reputation. Attach yourself to Lady C.; through her you can find out everything about Lady Sternheim's intentions. I shall give you news of the negotiations Count F. has undertaken. The lady's character gives me hope for a triumph of virtue, but it must be achieved before the eyes of the world."

My uncle made me wish to see the prince humbled, and I imagined the struggle of virtue as a delightful drama. These thoughts convinced me to conduct myself according to my uncle's wishes.

---

*I have already mentioned in my preface Lady Sternheim's little partiality to the English nation as a flaw that I would fain have erased from this excellent work, had it been possible to do so without too great alterations. If we are to believe the wisest Englishmen themselves, a lady of such a beautiful character as Lady Sternheim's is not any less rare in England than in Germany. Yet, here speaks a young Englishman (who may be justifiably prejudiced in favor of his nation), an enthusiast who has the right sometimes to argue faultily [Wieland].

Lord Derby has given me another motive to do so. As soon as he saw her, he felt a desire for her rare charms—for one cannot call his inclination love. He has anticipated me with his declaration. If he moves her, my happiness is lost, lost as surely as if the prince were to get her; for if she can love a profligate, she would never have loved me. But I am made miserable, most miserable, by the tenderest love of a worthy object which, unhappily, I see surrounded with the snares of vice. Confidence in her principles and fear of human weakness torture me by turns. Today, my friend, today she is being exposed to the eyes of the prince for the first time. I am not well, but I will be there even if it were to cost me my life.

I am revived, my friend: Count F. doubts that they will be able to prevail over the lady's mind! My lord ordered me to keep close to him during the performance of the comedy. The lady entered Countess F.'s box with her unworthy aunt. She looked so endearing that it hurt me to see her. I ventured to look at her only when my lord and I bowed toward the three ladies. Soon after, all the nobles and the prince himself were there, and his lustful eyes immediately turned to Countess F.'s box. The young lady bowed with so much grace that this alone would have made him take notice if her other charms had not done so. He spoke at once to Count F. and again looked at the young lady whom he now singled out for his salute. All eyes were fastened on her, but after a little while the young lady partially hid herself behind Countess F.

The opera commenced. The prince was seen speaking at length with F., who finally entered his wife's box to rebuke my lord and the countesses for taking up the young lady's place, although all of them had already seen the play often, whereas she had never seen it before.

"The ladies are not to blame, Count," said the young lady somewhat gravely; "I have chosen this seat. I can see enough and have the added pleasure of being seen less myself."

"But you rob so many of the pleasure of seeing you."

At this, he said, she merely bowed, showing nothing but disdain for his compliment. He said that he had then asked for her opinion of the comedy, upon which she had again said in a quite peculiar tone that she was not surprised that this diversion was enjoyed by so many people.

"But I desire to know how *you* like it, what *you* think of it; you look so grave."

"I admire the combined efforts of so many kinds of talent."

"Is that all? Do you feel nothing for the heroine or hero?"

"No, Count, nothing at all," he said she answered with a smile.

They dined at the Princess of W.'s with the prince, the envoys, and the other visitors, among them Lady Sternheim's uncle, Count Loebau. With much pomp Countess F. presented the young lady to the prince, who affected a wish to talk at length with her about her father. The young lady is said to have answered briefly and in a pathetic tone.

The seating order at table was mixed: a gentleman next to every lady. Count F., a nephew of the minister, sat beside the young lady who was placed so that the prince faced her. He looked at her incessantly. I took care not to look at the lady often, yet I noticed her discontent. Soon the guests rose from the table to play. The princess took the young lady with her, making the rounds of the tables. She sat down on the sofa with her and spoke very kindly to her. The prince joined them after he had played a round with my lord.

On the next day Count F. said to my lord that he cursed Loebau for having brought the young lady here. "She is destined to arouse a vehement passion;" he said, "but is a girl who has no pride in her charms. At a play she does not pay regard to anything but the 'combined effort of manifold talents'; at a choice table she eats nothing but an apple compote and drinks only water with it; at court she pines for the house of a country parson; and yet has great wit and sensibility—such a girl is hard to conquer!"

May God will it so, I thought; I cannot bear for long the distracted state I am in.

Write to me soon; tell me what you think and what I should have done.

Lady Sternheim to Emilia

Oh, my Emilia, how I need a comforting conversation with a loving and virtuous friend! I want you to know that I regret the day when I let myself be persuaded to come to D. Here I have been completely outside the sphere in which I used to move with such peace and contentment. Here I am of use to no one, least of all myself. The best of what I think and feel I may not tell because they find me ridiculously serious, and no matter how much I endeavor to speak the language of the people I am with in order to be obliging, my aunt is seldom satisfied with me; and I, Emilia, even more seldom with her.

I am not stubborn, my dear; truly, I am not! I do not demand that anyone here think as I do. I know too well that it is morally impossible. I am not offended that anyone spends the morning at the dressing table, the afternoon in visits, the evening and night in gaming. This is the grand world, and its members began the arrangement of their lives with these main divisions of time in mind. I have also ceased to wonder, as formerly, at the lack of well-founded knowledge in some of the persons who visited my sainted grandmama, though they seemed endowed by nature with many talents.

It is not possible in this deafening clamor of noisy diversions, my dear, for a young person like me to find one quiet moment to collect her thoughts. In short, everyone here is accustomed to this manner of living and the prevailing notions of happiness and pleasure. They love them as well as I love the principles and concepts that instruction and example have implanted in my soul. But they are not satisfied with my tolerance and fairness. I must think and feel as they do. I must be joyous at my well-turned finery, must be happy at the applause of the others and at hearing of plans for a supper or a ball. The opera (since it was the first one I have seen) was expected to excite me greatly, and heaven only knows what sort of miserable pleasure I was expected to find in the commendation of the prince.

During the performance I was asked every moment, "Well, how do you like it, ma'am?"

"Quite well," I answered calmly; "it is completely in keeping with the idea I had formed of these exhibitions." Then they were displeased and looked upon me as an uninformed person.

It may be, Emilia, that I am too sensible to love these shows. I consider it ridiculous and unnatural when a general sings on the battlefield and a dying lady love closes her life with a warble (which is what I read in an English author). But I cannot criticize anyone who loves these amusements. If one considers the combination of so many arts working together for the sake of our eye and ear, then it is very pleasant to see, and I find nothing more natural than the passion which an actress or a dancer inspires. The intelligence (allow me that word) with which the former completely enters into the character she represents, as she speaks soulfully of noble, tender feelings, herself becoming beautiful in doing so and having choice costumes, the affecting music, and all the decorations of the theater as concomitants in her task—how shall the young man escape who enters the hall with a sensitive heart and is there besieged by nature and art at once?

The female dancer, surrounded by lively graces, her every movement charming—in truth, Emilia, one should not wonder, not quarrel, if she is loved. Nevertheless, it seems to me that the admirer of the actress is nobler than he who admires the dancer. I have read somewhere that the boundaries of beauty are very precisely drawn for the painter and sculptor: if he oversteps them, beauty is lost; if he stays too far within them, his work lacks perfection. The line of what is charming yet moral in the dancer's art is, it seems to me, drawn as finely, for I thought it often overstepped. On the whole, I am content to have seen a play because my idea of it has been completely confirmed; but I shall also be content if I never see another.

After the comedy, I dined with the Princess of W., and there I was presented to the prince. What shall I tell you of him? He is a handsome man and very courteous; he greatly eulogized my dear papa; and I was displeased by that? Yes, my Emilia, I can no longer be so grateful for the eulogies they give him; their tone sounds to me as if they were saying, "I know that you have a high opinion of your father; therefore, I speak well of him to you." And in addition, my dear, I must tell you that the looks the prince threw at me would have spoiled the best things he could have said. What looks, my dear! God keep me from seeing them again! How I hate the Spanish fashion of dressing, which permitted me only a tippet. Had I ever felt proud of my figure, I would have done penance for it yesterday. The bitterest pain pierced me at the thought of being the object of such odious glances. My Emilia, I do not like being here any longer. I want to return to you, to my parents' grave. The Countess R. delays too long!

Today Countess F. told me with many pompous words of the prince's praise of my person and wit. Tomorrow the count is giving a great dinner party, and I am to be included. Since I have been here, I have never enjoyed a diversion to my taste. Lady C.'s friendship was the only thing that pleased me, but this too is no longer what it once was. She speaks so coldly, no longer visits me, and we do not play cards anymore; and if I approach her or my Lord Seymour (who are always talking together), they fall silent, my lord withdraws, sad and agitated, and the lady looks after him distractedly.

What shall I think? Does the lady not wish me to speak with my lord? Does he leave to show her his complete devotion? For he speaks to no one but her. Oh, my dear, what a stranger my heart is in this place. I, who would sacrifice my happiness to that of others—I cannot help noticing her fear that I might destroy their bliss. Dear Lady C., I shall relieve you of this fear, for I shall henceforth deny my eyes the pleasure of looking at my Lord Seymour. My glances, in any case, were only fleeting. I shall not visit you anymore when you are happily conversing with this amiable man. You shall see that Sophia Sternheim does not seek to preserve her heart's happiness through piracy!

Emilia, a tear filled my eye at this thought. But then the loss of a beloved friend, the only one I had here, the loss of association with a worthy man whom I value highly—that loss deserves a tear. D. will not cost me another! Tomorrow, my dear, I wish that I might depart tomorrow!

Why does your letter say nothing of my foster father? Why nothing of your journey and your companion?

Emilia, your letters, your love, and trust are all the good that I still hope for. D. holds nothing, nothing for me!

My Lord Derby to His Friend at Paris

Soon I shall silence your silly prattle. I have suffered it this long only to see how far you would go with your bragging to me, your master. Indeed, you should feel the lash of my satire today if I had not in mind to show you my design for a German love adventure, for which I am preparing myself. What signify your Parisian conquests, obtained only with gold? For what would even a Frenchwoman see in your broad face and spindly little figure? The conquests of the right honorables in Paris—what of them? A coquette, an actress—both pleasantly engaging, 'tis true, but they have been that for so many already that one must be a fool to congratulate oneself for receiving their favors. Was I not there, too, my fine gentlemen? And don't I know for certain that well-bred daughters of reputable families and honorable, charming married women are not allowed to make our acquaintance? Therefore, no more of your boasts, my good B., for victories like yours deserve no triumphal paean.

But to capture a masterpiece of nature and art which has been consecrated to the gods; to lull to sleep the Argus of prudence and virtue; to deceive ministers of state; to dash all the finely designed preparations of a rival beloved by her without his seeing the hand that destroys him—this deserves notice!

You know that I have granted love power only over my senses, whose choicest and most lively pleasure it is. Hence my eyes were always exacting; hence my objects always varied. Beauties of every kind have been subdued by me. I tired of them and next made ugliness my slave. After that, I conquered talent and character. How many observations could not philosophers and moralists make about the subtle nets and snares in which I caught women's virtue or pride, prudence or coldness, and even piety. I thought then, with Solomon, that there was nothing new for me under the sun. But Cupid scoffed at my vanity! From a miserable country hamlet, he brought hither a colonel's daughter whose figure, mind, and character are so new and charming that my former adventures would lack their crowning feat if she should elude me.

I must be watchful—Seymour loves her; but he is guided by my Lord G. because this rose is destined for the prince, to help win a lawsuit for her uncle. To cloak this scheme, Count F.'s son is offering to marry her; but if he sees that she loves him, he vows to dash Count Loebau's and his father's designs, the poor fool! He shall not have her! Neither shall Seymour with his melancholy tenderness that waits for the triumph of virtue; and the prince—he is not worthy of her! This flower blooms for me; I shall make sure of that! All my faculties are called upon to discover her weak side. She is sensitive; I saw it by the looks she sometimes cast on Seymour, even while I was talking to her. She is also frank, because she told me she thought my heart lacked kindness. "Do you consider my Lord Seymour a better man than me?" I asked her. She blushed and said that he was.

This remark filled me with raging jealousy, but it also showed me the way to her heart. I am now forced into a troublesome dissimulation in order to bring my character into harmony with hers. But the time will come when I shall mold her according to mine! I shall take that trouble with her, and

she will surely discover new pleasures when her enlightened and pure mind employs all its faculties to that end.

But praising her charms and talents does not move her. She is also indifferent to the usual signs of a passion she has aroused. Sublimity of mind and goodness of soul seem combined in her to an unusual degree; just as in her person all the charms of a perfect form are complemented by the grave bearing which lofty principles confer.

Every movement she makes, the mere sound of her voice make men desirous of her; yet one glance, one ingenuous glance, seems to drive that desire away because such a pure unspotted soul is reflected in her eyes. But wait, why do I babble like this? That is how poor Seymour's letters sounded when he was enamored of the beautiful Y. Shall this country maiden make an enthusiast of me? Let it be so—as far as it serves my purpose! But, by Jove, she shall compensate me for it!

I have won over my Lord G.'s undersecretary. The rogue is a very devil. He used to study divinity but because of some knavish deed has had to leave that pursuit. Ever since then he seeks to be revenged on all pious people. "It is pleasing when one can humble their pride," he says. Through him I intend to find out my Lord Seymour's intentions. He cannot abide the latter because of his moralistic preachings. You see that the theologian has undergone a severe metamorphosis; but I have need of such a fellow just now, as I cannot act openly myself.

Nothing more today—I am interrupted.

Lady Sternheim to Emilia

Emilia, I am almost crushed with grief: my fosterfather dead! Why did you not write to me, or at least to Rosina, when all hope was gone? My good Rosina almost expires with sorrow. I try to comfort her, but my own soul is afflicted. My dear friend, now the earth covers the best it had given us—loving, venerable parents! No heart feels your loss as mine does. I am doubly sensible of your pain. Why could I not myself hear his blessing? Why don't my tears fall on his sacred grave, as I am weeping for him with the same filial emotions as his daughters do?

Poor Rosina! She kneels at my side with her head on my knees, and her tears trickle to the floor. I embrace her and weep with her. May God give our souls wisdom from our sorrow and thereby grant the last wishes of our fathers, especially my dear fosterfather's wish for his Emilia when his trembling hand consecrated her marriage, giving her into the protection of a faithful friend. May virtue and friendship be Rosina's and my portion until the blessed moment of our mortal end. Then may some noble heart give thanks for the good example I have set, and may some poor soul which has found relief through me bless my memory! Then the wise man, the friend of mankind, will perhaps say that I knew the value of life.

I cannot go on writing, and our Rosina cannot write at all. She asks for the love of her brother and sister and wants to stay with me always. I hope you approve and thus strengthen the bond of our friendship. Magnanimity and kindness shall make it unbreakable.

I embrace my Emilia tearfully. You cannot guess how it saddens me that I must close this letter without adding something for my paternal friend. May eternal bliss reward him and my father! Let us, my Emilia, my Rosina, so live that some day we may face them as the worthy heirs of their virtue and friendship!

My Lord Seymour to Dr. B.

The lady becomes ever more dear to me and I become more wretched!

The prince and Derby seek to gain her esteem; both of them see that this is the only way to her heart. My passion's twofold obstinacy prevents me from doing the same. I merely strain to get a glimpse of her and to conduct myself irreproachably, whereas she avoids me and Lady C. and I no longer hear her talk, but the accounts of Derby (to whom she shows some regard) constantly convince me of her soul's nobility.

I believe she has brought about the first virtuous stirrings in his heart. Some days ago he told me that he had accompanied the lady to an assembly and what had happened when he went to her apartment: he had seen her chambermaid kneeling before her. The lady herself was only half-dressed. Her beautiful hair streamed over her neck and breast; her arms were thrown around the kneeling girl whose head she pressed to her bosom, while in her moving voice she spoke of the rewards of virtue and how death was a benefit for the righteous. Tears flowed from her eyes as she lifted them to heaven, blessing her father's and another man's memory for the instruction they had given her.

This sight amazed him, and when the lady noticed him she called out, "Oh, my lord, I cannot entertain you just now. Please give my excuses to my aunt. I shall see no one today."

Her solemn and pathetic appearance made him feel her reproof very keenly, for he had sensed the contempt she had for his opinions. He answered that if she knew how much respect he felt for her at this moment, she would consider him worthy of her confidence. But since without answering she laid her head on her maid's, he left and later heard from the Countess Loebau that this scene had to do with the death of the parson at P., who had in part raised the lady and who was her maid's father.

The Count and Countess of Loebau had expressed their satisfaction that the enthusiastic correspondence between the lady and man had come to an end, so that they could now guide her to think more in keeping with her station. They had gone with him to see the lady, he said, and had reproached her for her sadness and for her decision not to attend the assembly.

"Dear aunt," she had answered, "I have sacrificed so many weeks to the compliance I owe to you and the customs of the court that the duties of friendship and virtue may surely claim one day!"

"Yes," the countess replied, "but your love has always been confined to only one family. You are not sufficiently sensible of the respect and affection shown you here!"

To which the lady replied, "My gracious aunt, I regret that I seem ungrateful to you, but does not the man who filled my soul with good principles and my mind with useful knowledge deserve a greater measure of consideration than the polite stranger who obliges me to share his fleeting diversions?"

The countess: "You could more fittingly have used the words 'variable diversions.'"

The lady: "All these faults prove to you that I am unsuited for the court."

The countess: "Yes, especially today; and you shall, therefore, stay at home."

Derby told me this in an unconcerned tone but watched closely for signs of my emotions. You know that I can seldom hide them, and in this instance I could not do so. The lady's character moved me; I envied Derby's having seen and heard her. Dissatisfied with myself, my uncle, and the prince I blurted out heatedly, "This lady has the noblest and rarest character; woe betide the scoundrel who seeks to ruin her!"

"You are as rare a man as the lady is a woman," he countered. "You would have been the most fitting suitor for her, and I would have liked to have become her confidant and biographer."

"I do not believe, my Lord Derby, that the lady or I would have conferred that office on you," I said. At this answer I saw an expression on his face that entirely displeased me: it was smiling and pensive. But, my friend, deep in my heart I could not help feeling that Satan smiles thus when he designs a deadly plot.

Lady Sternheim to Emilia

Your silence, my friend, seems very long and unjust to Rosina and me; but I will not take revenge for the anxiety you have caused me but, when I next take a long journey, will instead write you when I have gone halfway. Because I know that you love me, I could not inflict on you the same concern I have felt. But your safe arrival at W. and your happiness at your future prospects have compensated me for that.

In addition, dear Emilia, I am happy to report that fate has presented me with a pleasant subject for several letters to you! For had I been forced to complain yet further about my disagreeable experiences, I would have disrupted your contentment, since your affectionate heart takes such a lively interest in all that concerns me and in the strange sensibility of my soul.

In this moral desert I have been traversing for three months now, I have found two pleasant springs and a piece of arable land where I shall tarry awhile to refresh my mind and heart at the former and to plant and cultivate useful fruits in the latter. But let me not speak in parables: you know that my education caused me to believe that simplicity and utility, rather than artifice and mere delight, constitute the means to happiness. I never saw my mother's affections so moved as when she heard of a noble, magnanimous act or of a deed inspired by duty, love of mankind, or other virtues. She never pressed me to her heart more lovingly than when, moved by charity or joy at the happiness of others, I said or did something on behalf of a friend of the family, a servant, or a dependant of ours. Further, I well remember that when I, like a thousand other children, made a remark or had a thought that was a subtle or apt (whereupon the whole company would burst out in admiration and praise), she merely smiled for a moment and at once tried to direct the regard her friends wished to show me to matters of active daily life, either by praising my diligence in the learning of a language, in practicing drawing, music, or other skills, or by mentioning that I had asked for a reward or favor for someone. Thus she made me realize that good deeds are far more deserving of fame than the choicest thoughts.

My papa conclusively proved this principle to me by pointing out that in the realm of nature those species of flowers which serve solely to delight the eye are much less numerous and fruitful than the useful plants which serve as food for man and beast.[*] All the days of his life were informed by this insight. How he tried to make his mind and his experiences useful to his friends! What did he not do for his inferiors and dependants! Well, my Emilia, with these principles, with these inclinations I entered the great world where most people live only to satisfy the eye and ear, where the excellent mind is not permitted to show itself except in a passing witty conceit—and you know with what diligence my parents sought to stamp out in me the inclination toward that talent!

---

[*]One can hardly say that there are species of flowers or plants which solely serve to delight the eye; and, as far as I know, not a single species is known that has not either an economic or a pharmaceutical use for man or that does not serve for the sustenance of some animals, birds, insects, or worms, thus having real utility in the design for the whole system of our planet [Wieland].

It has not completely left me and is never more noticeable than when I am displeased with or contemptuous of someone's ideas or acts. Judge for yourself: through my love of Germany I was recently drawn into an attempt to defend with some ardor the merits of my country. Afterward, my aunt said to me that I had given "perfect proof of being the granddaughter of a professor." This reproach stung me; the ashes of my father and grandfather were insulted—and so was my self-love. The last answered for all three: "I would rather prove my descent from noble souls through my convictions than have a fine name as the only evidence that I sprang from once noble blood!"

This caused a few days' coldness between us, but, insensibly, we came to feel more affectionate again. I think my aunt, feeling the pride of ancient nobility, knew how it wounds one to be reproached for a lack of noble ancestors. I, in turn, relented because I regretted that my spiteful answer had lowered me to my aunt's level when she had made the ignoble remark to me.

But it is time to lead you to the first of the two "springs," as I have somewhat picturesquely called them. The first showed itself during the private visits my aunt receives and makes. On these occasions I can make a multitude of changing observations about the infinite variety of the characters and minds revealed in the judgments, stories, desires, and complaints I hear. What trifles these people talk about! With what haste they strive to clear away another day of their lives! How often do court etiquette and fashion suppress the noblest impulses of a naturally excellent heart—and to avoid the hissing of the fashionable ladies and dandies urge one to laugh and agree with them.

This fills me with contempt and pity. The people at court are consumed with the thirst for pleasure, new finery, approval of a dress, a piece of furniture, a new, harmful dish—Oh, Emilia! How uneasy, how nauseated my soul feels because I am accustomed to value everything at its real worth. I pass over the false ambition that breeds so many low intrigues, that crawls before prosperous vice, looks upon virtue and merit with contempt, and makes others wretched without compunction. How fortunate are you, my friend! Your birth, your circumstances, have not diverted you from the moral goal prescribed for us. Without apprehension, without hindrance, you can practice all the virtues, exercise all the noble and useful talents. Now, in the days of your health and your strength, you can do all the good that most people in the great world ultimately wish they had done.

Nevertheless, religion and virtue receive a considerable show of respect here. The court churches are magnificently decorated, the best orators are appointed as preachers in them, and the services are properly and respectfully attended. Propriety in speech and manner is narrowly and anxiously observed, and no vice may appear without mask. Yes, even the virtue of loving one's neighbor receives a kind of tribute in the choice and subtle flatteries that each pays to the self-love of the other. All this has become a source of moral reflection for me. Through it I am even more deeply confirmed in the principles of my education.

My imagination often occupies itself with schemes for combining a court lady's duties, assigned to her by fate, with the duties imposed by perfect virtue, the necessary foundation for our eternal happiness. A union of the two may be possible, but it would be so difficult to keep them always in balance that I am not surprised that so few of these ladies try. I have often thought that if a man like my father had the post of prime minister, he would be the most venerated, the happiest among men. It is true, many cares would attend his days, but the thought that he could employ his talents and his heart for the welfare of many thousands now living and for their descendants—that prospect, the most gratifying for a truly good and noble soul, would have made all tasks easy and pleasant for him.

His knowledge of the human heart would show him how to win the prince's trust, thereby reinforcing the natural authority conferred by his righteousness, deep insight, and strength of soul. The other courtiers and placemen would then be as willing to submit to the rein of the wise and virtuous minister as they now are to the imperfect heads and flawed hearts of those from whom they expect fortune and preferment.

Thus, my Emilia, I often occupy my mind since becoming acquainted with the situation, character, and duties of this or that person. In turn, my imagination puts me in the places of those I judge. Then I weigh the universal moral duties our Creator's eternal and unchanging laws have imposed on every person, whoever he may be, against that person's ability to carry them out. In this manner I have been prince, princess, minister, court lady, favorite, mother of these children, wife of that man; yes, once I even put myself in the place of a governing mistress who guides all, and everywhere I found the opportunity to exercise goodness and prudence in various ways without letting the characters or the political circumstances fall into tedious monotony. In many of these people I have found ideas and actions whose justness, benevolence, and beauty I could not easily have matched or, much less, surpassed; but there were also many whose head and heart I liked less than my own.

After these fanciful journeys of my self-love, fairness naturally led me back to myself and my own duties. It dictated that I be as exact and strict in evaluating my talents and powers applied within my sphere as I had been toward others. By this means, my Emilia, I have become more observant of myself, have more deeply engraved my heart with wisdom, sensibility, and the conviction of what is good, and have daily convinced myself more thoroughly of what a great observer of human actions rightly asserted: "Very few persons use their moral and physical strength in full measure." For in truth, I have found many empty places within my life's compass, and even

some which were partly occupied by reprehensible things and worthless trifles. All this will now be cleared away; and because I am not naturally
prudent and good, I want at least to become wise and righteous by observing the harm others do themselves, and not to be one who can improve only
by experience and misery.

Lady Sternheim to Emilia

I thank you, my faithful friend, for reminding me of that part of my
education which urges me to put myself in the place of those whom I attempt to judge, merely to see what I would have done in their circumstances, but also to give me that humane gentleness "not to consider all
that runs counter to my principles as evil or base." You have reminded me
of this principle because my dissatisfaction with the people at court seemed
to you unfair, too severe, or even unjust. Taking your advice, I have discovered a second source of improvement: moderation in my dislike of the court
through the thought that just as in the material world all kinds of beings
have an appointed sphere within which they can find everything necessary
to their perfection, perhaps likewise in the moral world, a court may be the
only environment in which certain faculties of our minds and bodies can
attain perfect development. We find there, for example, the greatest refinement of taste in everything affecting the senses and depending on the power
of the imagination, such as the infinite number of art objects of all kinds
and almost all the necessities of sustenance and dress, tools and instruments, and all kinds of decorations for all categories of material objects.

The court is also the most proper stage for proving the extraordinary
pliancy of the human mind and body, a faculty which there expresses itself
in infinite, subtle turns of thought, expression, and gesture and—yes, even
in moral acts, depending upon prevailing politics and fortune or ambition.
Many of the fine arts receive their ultimate polish at court, just as language
and custom can be clothed in a rare and pleasing dress only by the graces
which reside there. All these are estimable advantages greatly affecting human happiness and certainly part of it.

The plant and animal kingdoms have their own beautiful and dainty
features in form, symmetry, and color combinations; and even the crudest
nations possess concepts of beautification. It is not for nothing that our
sight, taste, and touch are refined in comparing, choosing, rejecting, and
combining, so that it is quite proper to use these faculties fully. If only men
would not overstep the boundaries of things so lightly and eagerly. But who
knows whether even such excesses are motivated by the desire to perfect
our condition. This desire is the greatest proof of our Creator's goodness
because, though in our days of health and good fortune we use it wrongly
and badly, yet when our bodies meet with dissolution, this desire directs

our sights and hopes toward another world and the felicities and virtues that are everlasting and immutable there, affording us a comfort provided by no other aids.

You can easily see, my Emilia, how many hours of reflection and contemplation I have spent on all the subjects I merely touch on here; and you can also see that with these and the other diversions which my aunt's house affords me, there remains not one moment for boredom.

Now let me lead you to the "piece of arable soil" that I have found. This happened at Count F.'s country estate. The local mineral waters, which the countess uses, gave us the opportunity for a few days' visit. My aunt had asked the Countess B. and Lady R. to join us there, and chance brought us Lord Derby as well.

The lands, house, and garden are very fine. The ladies had many little feminine affairs to settle, and thus Lady R., Lord Derby, and I were sent on a walk. First we strolled through the entire house and garden where my lord was indeed a pleasant companion. He spoke to us of the differences which the national character of each nation produces in its architecture and decorations. He gave us descriptions and comparisons of English, Italian, and French gardens and houses, and even very prettily and with great facility drew one or the other of them. In short, we were so well satisfied with our walk that we agreed to go on an excursion in the open fields and through the village after breakfast next morning.

Those were two happy days for me. Country air, unobstructed views, the tranquillity and beauty of nature, the visible blessings of the Creator on meadows and cornfields, the industry of the peasants—with what tender feelings I fixed my eyes on them all! Many memories of bygone times, of past contentment were re-created in my heart. Ardently I wished that my tenants might be blessed in their labors and that my aunt R. might return. You know, my Emilia, that my face always mirrors the motions of my soul. I may have worn an expression of tender emotion, with the tone of my voice echoing that expression. But Lord Derby almost frightened me by the intensity with which he looked at me, seized my hand, and said in English, "Oh God, if love ever moves this breast, causing this face to show such an expression of tender sensibility, how great will be the felicity of the man who . . ." My confusion and the fright he gave me were just as visible as the former emotions had been. He immediately ceased speaking, withdrew his hand respectfully, and sought by his whole deportment to mitigate my impression of his impetuosity.

When we had gone halfway through the handsome village, we had to make way for a cart that came up behind us. It had sides of densely woven wicker, but a woman and three quite young children could be seen occupying it. The affecting sadness that I saw in the mother's face, the children's pale, gaunt appearance, the clean but very poor garments worn by all of them testified to the poverty and distress of this little family. My heart was moved; the thought of their need and the urge to help became equally strong in me. I was glad to see them alight at the door of the village inn and did not hesitate long. I pretended that I knew this woman and wished to speak with her, and I asked Lord Derby to entertain Lady R. until I returned. He looked at me with a grave smile and kissed that part of his sleeve where in my eagerness I had placed my hand. I blushed and hastened after the poor family.

On entering the house, I found them all sitting at the foot of the stairs. With tear-filled eyes, the woman was busy taking a silken kerchief and an apron out of a little sack and offering them for sale to the landlady, in order to pay the carter. Two of the children were crying for bread and milk. Deeply affected, I composed myself, approached, and assuming the expression of an acquaintance said to the poor woman that I was glad to see her again. I did this because a sensitive heart is embarrassed by witnesses to its misery, and because the unfortunate deem it a charity if the wealthy distinguish them with respect.

I asked the landlady to show me to a room where I could talk with the woman in private and gave orders to prepare a supper for the children. While I did this, the landlady opened a room, and the poor good woman stood there with her smallest child in her arms and looked at me with utter amazement. I took her by the hand and asked her to step into the room with the two older children. Closing the door, I led the trembling mother to a chair and asked her to sit down. I begged her to be calm and to forgive me for thus imposing myself on her. I told her that I intended no impertinence and that she should consider me a friend who merely wished to assist her in this strange place. A flood of tears prevented her from speaking, but she looked at me with a face full of hope and affliction.

Saddened, I gave her my hand and said, "You are suffering under a hard fate on both your own and your children's behalf. I am rich and independent; my heart acknowledges the duties that humanity and religion require of the wealthy. Allow me the satisfaction of fulfilling these duties and relieving your distress." While I said this, I took out some of my money, gave it to her, and asked her to tell me where she lived. The good woman slid from her chair to the floor and exclaimed with the utmost agitation, "Oh God, what a noble heart hast Thou let me encounter!" The two older children, running to their mother, threw their arms around her neck and began to cry. I embraced her, lifted her up, put my arms around the children, and asked the woman to compose herself and speak calmly. I assured her that no one there but myself should know her heart and her circumstances. I told her to believe that I would gladly be of service to her but that for now I desired nothing but to know her address and to give her my name. I did so with my pencil and handed her the paper.

She told me that she was once again returning to D. where her husband was, after she had visited a brother who had just asked her to leave. She asked permission to write down for me all the causes of her misfortune and to recommend herself to my goodness in judging her faults. After saying this, she read my paper. "You are Lady Sternheim? What a day this is for me! I am the unfortunate Councillor T.'s wife. If you mention me to your aunt, the Countess L., I may lose your compassion, but I beg you not to condemn me unheard," she exclaimed with folded hands. I gladly promised her that I would not, embraced her and the children, and took my leave, forbidding her to mention me and to let the landlady believe that we knew one another. Upon leaving, I ordered the landlady to give the mother and children good beds, food, and a decent carriage on the following morning; and I assured her that she should be paid.

My lord and Lady R. were in the garden of the inn. I found them there and thanked them for having waited for me. My face expressed delight at having done something good, but my eyes were still red from weeping. The lord looked at me often and gravely, and he rarely spoke to me during the remainder of our walk but instead entertained Lady R. This was the more pleasing to me as I could think of a plan to help this whole family as much as possible. And this, my Emilia, is the "piece of arable soil" I have found, where I shall sow care, friendship, and service. The harvest and the profit from it shall benefit the three poor children, for I hope that the parents will be faithful to the duties of nature and not use these benefits except for the good of their innocent and unfortunate children.

If I succeed as far as I wish and my heart dictates, I shall bless my stay here in D., for now I no longer consider the time I spend here wasted. In a few days I am to receive an account of this family's misfortune and then I shall truly know what I must do. Councillor T. is very ill and for that reason his wife has been unable to write thus far.

We returned the day before yesterday.

My Lord Derby to My Lord B. in Paris

You are eager to know the progress of the intrigue I announced to you. I shall tell you all. As everyone needs a confidant, you may occupy that honorable post and while doing so learn something for your own good.

Do not dare to burst into your stupid laughter at the wrong moment when I confess that I would have gained little had not chance, rather than my planning or subtle mind, advanced my intentions. I am well satisfied, for this puts my love affair into the same class as the affairs of state at our courts: in many of them chance contributes most to the outcome, and the wisdom of many a minister consists merely in making use (by knowing the history of past and present states) of this element of chance and then mak-

ing the rest of the world believe that the result was owing to deep insight.*
You will see how I have discovered this similarity and how I have availed
myself of an unforeseeable opportunity by using my understanding of the
passions and of the female heart.

For some days I was in an impatient quandary as to the best means of
winning Lady Sternheim. If she had only the usual wit and virtue, my plan
would have been easy; but since her thoughts and acts are dictated entirely
by her principles, every device which formerly pleased is lost on her. I
must have her—but with her consent! But to gain that I must first obtain
her trust and incline her toward me. Other than that nothing else remains
for me to do than, like the minister, make use of chance occurrences. I had
a sample of both these requisites at Countess F.'s country seat. I knew that
the lady and her aunt would go there for several days, and thus I made my
appearance there, too. Twice I succeeded in going alone on a walk with my
goddess and Lady R., and I used the first occasion to give some account of
my travels.

You know that I am a good observer and can chat pleasantly enough for
hours on end. The subject was buildings and gardens; and as the young
lady loves good sense and knowledge, I used her attentiveness to advantage. I have so fully obtained her respect for my knowledge that she kept
with her a sketch I made during my description of a garden in England,
saying to Lady R., "I shall keep this paper as proof that there are indeed
gentlemen who travel for their own improvement and for the delight of their
friends." This is an important step forward and will get me far enough. Let
me have no smirks of ridicule now, stupid fellow, when you see me as
elated over this trifle as I rarely was before over the final conquest; I tell
you, this girl is extraordinary! From her questions I perceived that she has
a great predilection for England which, by itself, will be useful to me without my doing anything.

I continued speaking cheerfully and calmly, for as she had become contented and trusting through the indifferent subjects of our conversation, I
took great care not to show her my love or any special regard. But I almost
lost my composure when I saw a change come over her voice and expression. We had just come to a mound in the garden from which we could see
the open fields. There we stopped. Our charming Lady Sternheim directed
her glance to a certain part of the landscape. She seemed moved, and her

---

*Nevertheless, it needs much insight to make such good use of chance, perhaps
more even than for a well-designed plan. But most people are not capable of com-
prehending that; and, therefore, they are usually encouraged to believe whatever,
given their understanding, reflects the greatest credit on those who govern them.
The world at large is deceived so much only because it wants to be deceived
[Wieland].

answers became fragmentary, but I continued as well as I was able to converse indifferently, keeping a close watch on the lady. A delicate blush covered her face and her bosom, which seemed to beat faster from a sensation
of pleasure. Longing was written in her face, and a minute later tears stood
in her eyes. B., everything charming I have ever seen in others of her sex is
as nothing compared with the enchanting aura of sensibility that was dif-
fused over her whole person.

I could barely resist the burning desire to clasp her in my arms, but to
be completely silent was impossible. My arm trembled with desire as I
seized one of her hands and said in English, I know not what anymore. But
the rage of love must have been discernible in my voice, for she was overcome by uneasy fearfulness, and the color drained from her face until she
was as pale as death. It was high time for me to recover myself, and I took
care to show myself respectful and calm for the rest of the evening. My
little dove is not yet tame enough to bear the fire of my passion close at
hand. All night its flames blazed in my soul; not a moment did I sleep. I
continually saw the lady before me, and my hand closed twenty times on
emptiness with the same ardor with which I had clasped hers. Beside myself, I thought I had seen longing and love for an absent object in her de-
meanor, but I swore to possess her with or without her consent. If she loves
me passionately, she may hold me—but even cold, she shall become mine!

Morning came and found me like a mad, burning fool at the window,
my face disturbed and my clothes torn open at the breast. The mirror
showed me a figure like the devil himself, a sight that would have caused
the dear, timorous girl to shun me forever. Maddened by her power over me
and determined to be compensated for my condition, I threw myself on the
bed and thought of how I might escape these confused, new sensations and
return again to my old principles. I knew I needed patience on the long,
tedious path that I saw before me; I could not foresee that the afternoon
would greatly advance my cause. When I came into her presence again, I
was all gentleness and respect and the young lady was silent and reticent.
After dinner, we young people were sent on another walk because the aunt
and Countess F. were still shuffling the cards by which they meant to deal
the young lady to the prince.

As agreed, we went into the village. As we approached the inn where
my men were quartered, we met with a small cart loaded with a woman
and children, which slowly passed us and hindered our progress. My Lady
Sternheim looked fixedly at the woman, turned red, pensive, sad (all seemingly in one moment), and looked after the cart with a melancholy expression. The vehicle halted at the inn and the people alighted. The lady's
glances were fixed on them, disquietude seized her, she looked at me and
Lady R., turned her eyes away, and finally laid her hand on my arm, saying
in English and with a tender expression and a suppliant, affectionate voice,

"My dear sir, please be kind enough to entertain Lady R. for a few moments here. I know this woman and want to have a few words with her."

I was startled but bowed in assent and kissed the spot on my coat where her hand had lain and gently pressed my arm. Seeing this, she blushed deeply, seemed confused, and hastened away. "What the deuce has the girl in mind with that woman?" I thought. Perhaps the latter was once a messenger or gobetween in a secret love intrigue. Yesterday, after my tender address, the girl was startled; today, all day long, she was prosaic and haughty and hardly looked at me. A beggar's cart brings a bawd here and her expression changes. She struggles to compose herself, and finally I am "my dear sir," on whose arm she lays her beautiful hand, pressing it with moving voice and look, in order to obtain an undisturbed interview with that woman. Well, well! How shall we look upon her strict virtue now? I would gladly have drowned Lady R. in the horse pond, to be able to conceal myself inside the inn and overhear what was said.

Lady R. looked after Sophia and said, "What is the lady doing at the inn?" I answered her briefly that Sophia had told me she knew this beggar woman and had something to say to her. She laughed and shook her head with an apish expression. She had long been envious of her friend's advantages, and having found nothing to criticize in her, was now feeling exultation at the seeming appearance of a fault. "It may well be a good old acquaintance from the village of P.," hissed this viper, trying to appear as if she was quite well informed.

I told her that I would have one of my people spy on the lady, as I, too, was utterly amazed at this occurrence. I sent one of them after her and sought meanwhile to draw out Lady R. as to what she thought about Lady Sternheim.

"She is an odd mix of the citizen and the courtier, constantly advocating delicacy which she herself does not know how to observe. What sort of conduct is it for a person of high rank to run away from a lady and a nobleman, in order—I know not how to say it better—to speak with a woman who looks most wretched. Perhaps that woman could show us better than anyone how to win that heart without the many arrangements and preparations that are now thought necessary." I said little to this, just enough to keep her engaged and prompt her to go on talking. Thus,the genealogy of the lady was next examined, her father and mother insulted, and the daughter ridiculed. I do not remember anything else; my head was in an uproar.

Lady Sternheim stayed away for a rather long time. Finally she returned with her face showing compassion but also contentment, her eyes somewhat reddened from weeping, she smiled quietly at us, and her voice was so tender, so affectionate that I was even more maddened than before and no longer knew what to think. Lady R. looked at her in an insolent way, and my goddess may have noticed our embarrassment, for she kept completely silent, as we did, until we had returned home.

I hastened away in the evening to get my report, and my man told me that he had found the landlady and the woman weeping at the kindness of the lady, that the woman was a complete stranger to the lady, had been amazed at being addressed by her, and had followed her with an anxious face into the room where the lady had led her and the children. There the lady had told her to be of good courage, asked pardon for accosting her, offered help and actually given her money. After learning that the woman was traveling to D. and that she resided there, she had written down her own name and address for the woman and lovingly assured her that she would continue to help her. She had also asked the landlady to order a decent coach to take the woman and her children home. It seemed to me that either my man or I must be a fool and I doubted everything he said, but he swore that his story was the truth.

I could not help thinking that this girl had the strangest character. Why the deuce did she turn red and grow confused when she wanted to do a good deed? Why did she lie to us that she knew this woman? Did she fear that we might want to share in her charitable act? Never mind! I will turn this discovery, this accident to my advantage. I shall seek out this family and do something good for them (as Englishmen are wont to do), and I shall do it without letting on that I know anything about her helping them. But you may be certain that I shall not take a single step without her noticing it. Through this act of charity I shall come closer to her character, and since we always attach ourselves with a certain affectionate inclination to the objects of our pity and generosity, she must necessarily form a good opinion of him who, without seeking recognition, helps to reinstate a family's good fortune. I will doubtless find occasion to say that her noble example has inspired me, and once having gained a hair's breadth on her self-love, I shall soon progress by leaps and bounds.

She watches me surreptitiously when I am conversing near her, but I counter her little artifice for knowing me completely by another: whenever she can overhear me I say something sensible, or I break off the discourse and assume a precocious expression. But although her reserve toward me has weakened, it is not yet time to talk of love; the scales are still tipped toward Seymour. I wish I knew why this healthy young girl prefers that pale, sad fellow to me with my fresh color and sprightly figure, why she would rather listen to his croaking tones than to my lively voice, and why she seeks his dead glances and avoids my speaking eye. Can it be that water runs in her veins? I will find out at the upcoming ball, for there any chink in her armor will show itself. At least, they have made all possible preparations to stir even the drowsiest senses into activity. Your friend will not miss the awakening of hers, and then I shall make sure they don't fall into slumber again.

Lady Sternheim to Emilia[8]

I have returned from the most pleasant journey I have ever undertaken with my aunt. For ten days we stayed at the Count of T.'s castle. There we found the widowed Countess of Sch. who permanently resides there, two other ladies of the neighborhood, and—to my indescribable joy—Mr.—. I had already read his superlative writings and through them improved my heart and taste. The unconstrained, quiet tenor of his conversation hiding his penetrating mind and great knowledge, and the calmness with which he tolerates being drawn into diversions and discourses that are entirely unworthy of his great genius and knowledge, stirred in me the same admiration for his affable disposition that all the world feels for his mind. I constantly hoped they would give him an opportunity to tell us something useful about the fine arts or good books (especially German literature) to improve our knowledge and taste, but I was quite disappointed in this hope, my Emilia.

No one thought of using the association with this great and benevolent sage for the benefit of our minds. They abused his patience and amiability by imposing on him the worthless topics of trifling minds, or newly arrived French romances, taking offense when he did not exult over them or praise other things as much as they thought he should. Oh, how I coveted every minute this estimable man gave me. He recognized my thirst for knowledge and my sensibility, and with great kindness answered my questions. He told me of excellent books and taught me how to read them for my benefit. He told me frankly that although I demonstrated the ability and thirst for knowledge in almost equal measures, I was not born to be a thinker. He said I should be content that nature had fortunately compensated me with the talent to fulfill the real purpose of our existence. This purpose was action, not speculation.[*] Further, because I was so readily and acutely sensible of the deficiencies that others allow in their moral lives and in the use of their days, I should strive to show the effect of my reflections on this topic by the noble actions of which I was so obviously capable.[**]

Never, my Emilia, have I been happier than when this understanding observer of the human heart's most secret corners thought me capable of

---

[*]Be it understood that when scholars' speculations have once become useful to society, they attain through that usefulness the value of noble actions [Wieland].

[**]Mr.—, whom we have the honor of knowing, told us upon being asked that his real meaning was this: He had observed in Lady Sternheim a certain inclination to reason about moral issues from general principles, to be discriminating, and to give her thoughts a kind of systematic form; and he had found at the same time that in this she succeeded least. It had seemed to him that her strength lay in her delicacy of perception, her power of observation, and the concomitant eagerness with which all the faculties of her soul sought to employ the goodness of her heart at every opportunity, and that this was what he had really meant to say to Lady Sternheim [Wieland].

noble and virtuous inclinations. With tender delicacy he reproached me for my timidity and reserve in judging the works of the mind; and he ascribed to me a right perception which, he said, justified speaking my thoughts as freely as others do. But he begged me not to attempt a masculine tone in speaking or writing. He claimed that it was the effect of a false taste when people accorded exaggerated praise to certain masculine properties of mind and character in a woman. It was true, he said, that women had indeed equal claim with men to all virtues and to all such knowledge which fosters their exercise, enlightens the mind, or improves our feelings and moral conduct, but that in exercising that claim the differences of the sexes must always be observed.

Nature herself, he said, had provided us instruction in this when, for example in love, she made the man passionate and the woman tender; in insults, she armed the former with wrath, the latter with moving tears; in the pursuit of business affairs and the sciences, she had given the male mind strength and depth, the female one pliancy and grace; in misfortune, she had surpassingly apportioned steadfastness and courage to the man, and to the woman she had given patience and resignation; in domestic life, she had assigned to the former the responsibility for the means of family sustenance, to the latter the proper distribution of those means. In this manner, when each sex remained in its prescribed sphere, both were running the same course, though each in different tracks as it were, toward the final goal of their destiny, without by an artificial mingling of the characters disturbing the moral order.

He sought to reconcile me with myself and with the fate I complained about. He taught me always to see the good side of a thing, thus moderating the impression of the bad side, and not to dwell on the latter more than was necessary to appreciate more vividly the charm and value of what is beautiful and good.

My mind relished the days of my association with this man. I sense that they will not return, that I will never again be fortunate enough to live according to my wishes and inclinations, as simple and undemanding as they may be! Do not censure me for my pampered faintheartedness. Perhaps the cause is the departure of Mr.—, which leaves behind a terrible void. He comes here only rarely. He visits this house, as pilgrims visit a ruined shrine where formerly saints dwelt, to venerate the shade of the great man who lived here, whose superior mind and experienced wisdom he admired, who was his friend, and who knew how to value him.

On the day after his departure, an insignificant French author arrived, whom a lack of good fortune in Paris and the strange weakness of our nobility in preferring French to German literature had brought into this house. The ladies made much of a man who came straight from Paris, had spoken there to many marquises, and knew how to make up whole treatises about the fashions, manners, and diversions of the beautiful Paris world. He was able to assist in all the female tasks, and he prated to the elegant widow in all the tones and turns of his language about his amazement at the delicacy of her mind and the graces of her person and soul, which was, he said, not at all German.

It was entertaining at first to see such a perfect illustration of the "rented minds" with which the rich and great of France surround themselves and which I had often encountered in books. Yet, by the fourth day I was tired of the empty tales he constantly repeated, varying only the words, about Parisian furniture, finery, banquets, and assemblies. But the scene changed when Mr.—returned. He took the trouble to put this domestic spirit conjured up from France in his proper place.

The pomp, the slavish prejudice harbored by our nobility for France with which the Parisian was presented to Mr.—, the affectation, the self-satisfaction with which the Frenchman heard himself praised as the author of very pleasing and popular little works, would have annoyed you as much as it did me. In contrast, how beautifully did the modesty of our wise countryman shine forth! With the humanity with which the genuine philosopher suffers fools, he disguised the impression which the dull aesthete must have made on him; and yes, with true affability he even remembered that he had read one of his little writings.

The whole episode reminded me of the following fiction: With ridiculous pride, a poor braggart shows the noble owner of a gold mine a small piece of tinsel, cut out in the shape of a star, which he turns back and forth in his hands, making much of the rustling sound he thus produces, something to which the magnanimous rich man's store of pure gold is indeed but ill suited. But the latter smiles affably at the fool with his toy, telling him that, although it gleams and rustles quite pleasingly, he had better guard it from the fire of investigation and the water of adversity[*] if he wants his enjoyment to endure.

Mr.—asked the aesthete about France's great sons whose writings he had read and valued highly; but like the rest of us the Frenchman knew them only by name and instead of discussing some man renowned for his learning, he continually slipped back into naming the wealthy or prominent.

I had long been displeased at the abuse of Mr.—'s presence and complaisance, especially as they all crowded around him and, like enviously buzzing wasps, prevented me from gathering a little honey for myself, en-

---

[*]I have found in this simile so much that is true and at the same time in keeping with the peculiar character of Lady Sternheim's mind that I could not bring myself to change any of it, in spite of being fully persuaded that the "fire of investigation" and the "water of adversity" cannot find mercy before the critics and would be better placed in Bunyan's *Pilgrim's Progress* than in this book [Wieland].

couraging only the Parisian to speak. Finally, when I had a chance, I posed the question, what profit French ladies derived from the association with their scholars. I was told that they learned from them the beauties of language and expression and the rudiments of all the sciences, in order occasionally to add some words to the conversation and thus gain the renown of having wide knowledge. Further, they learned at least the names of all the famous books and to pronounce something resembling a judgment about them. They also accompanied their scholars to the public lectures on physics, where without much trouble to themselves they collected useful ideas. The same was true in regard to the artists' workshops, where genius was busily producing the appurtenances of splendor and pleasure. All this, they claimed, contributed much toward making French ladies' conversation so pleasing and varied.

With distaste I was struck by the surpassing cleverness of French self-love, which extends to such noble and useful abuses: apparently it is enough if one is eager to know the blossoms of the trees; soon enough one will also want to investigate their growth and the ripening of the fruits. How many advantages this nation has over us! Nothing is more readily generalized than a woman's tastes.

Returning from their Parisian visits year after year, why have not our noblemen brought back for their sisters and other female relatives among a thousand harmful fashion reports this one, which would have bettered all the others? But because they collect only ridiculous and harmful things, why should they search out for us that which is decent and useful?

Further, I calculated also the profit which even the scholar's genius derives from the questions of the ignorant who are thirsty for knowledge, often leading him to reflect on a new aspect of these objects which he had formerly overlooked as trifling or which, because they touched on the realm of feelings, were noticed sooner by a woman than by men. Certainly the endeavor to instruct others in an art or a science renders our own concepts finer, clearer, and more perfect. Yes, even the pupil's backward manner of grasping something, his most simpleminded questions can be the occasion of great and useful discoveries. This was the case when a gardener at Florence observed the rising and falling of the well in different kinds of weather, resulting in the excellent invention of the barometer.

But I digress too far from the amiable German gentleman whose fine and infinitely knowledgeable genius collects moral tones and colors and in his works combines them charmingly into pictures of the people in our society, which is composed of so great a variety of characters. (He told me this when I praised him for his condescension in the face of so many meaningless conversations.)

With delight I discovered in him the model of a true friend. He told me of a much-revered man who had been raised by the former owner of this house and could be named as living proof of the innumerable faculties of our minds because he combined in himself the cunning of the most subtle statesman with all the scholarliness of the philosopher, the physicist, and the aesthete; he was able thoroughly to judge all works of art; he understood the state economy and agriculture in all its parts, spoke and wrote several languages well, and was a master at the piano and a connoisseur of all the fine arts. With so many perfections of mind he combined in full measure the noblest heart and the great character of a friend of mankind.

You can see from this picture whether Mr.—does not have cause to look upon the friendship with such a man as the surpassing felicity of his life, and you will rejoice with me in his decision to take his friend's eldest son with him to his new place of residence. Separated by half the length of Germany from his dearest friends, he expends all his esteem for the parents on their son in order to raise him to be a virtuous man and thus, far from his friends, preserve the connection of his heart with theirs. Oh Emilia, what is gold, what are the honors which the princes sometimes distribute to the meritorious, when measured against the friendship Mr.—has for the son of his fortunate friends? My heart reveres him. May God keep him! How blessed must be his evening hours after days filled with such noble purpose!

My letter is long, but my Emilia has a soul that lingers with delight on the description of a practical virtue and is grateful for it. Mr.—departed in the evening, and because every part of the house and garden where I had seen him and now missed him painfully plunged me into abysmal sadness that will not abate at our court, to my delight we left on the second morning after his departure. But in keeping with his advice, I shall ever search for the beautiful side of my fate and also show it to you in future.

Now I must prepare for the fête which Count F. will give at his country seat. I do not like these perpetual festivities, but on this occasion there will be dancing, and as you know, of all the diversions I most incline toward this one.

My Lord Derby to His Friend B.

I write to express my heart's joy, for here I may show it to no one. It is amusing to contemplate that all the preparations being made to honor the prince must surely drive the beautiful, timorous bird into my hidden net. Count F., who acted the chief fowler on this occasion, recently entertained all the nobility at his estate very pleasantly, where we all had to appear in peasant dress.

We assembled in the afternoon, and our peasant clothes revealed perfectly who were naturally noble and who had merely appeared so through artful contrivance. Many among us lacked only a spade or plowshare to be

the farmhands we impersonated, and certainly there was also more than one
lady who, with a basket of chickens on her head or busy milking, would not
have retained the least sign of privileged birth or upbringing. I was a Scottish peasant and represented the bold and resolute character of the highland-
ers quite naturally, and I had hit on the secret of how to enhance it with the
elegance which you know I possess, without disadvantage to my assumed
character. But that enchantress of a Sternheim was all charm and beautiful
nature in her disguise. All her features were innocent, rustic joy. Her dress
of light-blue taffeta bordered in black gave her slender Greek form an even
more refined aspect, proving that she did not need any artificial finery. All
her movements were invested with magical powers, attracting the envious
eyes of the ladies and the desirous glances of all the men. Her hair was
beautifully braided and tied back with ribbons, in order not to trail on the
ground. It gave me the idea of one day seeing her in the shape of Milton's
Eve—when I shall be her Adam! She was very lively and spoke most oblig-
ingly with all the ladies. Her aunt and Countess F. showered her with caresses, hoping to keep the girl in a lively mood for the prince as well.

Seymour felt the full power of her charms, but in keeping with his
politic agreement with his uncle he hid his love under a fit of the spleen;
and, silent and restless, the peevish fellow walked now under this, now
under that tree, with Lady C. as his peasant woman following him like a
shadow. It was a Herculean effort to keep my passion reined in, but to be
silent was impossible. I seized every opportunity of walking past Lady
Sternheim and saying something admiring to her in English. But several
times I could have crushed her when her eyes, if only briefly, fixed on
Seymour with all the disquietude of love. Finally she slipped away among
the crowd, and we saw her hasten toward the door of the parsonage garden.
The others discussed her departure, but I remained standing at the corner of
the little dairy to observe her when she returned. She came out in less than
a quarter hour. A charming blush and the most delicate expression of delight were spread over her face. With affable kindness she thanked several
spectators for their efforts to make way for her. Never had I seen her as
beautiful as at that moment. Even her walk seemed lighter and more graceful than usual. Everyone's eyes were turned toward her. She noticed it, cast
hers on the ground, and blushed even more. At the same moment, the
prince, too, came out of the parson's garden and straight through the crowd
of people. Now you should have seen the looks of suspicion and malicious
judgment in the faces of every prudish coquette and subservient lackey
about their meeting. You should have heard the silly jokes of the men about
her blush when the prince looked at her with such obvious delight. These
signs were taken as proof of a pleasant tryst in the parsonage, and everyone
whispered in one another's ear, "We are celebrating the ceremony of surrender of this beauty who was considered unconquerable." They noted the

charm with which she brought the prince some refreshment, his emotion as he rose, went toward her, and with consuming glances looked now at her face, now at her figure. Having partaken of the refreshment, he was seen to take the plate away from her, giving it to young F. and making her sit next to him on the bench. The joy of old F. and her aunt's pride, which were already becoming visible—these confirmed our conjectures. Seymour was beside himself and in a fit of rage; I took him by the arm and talked to him about this scene. Extreme contempt colored his remarks about her pretended virtue and its wretched sacrifice, about her impudence in enjoying this display of herself before the entire nobility. This last part of his censure brought me to my senses. I reflected that such an act was, in truth, too uncharacteristically barefaced and stupid. I remembered the scene at the inn in F. A doubt then crossed my mind, and it made me call my man Will. I promised him a hundred guineas to find out what had really transpired in the parson's house between the prince and Lady Sternheim. In an hour's time, each minute seeming like a year, he came back with the intelligence that the lady had not seen the prince, but had spoken alone with the parson and had given him ten ducats for the poor of the village, earnestly requesting that he tell no one of this. The prince had followed her, wanting to observe from afar how the nobility diverted themselves, so that upon entering he would not disrupt their amusements.

There I stood, cursing the little enthusiast who had made fools of us. Yet in reality the girl was nobler than we who thought only of our own diversion, while she opened her heart to the poor inhabitants of the village to let the day's joyfulness extend to them also. But what was her reward for this? The basest judgments of her character, which the most wretched creature among us felt himself entitled to make. In truth, a fine encouragement to virtue! If you feel like telling me that inner satisfaction is our true reward, I can't help remembering that the very expression of this satisfaction on the angelic girl's face was taken as proof of her guilt when she returned from the parsonage. But how thankful I was for my eagerness to know the whole affair. This made me, a confirmed villain, the most virtuous soul in the whole company, for I alone wanted to get to the bottom of the thing before passing final judgment on her. And look you, I was at once rewarded for my virtue with the hope that the amiable creature would come to my arms completely pure. Only her death or mine shall now prevent that. Now all my talents and faculties are dedicated to the execution of that design.

Triumphantly I hastened back to the company after forbidding Will to mention his discovery to a single soul, promising him another hundred guineas for his silence. Perhaps you will claim that I should have announced my discovery for the good of the lady and that then my triumph would have been noble. But softly, my lord, softly! I could not proceed so fast on the path of good works, and even less could I have sacrificed all my satisfaction. And what purpose would my discovery have served, except to increase the prince's difficulty and mine? Of how much amusement would I have deprived myself if I had interrupted the discussions on the former subject! For while I was gone, a misunderstood answer made by the prince had cleared up the entire affair. When Count F. had asked the prince whether he had seen the lady in the parsonage garden, the prince had answered him briefly with a "yes" and had immediately turned his eyes to her. Then what had transpired became immediately clear: she was— because the parson had to be given some role in this scene—morganatically married, and many already showed her the special respect that belongs to the future distributor of favors. Count F., his wife, and the lady's aunt and uncle headed up the line of these fools. Even my Lord G. played the role, although with him it seemed somewhat forced. But Seymour, reduced to an unyielding rage because his love and his mind's ideal image of her had been insulted, could hardly muster enough common civility to dance a minuet with her. The cold and stubborn expression he returned to her friendly gaze finally caused her not to look at him any more, but at the same time her dejection increased the noble grace of her inimitable dance in an enchanting way. I was maddened by every visible preference which her heart gave him, but I redoubled my vigilance over everything that might serve my purpose. I saw that she perceived the extraordinary efforts and flatteries of the courtiers and that she was displeased with them. I showed her only noble, refined respect. It pleased her and, lively and obliging, she said in beautiful English that dancing was the only diversion she loved. As I praised her minuet, she wished that I could say the same of her English country dances whose gaiety and decency she approved. She said they did not permit the lady to forget herself, nor the gentleman to take arbitrary liberties, as was the custom with the German dances. My delight over this friendly little conversation was much increased by my noticing Seymour's visible annoyance. The prince, not being pleased either, approached us; and I withdrew to tell Count F. that the lady preferred to dance in the English manner. The music instantly began, and each one looked for his peasant woman. As Lady Sternheim's companion, young F. led her halfway up the row, and his father made all the couples step back to give the lady first place. She accepted it with amazement and danced through the line with unusual speed but perfect grace. I intentionally refrained from dancing the first set and strolled up and down the line of dancers with my Lord G. and the prince. The latter had eyes only for Lady Sternheim and repeatedly said, "Doesn't she dance like an angel?" Because Lord G. assured him that an Englishwoman born and bred could not have executed the steps and turns any better, the prince had the idea that the lady should dance with an Englishman. I stepped to a window to wait and see who would be chosen, and after an interval of rest the prince asked the lady to dance the second set, too, but with one of us two Englishmen. A gracious bow and her look around toward us showed her willingness to do so. How tenderly her glance invited the frigid Seymour, whom as Lord G's nephew Count F. invited first and who refused. A sudden blush of vexation colored her face and bosom; but she immediately had a friendly glance for me, and I offered her my hand with respectful eagerness. But this glance did not compensate me but forced me to think, "Oh Sophia, such feelings for *me* would have dedicated my heart to you and virtue forever! The effort of wresting you from others abates my tenderness; desire and revenge alone are left to me." But my face showed nothing of this. I was all reverence. She danced exquisitely, which the others attributed to her desire to please the prince. I alone knew that the beauty and vivacity of her dance was an attempt by her offended self-love to punish Seymour for his refusal. And punished he was! So full of vexation, he was glad to vent his complaints to me; and he cursed himself that, though she deserved all his contempt, he could not help feeling the tenderest sentiments for her.

"Why then did you not dance with her?"

"God forbid," he said; "I would have sunk to the ground at her side from the struggle between the love and contempt I have for her."

I laughed at him and said that he should love as I do. He would then gain more satisfaction than he could ever obtain from his exaggerated ideas.

"I feel that you are happier than I," said the fool; "but I cannot change myself."

"A plague on love," thought I, "that makes such miserable dogs of him and me." Cast adrift between his contempt for an adored object and all the charms of the senses, Seymour was unhappy because he did not know of her innocence and tenderness. I, who could not renounce my respect and love for her, was a prey to envy and the desire to avenge myself; but I found little joy in this, other than the joy of destroying others' happiness, whatever the consequences might be. I have much work to do, for as artfully and surely as I was wont to lay my snares, all my former experience does not serve me with her, because she is so far removed from all sensuous pleasures. At a ball, where nearly all women are coquettes and even the best consumed with the desire to please, she practices benevolence. Others are drugged by the assemblage of many people, the noise of celebration, and the magnificent costumes and decorations; they are weakened by the music and exposed by everything to the temptations of sensuality. She, too, is moved, but to compassion for the poor; and this emotion is so strong that she leaves the company and all pleasures to do a charitable deed. Ah! Once this strong and active sensibility of her soul is turned toward the enjoyment of pleasure, and the first notes are sounded for me—then B., then I shall be able to describe from experience the exquisite voluptuousness which Venus pours out in company with the muses and graces. But I shall have to

124 The History of Lady Sophia Sternheim

prepare for this. Just as those enthusiasts who want to associate personally with spiritual beings must spend some time fasting and praying, so must I, to please this enthusiastic soul, forego all my former pleasures. Already my accidentally discovered charity toward the T. family has served we well with her; now it remains for me to surprise her in that house. She sometimes goes there to instruct the children and comfort the parents. Nevertheless, all her morality has not been able to prevent the influence of my guineas. Through them I shall find the opportunity to see her at their house and take another step closer to her heart, while, on the other hand, I seek to weaken the magical sympathy which shared enthusiasms might arouse between her and Seymour in a moment, if they ever came in close enough association to perceive how perfectly their souls are attuned, one to the other. But I have pretty well prevented that, for to obtain intelligence Seymour is using his uncle's secretary, who is my own slave and who first obtains the intelligence from me without having to talk to me, for we only write to each other and put our notes behind an old painting in the upper passage of the house. This disciple of Lucifer gives me excellent service, but I must give Seymour his due: He facilitates our efforts as much as lies within his power. He flees Lady Sternheim as if she were a snake, though he inquires about all her movements; and these, owing to the coloring that my intelligences give them, appear sufficiently distorted and ambiguous to have the desired effect upon his already prejudiced mind. I do not fear the prince. Every step he takes will remove him farther from his goal. Of all that princes can give she loves nothing. The girl represents an entirely new species of character.

My Lord Seymour to Dr. B.

Four hours ago I returned from a splendid and well-contrived entertainment; and as I cannot find any sleep (despite the violent emotions which my spirits have suffered), I want at least to seek the tranquillity that conversation with a worthy friend affords a troubled heart. Why, my dear mentor, could your experience and wisdom find no means to arm me against the effects of mistaken impressions of goodness, just as you found one to protect me from the example and encouragement of malice. I shall tell you the cause of my condition, and you will see for yourself how happy a prudent indifference would have made me.

The prime minister gave for the nobility (or rather the prince, under Count F.'s name, gave for Lady Sternheim) an "entertainment in the country" which the art of imitation brought to the highest conformity with real life. The costumes, the music, the place where the entertainment was held—all these were typical of the country festival. Special peasant cottages and a barn for dancing had been built in the middle of a meadow. For the first two hours the idea and its execution delighted me because I saw nothing before me but the beauty of the festival and the surpassing amiability of Lady Sternheim. Never, my friend, never again will the picture of genuine innocence, of pure joy, shine forth so perfect as it did in Lady Sternheim's noble beautiful figure during these two hours! Cursed be the machinations that extinguished that image of her! But in a person of so much understanding, of such an excellent education, the will must have been a party to it. It is impossible that they could have bewitched her; it is also impossible that her senses were merely excited by the music, splendor, and noise. I know full well that under these conditions one may inadvertently deviate from one's moral convictions and lose sight of them. But when she rejected the last admonition of her good genius, when a few minutes later she hastened to the prearranged meeting with the prince and in doing so earned the contempt of even the most wretched among us—then I was hard put to hide the contempt and revulsion I felt toward her.

I must explain to you what I mean by "the last admonition of her genius." There was a picture booth there, where the ladies drew lottery tickets. Tell me now, was it merely coincidence or a last warning of providence that Lady Sternheim drew Daphne pursued by Apollo? The prince's party did not relish this; they thought it would reinforce her obstinacy. She liked it; she showed it to everyone and talked about it as one knowledgeable in drawing and painting. My joy was indescribable. I thought the apprehensions of the courtiers well founded, and the lady's joy strengthened my hope that through her virtue she would become a latter-day fleeing Daphne. But how painfully and basely was I betrayed by her false virtue when, soon after, she threw herself into the arms of Apollo!

I observed her walking back and forth for some time with her worthless aunt and Countess F. The two wretched procuresses were vying with each other in flattering her. At length I observed that with a tender and careful expression she looked now at the company, now at the door of the parson's garden, and suddenly, with the lightest, most joyful step, she pressed through the spectators and hastened into the garden. She did not stay long, but her going into it had excited attention. But how much was this increased by the expression of satisfaction and humility with which she returned and by the prince's coming out soon after her, unable to hide his delight in her and displaying his passion in its full force! With abject servility she offered him some sherbet, chatted with him, and to please him danced in the English manner with such spirit as she had previously shown only on the subject of virtue. And how charming, Oh God, how charming she was! How inimitable her dancing! All the graces were united in her, just as all the furies were united in my heart! For I felt it torn apart by the thought that I who had adored her virtue, who had wanted to make her my wife, was forced to witness her delivering up her honor and innocence and doing it, before God and men, with a triumphant expression. I am at a loss to understand what I felt on this occasion. You know that I once felt a violent passion for one of our actresses. I knew that her favors could be bought and that her heart deserved no respect, nor did I feel any. And yet my passion continued unabated. Now, however, I despise and curse Lady Sternheim and her image. Her charms and my love still live in the depths of my soul, but I hate both—and myself for being too weak to destroy them.

During the drive home my uncle counseled me like a man whose passions have long been satiated, and who (if as prime minister he can disregard a thousand victims of sacrificial slaughter for the sake of satisfying the ambition of his prince) must naturally look upon the sacrifice of a young woman's virtue to a great man's passion as a very insignificant trifle. Oh, if she were a *common* girl with a parrot's beauty and a parrot's mind, I could look upon it as he does! But to own the noblest soul, to have such knowledge, to claim the reverence of the whole world—and thus to throw herself away! She is said to be married morganatically. Wretched, laughable subterfuge to shield a dissembled virtue from shame! Everyone flattered her. You, my friend, know me well enough to know whether I did so. I shall not go to court until I have become calmer. I never wholly liked the court life; now I detest it! I shall endure the travels with my uncle, but my mother shall not force me to take up court service or marry. Lady Sternheim has caused me to renounce both these conditions forever. Derby, infamous Derby, holds her in contempt, too; but he helps to drug her, for he shows her more than usual respect—the villain.

Lady Sternheim to Emilia

Come, my Emilia, you shall for once have a sprightly tale from me. You know that I am fond of dancing and that F. was to give us a ball. This is now past, and I was so delighted by it that the memory of it still pleases me. All the arrangements for this pretty entertainment were completely to my taste and in accord with my very own ideas: rustic simplicity and the refined arts of the court were so pleasingly interwoven that one could not separate them without robbing one or the other of its best features. I shall try to see whether a description of it can reinforce this notion for you.

The count wanted to entertain us all at his country seat, where his wife had taken the waters and had received visits from all the nobility, to signify his joy over the countess' recovery and his thanks for all the regard that had been shown her there. We were invited eight days in advance and asked to appear as couples dressed in handsome peasant clothes, because he wanted to imitate a country festival. His nephew, the young Count F., was a country swain in the list; and I dressed as an alpine maiden: light blue and black, its form showing my figure off most favorably without appearing in the least contrived or forced. A dainty little straw hat, put on in a careless manner, and my simply braided hair did my face honor. You know that I have been imbued with much love for the simplicity and the artless virtues of the country people. This inclination was renewed when I saw my clothes. My elegantly simple finery affected me. It was even more agreeable to my heart, which loves tranquillity and nature, than to my figure, although that, too, appeared to my eyes in its best light then. When I was completely dressed and, delighted with my rustic appearance, cast a last glance into the mirror, I made the wish that even when I put off these clothes again, pure innocence and genuine goodness of heart should always give my soul tranquil and true felicity!

My uncle, my aunt, and Count F. continued to praise my endearing and charming appearance, and so we arrived at the estate where we alighted in the middle of the avenue of trees planted in a beautiful meadow. Here we presently heard the sound of the shawm, saw several couples of handsome peasant lads and maids, and upon advancing soon heard a Jew's harp and a little reed pipe or some other instrument of the kind announcing the rustic festival. Simply constructed wooden benches had been placed among the trees, and two handsome peasant cottages had been built on either side of the avenue. In one of these all manner of dishes prepared with milk and other refreshments stood ready in small porcelain basins. Each of us received his wooden trencher and a porcelain spoon. Countess F., dressed as the landlady of an inn, stood in the doorway of the cottage and welcomed the guests with charming courtesy. All the domestics of the house were dressed as cellar boys or tapsters, and the musicians, too, were dressed in the peasant manner. There were pastry cooks and picture sellers in another place where our "peasants" led us, and where each "peasant woman" would receive a pretzel or piece of bread made from fine pastry, which her companion would break in two and then would find in it either a piece of lace, a ribbon, or some other pretty trifle. At the picture shop were shown pretty miniatures that were selected as in a lottery. I drew one of Daphne pursued by Apollo, an elegant little piece! It seemed to me that others envied my getting it because it was considered the most beautiful. I also thought that some ladies' faces changed oddly when they saw it.

When all the nobility were assembled, we young ladies were asked to assist in serving the older ladies and the gentlemen refreshments. Our industry was pleasing to see, but for a stranger the searching, half-concealed glances which the ladies would cast on one another would have occasioned many little remarks. The grass on which I stepped, the trees in whose shade I drank a dish of milk, the fresh air I breathed, the cheerful open sky about me, a pretty brook running not twenty paces from where I stood, and well-cultivated, rich fields of corn gave me heartfelt joy. It seemed to me that the unlimited prospect over the kingdom of nature freed my vital spirits and sensations and transported them from the stifling confinement of a sojourn within the walls of a palace filled with artificial decorations and gilt orna-ments into their natural freedom and native element. I also talked more, and more cheerfully, than usual and was among the first who formed the lines for the dance among the trees.

This drew all the inhabitants of the village out of their cottages to watch us. After some skipping about, I walked up and down with my aunt and Countess F., who praised and caressed me. Then I noticed the merry and brilliant throng of peasants that we represented with the addition of those who made up our spectators. Among the latter I saw many poor and sorrowful figures. I was much moved by this contrast and their good-natured enjoyment in watching us; and as soon as I felt myself least ob-served, I slipped into the parsonage garden directly adjoining the meadow where we were dancing. I gave the parson something for the village poor and went back to the company with a happy heart. My Lord Derby seemed to have listened for my steps, for when I came out of the parson's garden I saw that he stood at the end of the dairy and had fixed his eyes unwaver-ingly on the garden gate. He looked at me with searching and passionate glances and hastily approached me to tell me some extraordinary, yes, even infatuated, things about my face and figure. This and the curious way in which everybody looked at me made me blush and lower my eyes to the ground. When I lifted them up again, I was very close to a tree on which my Lord Seymour leaned, looking so sad and tender that I thought he must surely have heard everything that my Lord Derby had told me. I do not quite know why this thought somewhat confounded me, but I became really dismayed when I saw everyone rising and taking their positions because the prince was just coming out of the parsonage garden. The thought that he might have encountered me there gave me a kind of horror, so that I ran to my aunt's side as if afraid to be alone. But my inner satisfaction helped me regain my composure, so that I calmly made my bow to the prince. He looked at and praised my dress in very lively terms; but Lady F., urging me to offer him a dish of sherbet, caused me some embarrassment because quite unwillingly I was made to sit next to him on the bench. There he told me I no longer recall what strange things about myself and the rest of the nobility. Most of the guests now began singly strolling about. When I looked after them attentively, the prince asked me whether I, too, would rather walk about than be with him. I told him that I thought there would be more dancing and that I wished to take part in it. He immediately rose and conducted me to the others. I congratulated myself on my idea and quickly mingled with a throng of young people who were all standing to-gether. They smiled at my joining them but were almost too polite, except for Lady C. who turned her head aside in a surly manner. I also turned and saw Seymour and Derby who had linked arms and were walking back and forth with hasty steps along the brook. Meantime, darkness was setting in, and we were asked to a supper that stood ready in the other peasant cottage. We did not remain long at table, for everyone hastened into the ballroom concealed in a specially constructed barn. No one could have been more glad to leave the table than I, for when the lots were drawn for seating, my adverse fate placed me next to the prince who constantly talked to me and every minute made me taste some dish or other. This chance preferment[*] showed me the courtiers in a new but very diminishing light, for they conducted themselves toward me as if I had acquired great rank and they wished to make themselves pleasing to me. Everyone offered me becoming or unbecoming flattery, excepting Seymour who said nothing.

His uncle G. and Lord Derby, on the other hand, paid me most delicate courtesies. The latter especially showed the most obliging respect in his whole conduct toward me. He spoke of dancing in a tone proper to the subject, so that once again he filled me with respect for his talents and regret at the poor use he made of them.

During the dancing I was persuaded that it is not advantageous for *everyone* that the dance begins with a minuet, because that dance calls for so much grace in the turns and such precision of step that many find it difficult to satisfy these demands. The extraordinary applause I received put me in mind of my dear parents who, among other loving exertions for my education, insisted on my early and frequent practice in dance. The rapidity of my growth indicated that I would grow tall, and my father said that early instruction in dancing was most necessary to a tall person to make her movements harmonious and pleasing through the effect of music, because people had always thought that the graces ally themselves more readily with a person of medium height than with one of more than usual stature. This was the reason for my having to dance every day and during my needlework having to sing a minuet aria, for my father claimed that through this practice all my movements would insensibly attain a natural grace. If I were to believe all the praise they give my dancing and my poise, then all his theories would be proved true, just as I have found true his dictum that grace is preferred over beauty. I believe this because I have seen that the surpassingly lovely expression of the Countess Z., who was endowed with but very little beauty, attracted the envy of more women than did Lady B. with her Venus figure, even though the envious ladies were themselves well

---

[*]Few readers will need to be reminded that it was quite natural for Lady Sternheim's innocence and inexperience in the ways of the world to take as an effect of chance what was intention and design. At courts they understand no art better than how to create "chance events" when the intention is subtly to advance the passions of the sovereign [Wieland].

endowed. Why should this be so, Emilia? Do persons of sensibility perhaps feel more strongly than others the advantage grace has over beauty? And are they, therefore, more eager to possess the former? Did this envy come from the observation that the graceful Countess Z. attracted the most respected gentleman to herself? Perhaps artful self-love dares to attack individual charms that are pleasing rather than a perfect beauty, because the former are not immediately noticed by all eyes and because the lack of utmost perfection is readily associated with a faulty character or understanding and might, therefore, earn the critic a reputation for a keen eye. The smallest aspersion cast on a perfectly beautiful woman, on the other hand, is considered mere envy by everyone who hears it. Proper and prudent self-love should always desire for itself the favors of the graces because they never take back their gifts, and neither time nor incident can rob us of them. I confess quite openly that, had I been born in the glorious time of the Greeks, I would have dedicated my best sacrifices in the temple of the graces. But I can see my Emilia before me; I can guess what she thinks. While she reads this letter, the expression in her face asks, "Is my friend Sophia herself quite faultless, as she so confidently describes the faults of others? She may not have felt envy, for the plan her vanity had suggested apparently met with no obstacles. Her gratitude for having received dancing instruction as part of her education shows this. Often merely a high degree of self-satisfaction saves us from harboring envy, whereas true virtue should do so."

Be easy, my dear and stern friend! I see that you are right. I thought of myself as quite amiable, but I was not in the eyes of him who I so ardently wished would consider me so. I was vain and much satisfied with myself, but I have been punished for it. I tried very hard to dance well in the English manner, so that my Lord G. and Derby said to the prince that a native Englishwoman could not have observed the steps, the turns, and the measure more properly. They asked me to dance a set with an Englishman. My Lord Seymour was asked to oblige, and, Emilia, he refused! He did so with such an unfriendly, almost contemptuous face, that I felt hurt. My pride sought to cover up this wound. And yet his somber looks toward all the world disquieted me most of all. He talked with no one, except his uncle and Lord Derby, who eagerly obliged. I sought to reward him with my best dancing skills and, at the same time, to show Seymour by my liveliness that his reluctance had not affected me. You know me; you must surely guess that this moment was not pleasant for me, but my hasty inclination deserved chastisement! Why did I let the praises of a woman who loves my Lord Seymour prejudice me so much in his favor as to forget justice toward others and almost forget the respect I owe myself? But I owe him thanks for guiding me back to reflection and consideration. I now feel more tranquil within myself, more just toward others, and have, therefore, new cause to be pleased at the past entertainment. I have practiced charity toward my neighbor, and for myself I have learned a lesson in prudence. I hope that now my Emilia is satisfied with me and loves me as much as ever.

Lady Sternheim to Emilia

Now I have the letter poor Mrs. T. promised me at Count F.'s estate. In it she tells me the causes of her misfortune, but it is so detailed and written on such thick paper that I cannot enclose it. From my summary you will gather most of it, and I will here remark on some of the main points.

She comes from a reputable but poor councillor's family. Her mother, a virtuous woman and careful manager of the household, restricted her daughters to very simple food and clothes, permitted them only rarely to leave the house, and exhorted them to constant industry. She also continually told them that the family's small means prevented their imitating others, more prosperous and fortunate, in the richness of their dress, table, and other luxuries. The children reluctantly submitted. Then the mother died, and Councillor T. applied for the hand of the second daughter, which he received readily because they knew that he had inherited a considerable fortune from his parents.

And now the young man wanted to show his wealth; he made his wife fine presents; the furnishings of his house were handsome, too. They paid and received visits, invited guests, and the latter were entertained in the manner of wealthy folk. Thus they acquired a number of "table friends," and the young woman who all her life had known nothing but the lack of these felicities of wealth, eagerly devoted herself to the enjoyment of luxury, the diversions to be found in assemblies, and the delight in beautiful and varied clothes. She bore children, and they began to educate them also in keeping with their station. Their fortune was consumed; they incurred debts and continued in their accustomed luxury with borrowed money until the borrowed sum became so great that the creditors lost all patience and were forced to pay themselves by seizing the furniture and the house. Now all their friends vanished. The habit of a fine table and the love of beautiful clothes robbed them of what was left. The income from his post was consumed in the first few months of the year, and the remaining months were spent in want and sorrow.

Time passed, and the husband could no longer gratify his vanity, nor the wife her love of ease. He lacked the will and she the prudence to adjust themselves to their circumstances. They searched for benefactors and some were found, but their assistance did not suffice. The husband became embittered and reproached those who had been his friends. He insulted them, and they revenged themselves by causing him to lose his post. Now despair and misery in equal measure were their portion, both being increased by the sight of their six children. All their relatives had withdrawn their help; and since their distress frequently compelled them to resort to various little tricks, often of a low nature, as a means of helping themselves, they finally became the object of contempt and hatred. They were in this condition when I came to know them and offered them my assistance. Money, clothes, and linen, as well as other household necessities were the beginning, but I can plainly see that this will not be sufficient if the evil is not pulled up by the roots and their thinking cured of false notions of honor and happiness.

I have formed a plan of how this might be done and would ask your worthy husband, who has such great insight, to complete and improve it. For I can well understand that the experience and reflection of a girl of twenty is inadequate to give this family the necessary instruction on all points. You, my Emilia, will see that my thoughts are mostly excerpts from the writings used in my education, which I have tried to adapt to this case. It is difficult for the rich to give the poor advice that will please, for the latter will always question the sincerity of the former's moral ideas and will consider his exhortations to industry and frugality as a sign that his bene-factor is weary of being charitable. This suspicion will prevent any good effects.

Two days of diversion have interrupted my letter where I had stopped about Councillor T. I wish to God that I had been able to make him rich with the sole proviso that his wealth be used with prudence. The welfare of this family has cost me more than if I had given them half my fortune: I have sacrificed some of my principles! Councillor T. implored me to obtain another appointment for him through my uncle. I applied to the latter, and he said he could not use his new-found favor with the prince for anyone but his own children, and that he must do so by seeking to win his lawsuit. This saddened me, but my aunt told me that I should speak to the prince at the next opportunity; I would find that he delighted in doing good if one showed him a worthy object, and I would certainly not ask him in vain. In the afternoon Count F. and his wife visited us. I discussed this with them, too, and asked both to use their good offices with the prince on behalf of this poor family; but they, too, told me that because it was the first favor I sought, I would obtain it most easily by asking for it myself. In addition, because of the rarity of this case, so to speak, since never before had a vivacious young lady dedicated herself with such zeal to an unfortunate family, this newly discovered side of my character would increase his re-spect for me.

I became annoyed that I could find no helping hand in this work of charity. I did not like speaking to the prince, although I knew I could count on his willingness, for I had clearly perceived his inclination toward me. But it was precisely that perception which caused my hesitation, for I wished always to maintain distance from him. Yet my supplication, his acquiescence, and my gratitude would bring me closer to him, his compliments, and the tales he has already twice told me of those new, thus far unfamiliar feelings that I inspired in him. I struggled with myself for several days, but when I made a visit at the gloomy house of the T. family, witnessed the parents' happiness at receiving my gifts, but saw the house still empty of necessaries and occupied by six children, some grown and some still small—then I felt my peace of mind and my convictions should give way to the welfare of these children. Should not my self-loving delicacy make way for the duty of helping my needy neighbor? Should my vexation with the prince's growing passion prevent the picture of this family's joy if they received a post and an income? After all, I was sure that the prince respected my reluctance—and other such thoughts occurred to me. Everyone had assured me of the prince's certain assistance; my heart knew that his passion could not harm me without my consent. On the very next day, therefore, I carried out my resolution.

We were at a concert at the Princess of W.'s, and I was obliged to sing. The prince seemed ecstatic and begged me to walk with him up and down in the hall a few times. You can imagine that he said many things about the beauty of my voice and the skill of my fingers, and that I countered these compliments with some modest answers. But when he uttered the desire to show his respect through something more than words, I said that I was convinced of his noble and magnanimous thoughts and took the liberty, therefore, to ask his assistance for an unfortunate family who were much in need and worthy of the help of the father of their country. He stood still, looked at me in a lively and tender manner, and said, "Tell me, my amiable Lady Sternheim, what is this family? What can I do for them?"

I briefly told him, as clearly and movingly as I was able, about the whole misfortune in which Councillor T. and his children found themselves; and I asked him for the sake of the latter to show mercy and forbearance to the former who had already expiated his carelessness long ago through his great sorrow. He promised me that all would be well, praised me for my zeal, and added that he gladly came to the aid of the unfortunate, but that he well knew that those who surrounded him always cared first for themselves and theirs. I would give him much joy, he said, were I to show him more objects for his benevolence. I assured him that I would not misuse his goodness and once again briefly repeated my plea for the T. family.

He took my hand, pressed it between both of his, and said feelingly, "I promise you, my dear zealous intercessor, that all the wishes of your heart shall be fulfilled, if I can but keep you thinking well of me."

At this moment I almost hated my compassionate heart and the family of T., for the prince looked at me significantly; and when I wanted to take my hand away he held it faster and pressed it to his breast. "Yes," he repeated, "I shall do everything to make you think well of me."

He said this loudly and with such an ardent and passionate look on his face that many eyes turned to us, and I was sensible of a cold shiver passing over me. I snatched my hand away and said in a half-broken voice that I could not but think well of a prince who was so willing to show paternal kindness to his unfortunate subjects. I then made him a low bow and, feeling some discomposure, went and stood behind my aunt's chair. The prince is said to have looked after me and to have wagged his finger at me threateningly. Let him threaten! I shall never again walk with him and shall thank his beneficence toward the T. family only within the circle that forms around him whenever he makes an entrance at court.

All faces were watchful, and I have never heard such a general voicing of complaints at the gaming tables about absentminded players. I felt that their attention to me and the prince was the cause, and I could hardly recover from my confusion. My Lord Derby looked somewhat sad and seemed to observe me with some concern. He was leaning against a window, and his lips moved like those of a man agitatedly talking to himself. He approached my aunt's table just at the moment when she said, "Sophia, I am sure you have spoken to the prince about poor Councillor T., for I see by your face that you are moved."

Never did I like my aunt more than at this moment when she fulfilled my wish that all might know the subject of my conversation with the prince. I said quite cheerfully, therefore, that he had listened to my request with favor and promised to act upon it. My Lord Derby's gloom disappeared, and he remained merely pensive but quite cheerful. The others showed their approval of my solicitation with words and gestures. But, my Emilia, you can imagine what I felt when, having taken off my fine clothes after the assembly, I went with my Rosina in a sedan-chair to Councillor T.'s, who lives not far from us. I wanted to give the good people a tranquil night's rest by assuring them of the prince's goodness. I had seated myself near a window that looks out onto a small lane next to a garden. Parents and children were gathered around me; and upon my urging him, Councillor T. had taken his place next to me on the bench. I drew the wife toward me with one hand, while saying to them both, "Soon, my dear friends, I shall see you with happy faces, for the prince has promised the councillor a post and other kinds of assistance."

The woman and the two oldest children knelt down before me with exclamations of gratitude. At the same moment someone knocked upon the window shutter. Councillor T. opened window and shutter, and a packet with money flew into the room, falling heavily to the floor and startling us all. I hastily put my head out of the window and quite clearly heard the voice of my Lord Derby saying in English, "God be thanked; I have done something good! Now let those who will, take me for a villain because of my revelries!"

I confess that his action and his words moved my soul, and my first thought was, "perhaps my Lord Seymour is not as good as he appears, and my Lord Derby not as bad as he is thought to be."

Mrs. T. had run to the front door and called out, "Who are you?" But he hurried away like a bird in flight.

The package was opened and fifty carolines found in it. You may guess the joy this gave them: parents and children wept and squeezed one another's hands in turn. They almost would have kissed the money and pressed it to their hearts. I saw then the difference between the hope of happiness and the real possession of it. The joy over the promised post was great but clearly mingled with fear and distrust, whereas fifty carolines that one could hold in one's hands, count, and be sure of, transported them with delight. They asked me what they should do with the money, and I answered them tenderly, "My dear friends, use it as carefully as if you had earned it yourselves with much effort and as if it were the whole remainder of your fortune, for we do not yet know when and how the prince will provide for you." I then went home, satisfied with my day's work.

Through my intercession, I had fulfilled my duty to humanity and had persuaded the prince to an expenditure in behalf of benevolence, whereas others had seduced him into spending money on voluptuousness and luxury. I had filled discouraged hearts with joy and had experienced the delight of witnessing a good and noble act performed by a man whom I had thought malicious. How eagerly my Lord Derby has grasped the opportunity to do good. At my aunt's gaming table he hears, by chance, of the pitiable family and immediately inquires about them with an eagerness that causes him to give them, that same evening, such generous assistance in a true English manner.

He probably did not think I was present, but that I was at home at the table; otherwise he would not have spoken in English. In company I often heard him utter good sentiments, but I thought they were the hypocritical words of a subtle villain. But this act, freely done and unknown to anyone, could not possibly be hypocrisy. Oh, if he could only develop a taste for and consecrate his talents to virtue! He would become a man most worthy of respect!

I cannot help feeling some esteem for him now because he deserves it. I would never have given it to his subtle flatteries, his wit, and the respect he shows me. It can often happen that outward attractiveness obtains for us the homage and perhaps the most ardent passion of a great villain. But how despicable is a woman who shows pleasure in that and feels obligated to be grateful for this poor tribute to her vanity! No, none but the estimable shall hear from me that I esteem them. The whole world is entitled to my courtesy, but greater tribute than that must be earned through virtuous acts.

Now I believe it necessary to say that my whole plan for the T. family must be newly cast as soon as they receive a secure income. I leave it to your husband, a man who is well-intentioned and conversant with all varieties of morality and prudence, to make this plan usable. I ask that he do so quickly. And since my eyes are closing from lack of sleep, I wish you, my faithful Emilia, "Good night!"

Lady Sternheim to Mrs. T.

I thank you, dear madam, for the joy you have given me by being so frank; I assure you, in turn, of my true friendship and of my unabated eagerness to serve you.

You know from my last visit that Mr. T.'s wish for a post will be satisfied by the gracious benevolence of the prince. You know my joy in seeing you soon removed from the distress in which you languish; but may I also say that this joy is accompanied by the wish that you would endeavor to secure your future prosperity and that of your children. The comparison of your former good fortune with the sorrowful years that followed could become the basis for a plan which you and your children might now follow. My Lord Derby's present has enabled you to supply yourself with the necessary clothes and household supplies, so that the income from your husband's post can be devoted completely to the support and education of your children.

Feeling certain that my immature judgment was unequal to the task of formulating such a plan, I have asked a friend of mine, a man of the cloth, to do so, and he has written me as follows.

"As I see from your communication, reason and feeling are mature enough in the three oldest children to understand the power and usefulness of the comparison you mention. If you then calculate their income and necessary expenditures, they will be glad to be guided by your plan. Then tell them this:

"God has intended two kinds of happiness for us, of which the first is promised us for our souls and is eternal. We become worthy of this happiness through virtuous acts.* The second concerns our life on this earth. This one we can attain through prudence and knowledge.

"Talk to them of the order which God has established among men through differences among estates. Show them the higher and wealthier

---

*The editor leaves it to the cleric with whom this distinction is said to originate to justify the same. In his opinion (which is by no means new), in this life, too, neither public nor private felicity can be gained without virtuous conduct; and according to the principles of the Book of Revelation, something more than mere virtue is needed for the attainment of eternal bliss [Wieland].

one, but also the one that is lower and poorer than theirs. Talk to them of the advantages and burdens which each class has, and then guide your children into a reverent satisfaction with their Creator, who has appointed them to a certain estate through the parents He gave them. Within that estate He has given them each a measure of special duties to fulfill. Say to them that the duties of virtue and religion are as binding on the prince as they are on the least of men. Those who by birth hold the first rank have the noble duty of contributing to the common weal through useful knowledge and learning in public service or at the higher levels of the commercial estate.

"You can demonstrate this principle by pointing out to your sons that through the position of Councillor T. they belong to the first rank of private persons, in which, after they have fulfilled the duties for their eternal felicity, they must also fulfill those tending to cultivate the faculties of the mind through diligence in learning and studying, so that one day they can take their place in society as skilled and worthy men. Tell them that the origin of nobility is not a special gift of providence, but the reward of surpassing virtues and talents, exercised for the benefit of the fatherland. Also say that wealth is a fruit of untiring industry and skill, that it is up to them to rise above their equals by these means because virtues and talents have always been the cornerstones of honor and fortune.

"To your daughters you should say that besides the virtues of religion they must also possess the accomplishments of high-minded, amiable women, and that they can acquire and retain these without the help of great wealth.

"Our hearts and minds are not subject to fate. Without noble birth we can have noble souls, and without great rank we can have a great mind. We can be happy and joyous without riches; and without costly adornments, merely by virtue of our hearts and minds, we can be very amiable. Thus, through our good attributes we can win the respect of our contemporaries as the first and surest step toward honor and happiness.

"Then you might tell them of your income and the use you intend to make of it in keeping with your duty to supply the needs of their bodies for food and clothing and the needs of their minds for cultivation and diversion, such as masters, books, and companions. Mention also the obligation of prudence to put by a small sum against future unforeseen events.

"We need nourishment to maintain the strength of our bodies. We can most easily satisfy this need with the simplest foods. These will not take away much from a small income, and we are thereby heeding the voice of nature for our good health and, at the same time, we are living in accord with circumstances that do not permit us to indulge the excesses of our imagination in any case. And since the rich man, after overindulging, must have recourse to simple food and plain water to repair his injured health, why should we, being healthy, complain because we are forced by fate to live in keeping with the simple demands of nature? We need raiment to protect ourselves from the attacks of the elements. This service we obtain as well from lowly and inexpensive materials as from costly ones. The color that becomes my face and the beauty of form must be sought out in the latter as well as in the former, and if I have these, I have the foremost ornament of dress. A genteel walk, good bearing, the form which nature gave me, can give my simple, pretty dress a distinction which the rich man with all his expenditures cannot always obtain, and I shall earn as much respect from the sensible man because of my moderation as the rich man can obtain through his everchanging ostentation.

"If the furniture of our house lacks beauty and comfort, let us compensate with the utmost cleanliness for the lack of costly things; let us strive like the wise Arab to acknowledge joyfully that to be happy we do not need superfluities. Further, how nobly can the daughters of the councillor in time adorn the outward honor of their house, when the rooms are dressed up with beautiful drawings, the chairs and benches with tapestries by their skilled hands! If after this noble submission to their lot, the sight of the rich man should tempt them to a gloomy comparison between his circumstances and theirs, they should think not only of the pleasure he derives from his luxury and voluptuousness but also consider how the merchants, artists, and artisans benefit from them. At first they may feel nothing but painful dissatisfaction with the fate that cheated them of all these pleasures; but on further reflection, they will feel the pleasure a noble soul takes in the well-being of its neighbor. The smaller one's share in the general good fortune, the nobler is this joy!

"Examine the measure of your children's capacities, and leave none of them uncultivated. However modest you may be in dress and other expenditures for a person of your rank, consecrate all you have to your children's education. Let your daughters learn drawing, music, languages, and all the skills proper for women; let your sons acquire all the knowledge that is demanded of well-educated young men. Inspire both with the love and taste for the noble occupation of reading, which is so useful to our minds, especially the works that advance our knowledge of the physical world. It is one of our duties as virtuous creatures to know the works of our Creator, from which at every moment we receive so many benefits. The whole physical world contains testimonies to the benevolence and goodness of our Creator. The sight and knowledge of them pours the purest and most perfect pleasure into our souls, which is subject neither to men nor accidents of fortune. The more joy your children find in the natural history of our earth, the more knowledge they acquire of its plants, its utility and beauty, the more gentle will be their dispositions, passions, and desires, the more will their taste for nobility and simplicity be strengthened and confirmed, and the farther removed they will be from the idea that luxury and voluptuousness are the greatest means to man's happiness.

"Your children must also know the history of the moral world. The changes in fortune which elevated persons and entire kingdoms have suffered will lead them to observations that will increase their contentment with their restricted circumstances and their zeal for increasing their souls' virtue and their minds' knowledge. They will find throughout history that virtue and talents alone are the only goods of which fate and men cannot rob them."

This very evening your children shall receive all the books which are necessary to attain these goals. Accompanying them are my heart's best wishes that these works of benevolent and amiable men may be, for all of you, a source of useful knowledge and the greatest enjoyment of your lives, as they are for me.

One more thing I would ask, dear madam. Seek no more friends of the table. Prove your gratitude, respect, friendship, and all honorable sentiments to those who have served you in your misfortune; do good to other persons to the extent that your means permit; and with your children live quietly and in seclusion until your company is sought by worthy persons. The more beauty and accomplishments your daughters have as they grow up, the more you ought to keep them at home. The praise of their teachers and the modesty and prudence of their conduct will spread their fame even before their faces are well known. I am convinced that one day you will be very content to have followed your friend's advice!

Lord Derby to His Friend at Paris

"Heigh-ho, little brother," the countrymen of my Lady Sternheim shout to one another when the real fun is about to begin. And because I have spread my English nets on German soil, I, too, will say it to you: Heigh-ho, little brother! The wings of my little bird are entangled, though her head and feet are still free. The hunt for her which the other side has mounted shall soon drive her completely into my slings and even force her to look upon me as her deliverer. How excellent was my idea to adapt myself to her benevolence and yet maintain the appearance of indifference and secrecy. Not much was lacking and I would have waited too long and missed the best opportunity to appear to her in an advantageous light, but the gabbiness of her aunt helped me to recover everything.

During the last assembly at court, we all particularly noticed a long conversation between Lady Sternheim and the prince. I had overheard her sweet and captivating tone; and while I was wondering what the girl might be up to, I saw the prince take her hands and, it seemed to me, kiss one of them. My head was reeling! I dropped my cards and full of spite leaned against a window; but when I saw her hasten to her aunt's table and, seeming filled with emotion and somewhat confused, fix her eyes on the game, I approached her. She threw me an impetuous, half-timorous look. Her aunt said she could tell by her face that she had just spoken to the prince on behalf of Councillor T. The lady acknowledged it and said cheerfully that he had promised to aid the family, adding something about the distress these people were in. My mind fastened upon this, and I decided to do something for them the very next day, before the prince fulfilled Lady Sternheim's request.

As I was wont to do, I dressed in the overcoat of my fellow and crept to a spot near Count Loebau's dining room windows because I wanted to know each day with whom my beauty was dining. I had hardly reached the lane when I saw two sedan chairs approach and stop at the house. Two well-disguised ladies came to the door, and I clearly heard Lady Sternheim's voice saying, "To the Councillor T.'s at S. Garden." I knew the house; I ran to my room, fetched some money, and—while she was still there—threw it through the window at which the lady was sitting. I murmured a few words about the joys of charity and hearing them come to the door, I hurried away. There was magical power in my words, for when two days later I walked toward the lady at Count F.'s, to assure her of my pretended reverence, I noticed that her beautiful eyes rested on me with an expression of esteem and satisfaction. She began to address me in English, but as she had arrived very late, young Count F. immediately asked her to draw a card. She looked about her indecisively, as if she had a premonition, and drew a king, which made her one of the prince's party.

"Did I have to draw this one?" she said in an angry voice; but she could have drawn many times, she would have drawn nothing but kings, for Count F. had no other cards in his hand, and her aunt had purposely come late, when all card tables were occupied. The prince had just arrived in the company as if by chance, and being too polite to want to disturb anyone's game, had left it to chance—under the direction of the discreet F.—to supply him with a partner. The French envoy and the Countess F. completed the party. Sometimes my faro game permitted me to stand behind the prince's chair and let my eyes speak to the lady. Enchanting, inimitable grace accompanied everything she did. On one occasion, when she gathered up the cards with her beautiful hands, the prince felt it so vehemently that he hastily reached out with his own, seized one of her fingers and exclaimed passionately, "Is it possible that all these graces were reared at P.? You must agree, M. le marquis, France cannot show us anything more amiable."

The envoy would have been no Frenchman and no envoy had he not seconded the compliment, even without being convinced of its truth; and my Lady Sternheim simply glowed with beauty and annoyance, for the prince's glances were perhaps even more lively than his tone of voice. My girl continued shuffling the cards with downcast eyes. When she dealt them, I turned around; she glanced at me. I showed her a pensive, sad face when I looked at her. I fixed my eyes on the prince, and quickly walked to the faro table where she could see me play. I bet high and played distractedly; my intention was to make Lady Sternheim think that my observation of the prince's love for her was the reason for the neglect of my own interests and the apparent distraction of my thoughts. This she could attribute only to the vehemence of my passion for her, and it went as I would have it go. She observed all my movements. When the games were finished, I went with a melancholy air to the piquet table, just when the lady gathered up the money she had won. It was a large sum and all from the prince.

"Even today," she said, "the children of Councillor T. shall receive it, and I shall say to them that Your Highness has generously lost it on their behalf."

The prince looked at her smiling and cheerful, and I reluctantly quit the room, resolved to lie in wait for her when she should go to the T.'s, to force my way in there and speak to her of my love. She had observed me all afternoon as I seemed possessed in turn by dejection and agitation. My intrusion there would be put to the account of my vehement passion. In any case, I have found during my stay in Germany that they are favorably predisposed toward us, and therefore judge our most extravagant actions with the greatest forbearance—yes, sometimes they even consider them proof of our great and free souls.

By making use of a momentary opportunity, I have won more than by a whole year of sighing and whimpering. Read the following scene, and admire my presence of mind and the control that I maintained over my usually so ungovernable senses during the entire half hour I was alone, completely alone, in a room with my goddess and saw before me her beautiful figure in a most charming state. She had returned home to take off her robe and headdress, and had put on only a large cloak and a cap before being carried to the Councillor T.'s. The cap she had taken off had removed all the powder from her chestnut hair and put her locks in some disorder. A short undergown and the lovely heightened color which my presence and conversation gave her made her inexpressibly charming.

A few minutes after she entered the house, I knocked and called softly for Mrs. T. She came to the door and I told her that I was secretary to my Lord G., who had sent me here with a present for her family, which I was instructed to give to Lady Sternheim in person and talk with her about it. The woman let me wait for a moment and ran off to take her husband and children into another room. Then she beckoned to me, and, like a fool, I almost trembled when I took the first step through the door; but the anxiety which the girl obviously felt reminded me in the nick of time of the superiority of the male mind, and I used my remaining confusion to gloss over my forced entrance. Before she had recovered from the surprise of seeing me, I knelt at her feet and made some vivid excuses in English for this invasion and the fright into which I had thrown her. I said that it was impossible for me to go on living without making confession to her of the lively esteem I felt for her. I added that, because my Lord G. had prohibited my making frequent visits to her uncle's house and because I had seen with my own eyes that others were bold enough to show her their feelings, therefore, I would merely ask the privilege of telling her that I revered her for her rare mind. I said that I had witnessed her virtue in action and that she alone had reminded me of a certain maxim by a wise man. He had said that if virtue were to appear in visible form, no one would be able to resist the power of its charms. I told her that I looked upon this house as a temple, where, at her feet, I made a vow to dedicate myself to virtue, which I had come to know through her in all its beauty. I said that I did not feel worthy to speak to her of love before I had completely reformed myself, an endeavor in which her example would serve as my model. My appearance there and the heat of passion in which I addressed her had, as it were, numbed her and at first also made her a little angry; but the word "virtue," which I repeated several times, was the charm with which I appeased her anger and gained as much of her attention as I needed to make her vanity my ally. I also observed how, even while she was frowning with displeased maidenly modesty and several times attempted to interrupt me and hurry away, my acting the Plato with his "virtue become visible" notably lightened her serious countenance, and the most delicate moral pride was expressed by her lowered eyes. This observation sufficed for the present, and I concluded my speech, which had become most tender, by repeating my humble pleas for forgiveness on account of my startling her.

With a somewhat tremulous voice she said that my appearance and address had admittedly been very unexpected and that she wished the feelings of which I had spoken to her had prevented me from thus surprising her in a strange house.

I made some moving presentations and my face was marked by the fear of having offended her. She looked at me cautiously and said, "My lord, you are the first man who speaks to me of love and with whom I find myself alone; both of these facts make me uneasy. I would ask that you leave me and thereby show me proof of the esteem you purport to feel for my character."

"Purport! Oh Sophia, if these were feigned sentiments, I would have used more prudence to avoid your anger! Adoration and despair emboldened me to come here. Say that you forgive my rashness, and do not reject my reverence."

"No, my lord, I shall never reject the true esteem of a worthy man; but if I have obtained yours, you will leave me."

I seized her hand, kissed it, and said tenderly and with eagerness, "Divine, adorable girl! I am the first man who speaks to you of love—Oh that I were also the first man whom you love!"

I remembered Seymour, and it was well that I withdrew. At the door I put down my packet of money and, looking back, said, "Give it to the family."

She looked after me with an expression of affability, and since then I have twice seen her in company, where I always keep a respectful distance and only very rarely utter words of adoration, sorrow, or some such. Whenever she can see or hear me, I conduct myself very prudently and modestly.

I know from my Lord G. that at court they are laying several plots for beguiling her head; her heart they think they have already because she likes to do good and because the prince will oblige her in everything. In her presence they constantly talk about love and gallant connections, which they treat lightly and—as they say in the great world—"philosophically." All this is to my advantage. For the more the others endeavor to weaken her ideas of honor and virtue to tempt her to forget them, the more her female obstinacy will make her defend her principles. My Lord G.'s formal courtesy and Seymour's cold and suspicious countenance offend her conviction of her virtue's value. *I* show her reverence; *I* admire her rare character and do not deem myself worthy to speak to her of love until I shall have been reformed by her example. Thus hemmed in by the armor of her virtue and entangled in the bonds of her vanity, she will be rendered unfit for combat with me, like the knight of old, dressed in fighting panoply, who finally collapsed under its weight and was trapped in his beautiful, tight armor.

Say no more about my being so quickly satiated after my long-sought possession of the beautiful, pious—; and that after all my efforts the same fate awaits me with this paragon of virtue. You are far removed from having the right idea of the rare creature of whom I write. It is true that any passionate devotee has as many exalted ideas of virtue as does my Sophia (and it is indeed pleasant to rid an amiable person of all these hobgoblins), but the difference between them is this: just as the devotee, simply from self-love, strives to escape the terrible pains of hell and gain the enjoyment of eternal bliss through piety (that is to say, she is virtuous out of self-interest, and the fear of hell and desire for heaven spring solely from the intimations of her sublimated senses), in the same way her surrender to a lover may also result from imagining the pleasures of love. For if the senses did not count for so much with pious people, how do we account for the sensuous descriptions of their celestial joys and for the ecstatic expression with which they relish the choicest morsels at the table?

But my little moralist is tuned quite differently. She sees her virtue and her bliss solely in actions for the good of her fellow man. Splendor, ease, delicate dishes, shows of respect, diversions—nothing can equal for her the pleasure of doing good, and from this motive she will one day fulfill the desires of her lover. The same thoughtfulness she employs in relieving the objects of her beneficence and supplying them with a new happiness—this same thoughtfulness she will also use to increase my pleasure. I deem it impossible that one can become tired of her! However, in but a little while I shall be able to give you news of that. The comedy is fast drawing to a close because the prince's passion is becoming so violent that the preparations for her undoing are pursued more avidly, and festivities upon festivities are staged in rapid succession.

Lady Sternheim to Emilia

Would you, dearest Emilia, ever have believed that there would come an hour in my life when I should be sorry to have done good? That hour has come; I am dissatisfied with my heart's warm eagerness for the improved well-being of my fellow man, and I am sensible of the strife between "mine" and "thine." You know from my earlier letters what it cost me to importune the prince on behalf of the T. family to grant them a favor. You know the motives for my reluctance and for my overcoming it. But the redoubled perplexity which the prince and my Lord Derby have given me because of my appeal is so unpleasant that they have made me dissatisfied with my heart. The prince pursues me more than ever with his looks and his discourse, and during a game of piquet that I played with him, he did not scruple to exclaim so passionately on my charms that everyone took notice. My Lord Derby had just left the faro table and joined us. Amid the confusion that overcame me from anger and embarrassment over the prince's conduct, I directed my eyes perchance to Derby; and I clearly saw the expression of violent emotion in his face. I noticed also that after casting some wild looks at the prince he went away and seemed quite confounded. I had no way of foreseeing that he would disquiet me utterly that very evening.

The prince lost much money to me. I had noticed that he played badly on purpose when he was alone against me. This displeased me. Whatever his intentions, I did not want his money, and I said that I would give it to Councillor T.'s children that very evening. Derby must have heard that and decided to watch me and speak to me at Councillor T.'s. He contrived it cunningly, for when I had been there but a little while, he came to the house, asked for Mrs. T., and said to her that he was secretary to my Lord G. and had orders to give me something for her family. In hopes of receiving a large present, the woman made her husband and children, as well as

Rosina, leave the room where I was. Before I could ask her what she wanted, she entered with my Lord Derby, announced him as secretary, talked of the present he had for her, and went away. Surprise and vexation stunned me long enough for my lord to kneel at my feet, make his apologies, and ask forgiveness before I could complain about his intrusion. When I did so, it was with few and serious words, upon which he began to talk of a long-hidden passion and of the despair into which my Lord G. had plunged him when he forbade him ever again to come to our house, when, all the while, he was forced to observe that others spoke to me of their love. My Lord G.'s prohibition took me aback and made me thoughtful. Derby talked on in a state of the most violent emotion, and my distress grew as I recalled the agitation in which I had seen him all evening among the company. I asked him to leave me, and at the same time I tried to walk toward the door. He opposed me with very respectful gestures but with a voice and looks so fraught with passion that I became fearful and felt faint. This was the moment when I grew angry with my heart for urging me to bring the children my card money that evening and thereby exposing me to this distress.

I finally recovered when he implored me, in the sacred name of virtue, to let him speak for one more moment. I cannot repeat any of it, but he spoke well. He said little of my outward graces, but he claimed to know my character, which he considered rare, and in the end, in a most affecting manner, he made a solemn vow of virtue and love.

Dissatisfied with him and with myself, dismayed and moved, I begged him to give me proof of his sincerity by leaving me. He immediately left with renewed apologies for his startling me and at the door put down a heavy packet of money for the poor family.

An unusual feeling of grief oppressed my heart; the greatest happiness that I wished for at that moment was to be alone. Mrs. T. came in, and I gave her the present, together with the money I had won. Her joy relieved me a little, but I hurried away with the firm resolution never again to enter this house as long as my Lord Derby was in D. When I returned home, my uncle and aunt were still playing cards, and I retired to bed. Through the loss of my parents and friends I had known melancholy nights before, but never had sleepless hours filled my soul with such restlessness and pain as they did realizing that my lot and my circumstances totally opposed my wishes and character. My principal care has always been to conduct myself irreproachably; and now through my Lord Derby's behavior, I am exposed to the suspicion of a private meeting with him. My Lord G., whose esteem I believed I had earned, expressly forbids his relative to have contact with me! I had wished for the friendship with a virtuous man, and he shuns me, while at the same time the prince and Count F. begin to pursue me. And what shall I say of my Lord Derby? I admit, the idea of being loved by an

Englishman is singularly pleasing to me, but—and yet, why did I choose
the one and reject the other before I knew them? I was certainly precipitate
and unjust. Derby is impetuous and imprudent but has great wit and sensibility. How quickly, how eagerly he does good! His heart cannot be corrupt
because he is so keen on doing good. (I almost want to add, because he can
love me and my principles.) But everyone considers him a wicked man; he
must have given cause for an opinion so generally held. Yet virtue lays
claim to his heart! Oh Emilia, what if love were capable of completely
retrieving him from the paths of error! What if I were the cause—would I
not then owe love the sacrifice of giving Derby the preference that I had
given to another who did not desire it? But at present I wish that I were
spared a choice and that my aunt R. would come soon. Vain wish! She is at
Florence and remains there for her lying-in. So you see, everything is
against me! The rustic peace, the quiet, the noble simplicity which dwell in
my remote S. would be as refreshing to my poor head and heart as a view
of the open plain would be to a courtier who has long wandered about in
artificial gardens and whose eyes have been tired by looking upon the rare
and forced beauties there. How gladly would he set his feet, tired from
walking upon crushed marble, on a piece of earth covered with moss; how
gladly would he look about him in the unlimited, beautiful panorama of
field, forest, brook, and meadow where nature spreads out its best gifts in
charming disorder! On such an occasion I observed in many of these courtiers the power of the pure, first impression of nature. Even their walk and
their gestures became freer and less forced than in the so-called pleasure
gardens; but a few moments later I also observed the force of habit which,
awakened by a single thought, disturbed the gentle tranquillity that had cap-
tured their hearts. Judge for yourself, my Emilia, how tired my moral eye
must be of daily looking upon artificiality in the mind, in the sensations, in
the pleasures, and in the virtues! Add to that the proposal of a union with
young Count F., which I would not accept even if I liked the man, because
it would chain me to the court. For no matter how these fetters were gilded
and strewn with flowers, they would chafe my heart all the more. I suffer
by the thought that I am robbing someone of a hoped-for happiness, the
fulfillment of which it is in my power to give; but why will not people
make a comparison between their way of thinking and mine? They would
then see quite clearly the impossibility of leading me into the way of their
principles. My uncle and aunt astonish me. They, who knew my parents
and my upbringing, they, who must be convinced of the firmness of my
ideas and sentiments—did they think they could induce me through the
glittering toys of rank, splendor, and diversions to surrender my hand and
my heart? Yet I cannot be angry with them. In accordance with their ideas
of happiness, they seek to make me happy through a distinguished union,
and they take all conceivable trouble to present the court to me in its most

seductive light. They have even tried to use my love of benevolence as a motive. Because Count F. assured them that the prince greatly esteemed me, that he would with pleasure grant every favor I might request, they have, I believe, hired people to apply to me for intercession with the prince on their behalf. Their supposition that this would be the greatest temptation for me is quite correct, for the power to do good is the only happiness I desire.

To my delight, the first request I received proceeded from vanity, and they desired something that they could very well do without, so that, without compunction, I could deny them my recommendation.[9] In doing so, I announced my decision never again to importune the prince and that only the extreme distress and helplessness of the T. family had urged me to do so before. Had it been a person truly necessitous who applied to me to speak in his behalf, my heart would once again have fallen into sad perplexity in trying to decide between my duty and desire to serve that person and my reluctance to be obligated to the prince for a favor. Yet I must speak to him once more, about my uncle's lawsuit, and this shall take place at the masked ball, for which many preparations are being made.

A general exertion of everyone's powers of invention is the result of that undertaking. Each person wants to be attired pleasingly and in character. Courtiers and burghers are invited; it is to be an imitation of the English masked balls at Vauxhall. I must confess that the entire plan pleases me. First, because I shall see the whole representation of the Roman saturnalia that I might call "feasts of equality" and further because I expect grand entertainment from observing the degree of power and beauty of so many persons' imaginations manifested in their different inventions and choices of dress. Count F., his nephew, my uncle, my aunt, and I shall represent a troupe of Spanish musicians who are strolling the streets at night and singing in front of the houses. The thought is pleasant. Our clothes of scarlet and black taffeta are very beautiful; but to let my voice be heard in front of so many people will ruin my pleasure, for it must make me appear overly confident of its beauty and too desirous of praise. But they want to please the prince, who likes to hear me sing, because they believe my uncle's lawsuit would benefit; and I would rather sing for him before all the world than once more in our garden, like yesterday, when I was obliged afterwards to walk with him and hear him speak of love. 'Tis true, he clothed his remarks in expressions of admiration for my wit and adroitness, but he said that my eyes, my figure, and my hands had wrought much confusion at his court; that it was impossible for him to escape it because the power of my charms had not spared the master any more than his servants.

"Then my removal will be the best remedy for this disorder,"[10] I said.

"That you shall not do! You shall not rob my court of the adornment it receives through you. You shall choose and make one man happy, and you shall never, never depart from D."

I was grateful that he added this. He must have done it because he noticed that I was confused and suddenly looked sad and grave. For when he talked of my choosing one fortunate man, he turned to me and looked at me so longingly that I was afraid of his further declarations. He inquired tenderly after the cause of my seriousness; I recovered myself and said to him in a quite lively manner, "It is the thought of a choice because I cannot imagine making a choice here in D. that would be in keeping with my ideas."

"None at all? Take the one who loves you most and can best prove his love to you."

While thus talking, we had reached the company. Everyone tried to read something in the prince's face. He was courteous to them but soon went away, saying to me with a smile that I must not forget his advice. I spoke earnestly to my aunt of the sentiments I had discovered and said that I would not acknowledge and encourage any person's love that I could not return; I would, therefore, not sing at the ball and I asked her to let me return to Sternheim.

Then there was an outcry at my exaggerated, phantastical ideas that could not tolerate even a tender courtesy; she said that for the sake of heaven and her children, I must not refuse to go to the ball. If I was dissatisfied after it, she promised to accompany me to Sternheim and remain there for the rest of the year. I said that I would hold her to this promise and renewed my own of compliance to her. Thus, this will be the last act of tyranny to which my complaisance toward others shall subject me, and then I will see my Sternheim once more. Oh Emilia, with what transports of delight shall I enter the house where every corner reminds me of my parents' practical virtues and invites me to follow their example. The virtues and faults of the great are not for my character; the former are too splendid, the latter too dark for me. A round of peaceful employments for my mind and my heart is the kind of happiness I am destined for, and that I shall find on my estates. Once, that happiness was increased by the amicable companionship of my Emilia, but providence intended to let her virtues shine elsewhere and left me only her letters.

I am glad that I have come to know the great world and its splendors. I now know how to evaluate it more justly in all its parts. I owe to it the refinement of my taste and wit because I have come to know what is perfect in the arts. Its luxury, its noisy, tiresome diversions have made the noble simplicity and the tranquil joys of my father's house more pleasing to me. The lack of friends that I suffered has taught me to value the worth of my Emilia more highly. Though I have felt love's power over my heart, I am glad that it can be wounded by the son of heavenly Venus alone and that virtue has preserved its domain within it undisturbed. I am certain my affection will never choose an object seeking to displace it from there.

Beauty and wit have no power over my heart, though I know the value
of both; neither do flaming passion and tender speeches, but least of all do
praises of my personal attributes, for I see in them nothing of my admirer
but that he loves his pleasure. Esteem for my heart's good inclinations and
my mind's exertions to acquire talents—this alone moves me because I take
it for a sign of a kindred soul and of true, lasting love. But no one from
whom I wished to hear it has told me that. Derby's protestations had this
tone; but not one string of my heart has answered to it. This is another man
whose love, or whatever it is, increased my longing and impatience for
tranquillity and solitude.

The ball is a week from today. Perhaps, my Emilia, I shall write you
my next letter in the study of the Sternheims, at the foot of my mother's
picture, the sight of which will inspire my pen to write on a different
subject.

Lord Derby to His Friend

The comedy of the prince and my Sternheim, of which I lately wrote
you, has, through the romantic freaks of Cousin Seymour, risen to such
tragic heights that nothing but the death or flight of the heroine can develop
the plot further. The goddess of youth shall, I hope, prevent the former; and
Venus may well provide for the latter through my intervention.

As the lady likes dancing, they hope through the amusements of the
ball to make her pliant and yielding sooner; and as she has never seen a
masked ball, preparations are being made for giving one on the prince's
birthday. She was persuaded to sing on this occasion, and she had the
charming idea to impersonate, with others, a troupe of Spanish musicians.
Hearing news of this, the prince desired Count Loebau to permit him the
pleasure of providing the lady's dress, to make her a present of it without
her knowledge. The uncle and aunt consented to it because their masks
were obtained at the same time, but two days before the ball it became
known to the court and the town that the prince would give the lady the
dress and jewels and would himself wear her colors, too. Seymour was
filled with the utmost rage and contempt; I myself became doubtful and
determined to observe Lady Sternheim more closely than ever before.

Nothing could have been more charming than their entrance into the
ballroom. Countess Loebau, dressed as an old beldam, preceded them with
a lantern and some scrolls of music. Following them were old Count F. with
a bass viol, Loebau with a transverse flute, and the young lady with a lute.
They took up a position before the prince's box and began to tune up. The
dance music ceased, and the young lady sang an aria. She was dressed in
scarlet and black taffeta, with her beautiful hair spread out carelessly in
flowing locks, her breast decently, yet rather less fully, covered than usual.

In general, she seemed to be dressed with much care, in a manner that displayed by turns all the charming beauties of her figure. The wide sleeve was certainly designed for the sole purpose of falling back while she strummed the lute to display fully her perfectly formed arm. Her half-mask revealed the most beautiful mouth, and her self-love endeavored to elevate the beauty of her voice and give it the magic power of true art.

Dressed in a black domino and leaning against a window, Seymour looked at her with intense emotion. The prince, in a Venetian cloak, was seated in his box. Desire and hope were written in his eyes. After having lavishly praised the skill of her fingers, he clapped his hands merrily and came to dance a minuet with her. My head began to grow warm, and I advised my friend John, Lord G.'s secretary, to redouble his attention, because my boiling blood prevented me from doing so myself. Nevertheless, I had time to reflect that the face and what one calls the physiognomy are the true expression of our soul. For without the mask my Lady Sternheim had always been the picture of moral beauty, in that her expression and the look of her eyes seemed to pour an aura of nobility and spiritual purity over her entire person, keeping all desires she inspired within the bounds of respect. But now her eyebrows, temples, and half her cheeks were covered and this made her soul, as it were, invisible. Thus she lost the characteristic moral aspect of her charms and descended to the general idea of what constitutes a woman. The thought that she had been given her costume by the prince, had sung in his honor, and had been loved by him for a long time already made her appear to us as his true mistress. This impression was confirmed when, a quarter hour later, the prince appeared in a mask of the same color as hers. As people were just then dancing in the Greek fashion, he took her from the side of her aunt with whom she had been talking, put an arm around her waist, and danced the length of the hall with her. This sight angered me to the point of fury, but I noticed that she often resisted and strove to disengage herself. Yet with each of her efforts he pressed her more closely to his breast; and when he finally led her back, Count F. drew him to a window and spoke to him eagerly. Sometime after that, a white mask *en Chauve-Souris*,[11] was seen standing next to the lady, who suddenly gestured violently with her right arm toward her breast and then a moment later stretched out her left hand imploringly toward the white mask. He disappeared in the throng, and with the utmost swiftness the lady ran after him through the hall. I followed the white mask to the corner of a passage where he dropped the costume and revealed himself to be Lord Seymour in his black domino. He ran down the stairs in the greatest agitation and left me utterly perplexed about his conversation with the lady. John, who had not lost sight of her, followed her and saw that she entered the room where her uncle and Countess F. were. He said that immediately upon entering she tore off her jewelled headdress and with contemptuous and painful exclamations threw it to the floor. She looked with disgust at her uncle who had approached her, and asked him in the most sorrowful voice, "How have I deserved your sacrificing my honor and good name to the prince's hateful passion?"

With trembling hands she untied her mask, tore the laces of her collar and cuffs into pieces, and scattered them about her. John had pressed to the door immediately after her and witnessed all these agitations. The prince, Count F., and her aunt hurried in, the others withdrew, and John hid in the curtain of the door which they had immediately locked. The prince threw himself down at her feet and, with the most tender expressions, asked her to explain her sorrow. She shed a flood of tears and tried to get away, but he held her and repeated his entreaties.

"Why do you abase yourself? It is no compensation for the abasement of my good name. Oh my aunt, how miserably, how maliciously, you have treated your sister's child! Oh my father, to what hands you have entrusted me!"

Her solemn tone of agony must have moved his innermost soul. Her aunt pretended that she did not understand a word of her complaints and her displeasure and told her that she wished never again to be burdened with her.

"Grant me this last favor and send me home! You shall not long be burdened with me."

My Lady Sternheim said this with a stammering voice. A violent trembling had seized her; she leaned upon a chair and was scarcely able to stand. With all the tenderness of a lover, the prince was at pains to calm her. He assured her that, loving her, he would do for her everything in the world that was in his power to do.

"Oh," she cried, "it is not within your power to restore the peaceful life of which you have robbed me. My aunt, have mercy on me—take me home!"

Her trembling increased, the prince became alarmed, and he went into the next room, to have a coach readied and to send for his physician.

Countess Loebau had the cruelty to reprimand the young lady for her behavior. The lady answered with nothing but a flood of tears, raised her eyes to heaven, and wrung her tear-moistened hands.

The prince arrived with the physician who looked at the lady with astonishment, felt her pulse, and pronounced that she had a most violent fever with strong convulsions. The prince earnestly recommended her to his supervision and care. When the coach was announced, the young lady looked about her worried and frightened, fell down before the prince, and lifting her hands toward him, cried out, "Oh, if it is true that you love me, let me not be taken anywhere but to my home."

The prince lifted her up and said with great emotion that he swore he harbored only the most respectful sentiments toward her and had no thought of betraying her, that he begged her to compose herself, and that the physician should certainly stay with her.

Having put her kerchief round her neck, she gave the old gentleman her hand and with tottering steps left the room. Her aunt stayed behind and began to talk about the girl. The prince told her to be quiet and angrily said to her that they had all given him the wrong idea of the lady's character and had led him down the wrong path. With that he went away, as did the countess, and John was released from his confinement.

In the hall they had continued dancing, but meanwhile there was much whispering about this adventure. Almost everyone criticized the young lady's conduct as exaggerated coyness. "One can be virtuous without making such a big racket about it." "Doesn't it appear as if the prince had never loved a lady before her?" " . . . but there is a gentler and nobler way to defend one's honor without calling the whole world as witness," and other such remarks.[*]

Others took it for a delightful comedy and were eager to see how far she would carry her part.

I was convinced that Seymour must have caused this passionate welling-up of virtue, but exactly what he told her and what impression he made on her by it—that I wished I knew to plan my next steps accordingly. I concealed my uneasiness and bantered along with the rest while waiting for John, who had hurried home to spy on Seymour.

But imagine my surprise, if you can, when my good John told me that immediately after his return Seymour had left in a post-chaise-and-six, followed by a single servant. What the deuce could that mean but an arranged abduction! I drew John out of the hall by his arm, threw my mask down in the street, and put on his surtout. Thus attired, I hurried to the Loebaus' house to get news of my actress. Jealousy, rage, and love chased one another round my head; anyone who had told me just then that she was gone would certainly have been a dead man. But before a quarter hour had passed, someone ran from the house to the apothecary's. The door remained open; I crept into the courtyard and saw light in Lady Sternheim's chamber. This made me feel easier, but my doubts remained. These lights could be a deception. I now ventured into her maid's room. The door of my lady's chamber was ajar and I heard her say something. Seymour had, therefore, departed alone. I thought of a plausible excuse for my presence there and then bravely beckoned the maid to come to me. She did not recognize me, ran toward the door, which she immediately closed behind her, and asked hastily who I was and what I wanted.

---

[*]And those who said this were not entirely wrong with respect to themselves [Wieland].

I made myself known and asked her in plaintive and respectful words for news of her divine lady's health. I implored her on my knees that she would every day give one of my men news of my lady's condition. I told her that I had witnessed how noble and worthy of adoration the lady's character had shown itself to be, that I revered and loved her beyond all expression, that I was ready to sacrifice my life and all I owned in her service, but that I feared for her health, as I had heard the physician speak of a fever.

The girl was glad to hear my story of the evening's events because, she said, the young lady had done nothing but weep and tremble. I adorned the story as much as possible for the glorification of the lady and mentioned the white mask. The girl interrupted me, saying, "Oh, that white mask has made my lady ill! For he asked her quite openly whether she had trampled all the laws of honor and virtue underfoot, because she displayed herself in the dress and jewels that would prove to be the price of her virtue, that all the masks would tell her so, and that everyone despised her because they had expected better things from someone of her mind and education."

"And who was this mask?" I asked. She said that the young lady did not know, only calling him a noble, benevolent soul though he had pierced her heart.

I thought, "Heaven bless the benificent Seymour for his foolishness! It will serve my scheme well!" I promised the girl to try my best to discover his identity and told her what people were saying, with the addition that I would become the lady's defender, even if it should cost me my neck, and that she needed only to tell me what I could do for her. The girl was moved. (Young women like to see the power of love; they are so charmed by the dominion their sex has over us that they delight in helping to plait the garlands that are to crown our constancy.) She promised me a second interview on the following evening, and I went to bed quite cheerful and full of great schemes.

My chief care now was to conceal from the pedantic Seymour the lady's resistance and the heroic effects of his ill-mannered reproof; but because I could not find out where he was keeping himself, I had paid a postal official who promised to deliver to me all the letters addressed to the young lady, Loebau, and all Seymour's acquaintance. I am certain she cannot receive any letters in her own house. She wanted to return to her estates without delay, but her uncle declared that he would not let her travel. Her fever lingers; she wishes to die. She lets no one but the doctor and her maid come to her. I have won over the latter and see her every night, when I must submit to her rehearsing her lady's many virtues; for example, "She is very affectionate, but she will not love anyone but a husband." Do you get the hint?

The other evening I asked innocently, "Has she never loved?"

"No, I have never even talked to her about it or praised a gallant except, when we first started staying here, the Lord Seymour; but for a long time now she hasn't mentioned him. She thinks very highly of your Honor's benevolence."

I acted very modestly and discreetly towards the little creature; and as in the name of her lady she forbade me to defend her honor (which I had proposed to her), I added plaintively, "Will she also reject my addresses?" I said that though I would have to make my suit against Lord G.'s will, I would nevertheless venture everything to deliver her from the hands of her unworthy family and present her to a better one in England. I had to harp upon this string because she herself had set the tone for it and because I wanted to use her aversion toward D. and her predilection for England before Seymour's rage cooled and his enthusiasm carried him as far in rewarding her virtue as his contempt had led him in the other direction. She had formerly praised him extravagantly, but now she no longer spoke of him nor mentioned Lord G.—all these being signs of a glimmering love. I found means of sending her little satirical letters in which her sickness and the scene she had acted out at the ball were ridiculed. The disdain in which Lord G. held her was also noted in them. In addition, almost everyday I repeated the offer of my hand, while at the same time leaving it to her choice as to whether I should make an announcement, or whether she would entrust herself to my honor and love. Now let fate take its course with this plot. I cannot creep about here much longer. It has been a fortnight already; and without the preparations they are making at court for the arrival of two princes from—,I should have had to interrupt my work before now. John is an excellent fellow! If the need arises, he is willing to learn the marriage vows by heart and to impersonate the English envoy's chaplain. My latest proposals must bear fruit, for with all her shining perfections she is after all—only a woman! Her pride is offended, and it is difficult to abstain from opportune revenge. Not a soul, except myself, takes any interest in her. In addition, she thinks me generous and feels much gratitude for my sentiments. Never, she says, could she have anticipated this. But she does not wish to make me unhappy; no one shall be entangled in her misery. My reticence in not insisting on a visit in her chamber pleases her, too, perhaps because she does not wish to be seen flushed with fever.

Within a few days my mine must blow up, and I think it will turn out well. Wish me luck!

My Lord Derby to His Friend

She is mine, irrevocably mine; not one of my devices has missed its mark! But I needed a devilish deal of cunning to keep her favorably disposed and at the same time prevent others from exploiting her weakness. Her guardian angel must either have deserted her or be a phlegmatic, torpid creature, for in no direction has he done anything at all for her. Didn't I tell you I would catch her through her virtue? I have touched her magnanimity because I offered to sacrifice myself for her. Therefore, in order not to remain in my debt, she offered herself up. Would you believe it—she consented to a secret union, contingent upon a few conditions of which none but such an enthusiast would have thought. My satirical letters had told her that her uncle wanted to sacrifice her in the interests of his lawsuit, but this was of no great concern to anyone, as people were saying that her mother's mismarriage did not obligate them to treat her with the respect due a real lady.

Everything was called into play: her virtue, her self-love, and her vanity, and now I was given the whole bundle of satirical letters to read. She even wrote a summary and asked me whether my observation of her character had given me enough knowledge of her heart to be convinced of the falsity of those accusations. She said she knew that in England a man of honor would not be censured if he married according to his heart and the merit of his beloved object. She told me she could not doubt my generosity, as she had often seen me exercise it toward others. That was the reason she held me in high esteem; and now, when fate had made her an object of my generosity, she unhesitatingly accepted the aid of a noble heart. She said I could be eternally sure of her tender gratitude and high esteem. She assured me that she shared all my reservations with regard to making our union public, and that she herself would be glad if everything remained secret and I had no other expenditures on her account but the cares of love. She asked me to agree to only four conditions, of which the first was difficult to accomplish but unavoidable for her peace of mind; namely, that we must be married before she departed from her uncle's house because she did not want to leave it except on the arm of a worthy husband. The second condition was that I would permit her to make over the income from her estates for three years (the little dove!). Third, she asked that I immediately conduct her to her uncle, Count R., at Florence, because only to him would she disclose our marriage; indeed, her other relatives did not deserve her confidence. The moment we arrived at Florence she would be mine and for the rest of her life would have no other will but mine. The fourth and final condition was that I would let her keep her chambermaid with her.

I objected to the first article as it would be impossible because Lord G. or the prince would find out everything. I said that we should, therefore, be married at another safe place. But her decisive reply was that in that case she would rather remain where she was and await her destiny. Now John came to my assistance, and enabled me to write her two days later that I had won over the envoy's chaplain who would marry us. If she liked, she could send her maid that evening to speak with him herself. That is exactly what happened. The girl brought him a letter, written in English, in which my heroine confided the reasons for a secret ceremony, justified her decision, and commended herself to his prayers and care, enclosing a handsome ring.

"That devil, John, was wearing the doctor's canonicals and wig and spoke in broken but very pathetic German. The little wench crept up to him full of awe. I gave her a paper signed by John to take back and asked her to tell her mistress that the approaching festivities would provide the most favorable opportunity to carry out our desires because her illness would prevent her from being invited or observed.

Everything went according to my wishes; she was pleased with the paper and my compliance with her demands. Tell me, why are good people so like sheep, and why are women so imprudent, despite their innumerable examples of our knavery? But vanity rules them unimpeded, so that each one believes she is an exception, too amiable for anyone to play her for a fool. So let them accept the proper and natural punishment for their folly, while we enjoy the rewards of our genius! Certainly, if my Sternheim is no exception, none exists on this earth! Meanwhile, her ruin is not yet inevitable. If she loves me, and if in possessing her I find every varied and lively pleasure that I expect, she shall be Lady Derby and make of me the founding father of a new and singularly constituted clan. It will be fortunate for my firstborn that his mother has such a gentle, pious soul. For if she were fired by the same spirit as I, the safety of society would make it necessary to strangle the little imp at birth. But this not being the case, all our offspring will be distinguished by a charming mixture of wit and sensibility. But how the deuce did I arrive at this piece of domesticity? My friend, if this goes on, the outlook is bad; but I will test myself to the last degree.

My girl had her medicines made up and her trunk packed with linens and some light clothes. John and I carried it away at night. In the high-flown tone of lofty virtue, she wrote a long letter declaring that she was fleeing from danger and malice with a husband worthy of her. She made over to her uncle the use of all her revenues for three years, so that he could finance his lawsuit. She said she hoped he would thus gain more benefit for his children than he had received through the cruelty to her. He would get news of her from Florence. She willed her sumptuous clothes to the poor of the parish. Then she sent copies of this "testament" to the prince and Lord G.

On the day of the grand country festival, all my preparations were made. I was at court all day and mingled everywhere with the crowd. When the bustle became disagreeable, I crept to my coach and hastened to D. John hurried with me to the Loebaus' little garden pavilion where I confess I waited for the first time with beating heart for my pretty girl. At last she entered, stumbling and leaning on the arm of her maid, dressed prettily from head to toe and, as it were, protected by her dignity and touching grace. She hesitated a moment at the door; I ran toward her. She took a step, and I knelt at her feet, moved by real tenderness. She gave me her hands but could not speak. Tears fell from her eyes though she tried to smile. I could feel her embarrassment acutely, for I myself was a little ill at ease. John told me later that I gave him the signal none too soon; he could not have answered for himself much longer, as his resolve had almost deserted him. But these were only empty echoes of the youthful ideals we had not yet quite put off.

I pressed my girl's right hand to my breast. "Is it mine, this blessed hand? Do you wish to make me happy?" I asked in the tenderest tone.

She answered, stammering, "Yes, yes!" and laid her left hand on her heart. Seeing my signal, John came forward, addressed us briefly in English, babbled the marriage vows, and consecrated our union. I lifted my half-fainting Sophia up, clasped her in my arms for the first time, and kissed the loveliest lips my mouth had ever touched. I felt an emotion of tenderness, unknown to me until then, and endeavored to inspire her with courage. For a few moments she remained wrapped in silent amazement. Then, with an enchanting air of confidence, she laid her beautiful head on my breast. Lifting it up again and pressing my hands to her bosom she said, "My lord, all I have on earth now is you and the testimony of my heart. Heaven will reward you for the solace you have given me; this heart will be eternally grateful to you!"

I embraced her and made all manner of avowals. Then it was time for her to retire with her maid and put on men's clothes. I left her alone to do this because I did not trust my passion, and besides, I had no time to lose. We got out of the house without being noticed because of the festivities in honor of the princes from—. Many carriages were coming and going, and mine was not noticed carrying my lady and her maid away. Having resumed his own identity, John was their guide. Agreeing with him that they should put up at the village of Z., not far from B., I returned to the ball where no one had noticed my absence.* With great merriment I executed the figures of the dance and had to laugh when the prince would not look at the English dancers because the memory of Lady Sternheim tortured him.

In another letter I shall describe for you the noise, conjectures, and pursuits of the next day. I shall now go on a week's visit to my lady who, as John writes me, is very depressed and cries much.

Heureusement (luckily)! [Wieland].

You see, my friend, from the letters of the despicable Lord Derby what abominable tricks were used to bring this best of young ladies to the brink of the greatest misery. You can also imagine how sad I was when she came to the ball, became ill, and was thrown from one distressing agitation of her soul to the next. Because she received no letters from anyone, we assumed that the prince and Count Loebau intercepted them. The manner in which her request to visit her estates was denied and the princes' visit assisted the intentions of Lord Derby. Unfortunately, that inhuman man deceived me, too, so that I helped to remove my lady from her uncle's care.

You see from his letters how much cunning and cleverness he had. Besides that, he is a very handsome man, and my lady was glad to have her longing for England satisfied.

Oh, you still have much to read that will astonish you! I will work as hard as I can so as not to keep you waiting very long.

✿

PART TWO

Seymour to Dr. T.

Two months have passed since I wrote you, since tortured by doubts and suspicions, I have shunned all society and finally, through a misplaced zeal for virtue, have made myself the most miserable creature on earth. Oh, if I alone were miserable, I would think myself fortunate; but I have driven the best, the noblest soul to a desperate resolve. I am the cause of my adored Lady Sternheim's misery. No one knows anything of her fate, but my heart tells me she is unhappy. That thought devours the very heart which nourishes it. But it must seem that I am writing nonsense; I must try to make myself understood.

You know how distraught I was upon returning from the festivities at Count F.'s, and that from that moment on I avoided all company. My love was wounded but not dead; I thought contempt and avoidance would cure me of it; I did not even want to hear the lady mentioned. Finally, my uncle tried to extinguish my passion all at once by telling me that a masked ball had been planned for the prince's birthday, that the prince would wear my lady's mask, and that she would receive her costume and jewels as his gifts. From this, he said, I could infer that she had sacrificed her virtue to him. He told me she asked favors of him before and had received all she requested, that the prince came into Count Loebau's garden at night, accompanied only by his darling, etc. My uncle succeeded; the force of my love dissipated with esteem for her and with the hope I had blindly continued to nourish. But I was not yet quite indifferent: my soul was grieved by the remembrance of her wit and virtue. "How happy, Oh my God, how happy she could have made me," I cried, "if she had remained true to her education and her nature!" However, I did not want to leave her without seeing her punished, and the masked ball seemed to me well suited for my intention. I made myself a double mask. Wearing the first, I intended to ascertain for myself whether she had forgotten her worth and her duties. She came into the hall as if accompanied by all the graces and wearing the jewels the court jeweler had shown my lord. She was so disgustingly complaisant as to let her beautiful voice be heard and to encourage the prince and the rest of the company to be joyful. If I could have robbed her of her charming figure and all her talents, I would have done it at that moment. It would have been easier for me to see her miserable, ugly—yes, even dead, than to be a witness to her moral destruction. My soul was in the deepest pain when she sang and danced minuets with the prince and with others. But when he put his arm around her, pressed her to his breast, cavorted with her in the shameless, indecent whirling-dance of the Germans[12] and engaged in a familiarity that broke all the bounds of good breeding—then my silent misery turned into burning rage! I hastily slipped into my second disguise, went up to her, and reproached her bitterly and violently about shamelessly exhibiting herself with such abandon in her vile ornaments. I added that all the world despised her, whom they had formerly adored. My first words completely astonished her; she could say nothing except to stutter "I—I . . . ," putting one hand on her breast and attempting to catch me with the other. But wretch that I was, I escaped, not wanting to see the effect my speech would have. I hurried home, had six post-horses put to my chaise, took my old servant Dick with me, and drove for six days without knowing where, until I finally had to stop at a village, where I strictly charged Dick to tell no one about me. The state of my soul defies description. I was without feeling, mindless, unhappy, restless; and yet I denied myself the only aid my sufferings demanded—to get news from D. This fatal obstinacy laid the foundations of the deep sadness that will haunt me to the end of my life. For while I was hiding in a lonely village during the first days of the prince's supposed triumph, trying to get over my unconquerable love, the young lady had shown the noblest resistance, had almost lost her life from grief, and as she had been prevented from returning to her estates, had finally fled her uncle's house. A month after this event I returned, gloomy and emaciated. My lord received me with tender affection. He told me how I had worried him and also that he had thought I might have abducted the young lady.

"Would to God you had permitted me to do so," I cried; "I would not be so miserable now. But don't speak to me of her anymore."

He embraced me and said, "But dear Charles, you must hear what happened. She was virtuous after all; everything said against her was false, and now she has fled." Then my eagerness to know all was as great as my former fear of it.

It seems the young lady believed that her aunt had had her jewels newly mounted and was lending them to her for the ball. She had believed herself in the merchant's debt for her costume, her singing had been a forced favor on her part, and in a letter to the prince she had blessed the person in a white mask who had revealed to her all the malicious rumors that had destroyed her reputation.

"Oh, my lord," I cried; "I was that person. I spoke to her and heaped reproaches on her, but right after that conversation, I hurried away." He resumed as follows: "While still at the ball, the young lady threw down the jewels at the prince's feet and drove home in a state of the most extreme agitation. She was extremely ill for a week and did not receive anyone. On her recovery, she asked to be allowed to go to her estates, but her uncle did not let her go. A week later, when a fête was given at court in honor of the princess of Prussia, she and her chambermaid disappeared. The Count and Countess Loebau, who remained at the ball until morning, and their servants, who had not risen early either, gave no thought to the young lady until the afternoon when the table was laid for the count and they began to miss her and her maid. But when they forced her apartment open, they found only letters, one to the prince, one to my Lord C., and one to her uncle in which was enclosed a list of the clothes she had sent to the parson to be sold, the money from which he was to distribute to the parish poor. Briefly, but with dignity and emotion, she enumerated the complaints she had against her uncle and his wife and the reasons why she was leaving them. She said she was placing herself under the protection of a husband of her choice, whom she had married before leaving their house for Count R.'s at Florence, from where they would hear of her. Meanwhile, she was signing over to him the use of all the revenues from her estates for three years, so he could conclude the lawsuit that he had sought basely to finance by sacrificing her honor. She said that this was a present she was giving to his two sons, and that they would receive more blessings from it than from their designs for her perdition. To the prince she wrote that she had fled with a noble and worthy husband from the pursuit of his hateful and dishonorable passion, that she had left to her uncle the revenues from her estates for three years, but that she hoped that after that time was up, she would, through the sovereign's justice, once more receive them. To my Lord G. she declared that she had always revered his mind and character and had wished to have a small part of his respect, though it was probable that her circumstances would cloak her own character in so nebulous a light that he would be unable to form a proper opinion of her. She assured him, however, that she had never been unworthy of his esteem and had not deserved his contempt. She asked him to let his nephew read the letter also. After this discovery," my uncle continued, "Loebau hurried to the prince, who was greatly astonished and had wanted to send everywhere in search of her, if Count F. had not advised against it. They had merely sent a courier to Count R.'s at Florence, from where they have, however, until now received no news of the young lady."

While my lord was giving me this account, all my soul's faculties seemed suspended; but when he finished, they revived again. He was obliged to listen to my bitterest recriminations for preventing me from uniting myself with the noblest of hearts. Her magnanimous benevolence toward her uncle (a noble return for his despicable insult), her remembrance of the poor and of me, to whom she sought to justify herself—how many blows to my heart! How I hated staying at D., how difficult it was to hide my wrath when I saw her enemies or when someone wanted to speak to me of her! For the courageous step she had taken to save herself was criticized by everyone. All her excellent qualities were diminished, and flaws and follies of which she was quite incapable were falsely attributed to her. How base (and yet how common) is the pleasure of discovering flaws in a meritorious person! It is easier to find a thousand hearts, willing to debase themselves by discovering the weaknesses of human nature in an otherwise distinguished person, than to find one honest enough to acknowledge superior wisdom and virtue in another and sincerely to admire him.

I sent a courier to Florence with a letter to Count R., telling him the story of his worthy niece. From the answer I received, I learned that he did not know anything of her whereabouts. All his efforts to find her had been in vain. All this increases my self-reproach because of my precipitous departure from D. Why didn't I wait for the effect of my harangue? If one wants to make improvements, is it enough to dispense bitter recriminations? My heart would rebel at seeing an invalid beaten or mistreated, yet on the person I loved, whom I considered misguided, I rained such blows as must have deeply wounded her soul! But I saw her as a creature voluntarily throwing herself away and thus becoming unworthy of my respect, and I thought myself justified in treating her accordingly. Oh, how cruel my egotism was to this amiable girl! At first I did not want to speak of my love until I was satisfied that she had shown herself in the full glory of triumphant virtue. She proceeded on her own fair path; and because she did not follow my own idealistic plan, I assumed the authority to punish her most severely. All of us judged and damned her, but she—how noble, how great she became at the very moment when I thought her debased! When she blessed the white mask, she blessed me, the human fury that had almost driven her to the brink of an early grave. Oh, what can she say now of the wretch whose thoughtlessness threw her into the precipitous and certainly unhappy union she must already regret and can never break. And yet she wrote my name, she wanted me to think well of her! Oh Sophia, even in the misery I caused you, your magnanimous, innocent soul would weep at my tortured heart if you knew its first hopes, now mingled with all the pain of losing you that I have caused myself!

After an absence of eight weeks, Derby has returned from a journey to E. and is showing me special attentions. I poured out to him all my tender sorrows, but he laughed at me and maintained that with all his reputation for wickedness, he caused less damage than I through my virtuous zeal. He says his wickedness carries a kind of warning with it that puts people on their guard, whereas the severity of my principles leads me to judge apparent and inevitable human faults with such cruelty that the wicked become more obstinate and good people are driven to desperation. How could *Derby* utter this truth? I feel—yes, I feel that he was right, that I was cruel, that it was I—wretch that I am—who have made the best of women miserable!

Oh my friend, my teacher, the measure of my misery is full. All the hours of my life are poisoned. John, our secretary, departed two days before the young lady's flight and has not returned since then. Her chambermaid visited him once, and among his papers was found a torn page where, in the handwriting of my Sophia, the following appeared: "I approve of all the reasons you give for the secrecy of our union, but see to it that the marriage takes place. For I shall not leave here unmarried, though I prefer a union with an Englishman above all others."

Thus she has become the property of one of the worst men of any nation. Oh, I curse the day when I first saw her, when I found a sympathetic soul in her. And may God forever damn the scoundrel to whose arms she fled! What tricks that churl must have employed! He could not have succeeded, without affliction having disordered her brain. But the letters she left behind are written in such a benevolent, noble tone and with so much wit! Yet—I think I once read somewhere that when the artificial and acquired functions of the brain are disordered, the mechanisms that cause the brain to obey our best and most natural inclinations take charge.

Judge for yourself then the nobility of our young lady's principles.

Lady Sternheim to Emilia

Here lives your friend in a lonely village, unknown to all who see her and hidden from those who knew her. I find myself here, my self-love and excessive sensibility having led me far astray, making me enter a path from which I would have zealously shrunk with horror in my days of tranquil reasoning. Oh, if I could not tell myself, if my Rosina and my Lord Derby himself could not testify that all the powers of my soul had been weakened and suppressed through affliction and illness, where would I get one moment's peace and satisfaction, my Emilia, considering that I have engaged in an intrigue, that I have entered into a clandestine marriage, and that I have fled from the house into which my foster father himself had placed me.

It is true, I was cruelly mistreated in that house; it was impossible for me to remain there with feelings of trust and contentment. Certainly my

bitterness was just, for how can I think of my uncle and aunt basely sacrificing me to their own interests and helping to lay snares for my honor,
without the utmost anger?

I had no friend at D.; and my heart rebelled at the very idea that, after
regaining my health, I would again have to meet all those persons who had
long known why I was introduced at court and had laughed at my distress
and resistance. Yes, all of them knew of it, even my Lady C.; and even
after learning my character, not one of them was noble and humane enough
to give me the slightest hint. Yet I had offended no one; I had tried to hide
my sentiments whenever they tended to condemn theirs or to displease
them. How willing I was to excuse all their seeming faults! But they
thought the child of an unequal marriage to be of little consequence. Oppressed by the weight of so many insults poured on my character, my birth,
and my reputation, how could I reject the consolation offered me by my
Lord Derby's respect and love? The distance of Count and Countess R.,
their not answering my last few letters, the rudeness with which they denied me refuge on my own estates, and—my dear Emilia, I do not deny
it—my love for England and the distinguished rank to which my lord's
generosity would raise me; these two considerations also had great attraction for my forsaken and stunned soul. I was prudent enough, however, not
to leave the house without first being married; and I communicated that
fact to the prince, my Lord G., and my uncle. I did not name my spouse
although he generously left me free to do so, even though that would have
cost him the envoy's and his court's favor because people might have
thought that Lord G. had promoted this union; and such a suspicion could
have had unpleasant consequences. Was I not obliged then to be magnanimous, too, and by my silence prevent him who loved and saved me from
suffering their ill will and having to justify himself? It was sufficient that
he had won over the envoy's chaplain to whom I wrote the entire story of
my secret marriage and whom my lord gives a pension sufficient to live
upon if he should lose his position. Reinforced by all this, I departed with
a happy heart from D., accompanied by one of my lord's most faithful
servants. To evade all suspicion, my husband had to remain behind and
attend the festivities which had been arranged in honor of two foreign
princes. This circumstance pleased me, for I would have trembled and suffered at his side, whereas I made my way happily and peacefully with my
Rosina until we came to a small village where I took up residence and have
stayed for four weeks now without my lord finding the proper opportunity
thus far to join me safely. My first plan had been to continue my journey to
Florence and await my lord there, but I could not get his permission to do
so; and even now he wants to disengage himself completely from my Lord
G. and only then to take me to Count R. and after that directly to his
homeland.

In these four weeks of solitude I have kept myself confined indoors and have had no books other than some English writings belonging to my lord that I did not like to read because they are leftover testimonies of morals corrupted by example and seduction. On the first cold day of autumn that obliged me to have a fire, I threw them all into the stove because I could not bear that these books and I had the same master and abode. The days seemed long; Rosina asked for needlework from our landlady; and I, feeling my mental faculties increasingly restored, reflected on myself and my destiny.

These reflections are gloomy because the contradiction between my inclinations and my circumstances has existed ever since the death of my beloved and revered father and has increased since the moment of my entry into the great world.

Oh, that my father had remained with me until, with his blessing, my hand was joined to that of a worthy man! My fortune is adequate; and since my husband and I would have followed the example of noble benificence my parents set us, the blissful consciousness of a life well spent and my joy over the well-being of my dependents would have crowned all my days. Why did I not heed the voice that told me to remain in P. when, filled with anxiety, my soul resisted my uncle's and your father's persuasions? But I too finally thought that prejudice and obstinacy might be the roots of my aversion and agreed that the poor thread of my life, which until then had unwound so simply and uniformly, should henceforth be interwoven with my aunt's confused and uneven fate. I could not escape this web except by tearing off all connections. In addition, I learned of the conspiracy against my honor; and then my extreme sensibility, encouraged since early youth, fed my offended self-love. Oh, I have lerned to distinguish a sensibility that relates to others from one that has no object but ourselves!

The second kind is justified and comes naturally to all human beings, but only the first is noble. It alone makes it probable that we are made in our Creator's image, because this sensibility toward our neighbor's circumstances is the driving force of beneficence, the only attribute that bears a genuine (though imperfect) impression of the divine image. This impression the Creator has imprinted on all parts of the physical world, so that even the lowliest blade of grass is food for animals as beneficent as the mighty tree is for us. The smallest grain of sand serves its destined beneficence by lightening the soil to make it fruitful, just as the great rocks that fill us with wonder serve to fix our general abode, the earth. Are not the plant and animal kingdoms filled with gifts of beneficence for us? The entire physical world faithfully discharges these duties, and every spring they are renewed. Man alone degenerates and effaces that sacred impression which in us should shine much more strongly and beautifully because we have been empowered to reveal it in so many ways.

Here, my Emilia, you recognize my father's principles. My melancholy vividly recalled them to my mind, when in the quiet of my solitude I turned and viewed the path along which my sensibility hurried me and which has led me far from my destined place. Oh, I have indeed neglected the beneficent duty of setting a good example for others![*]

No one will say that sorrow and despair participated in my decision, but every mother will warn her daughter with the example of my mistakes; and every daughter will imagine that she would have found a nobler and more virtuous means to extricate herself. I myself know that these exist, but at the time I did not see them; and no one was kind enough to point them out to me. How unfortunate is he who is reduced to seek excuses, my Emilia, and how sad it is to find them so weak and insufficient! As long as I was sensible of others I offended only the prejudices of unfeeling souls. Even if it seemed that my ideas of beneficence were exaggerated, nevertheless, they were admirable and worthy of imitation because they bore the impression of the divine image. But when my sensibility was directed only toward myself, I offended against good conduct and all the social virtues of a well-born girl. How dark, oh how dark is this part of my past! What is left to me now but to fix my eyes on the path that lies before me and walk straight ahead in the clear light of day?

I first found comfort by occupying myself with teaching two poor nieces of my landlady to work and think. Emilia, you know that I like to keep busy. My reflections and my writing saddened me. I could not change what had happened in the past; I had to accept criticism as the just consequence of my erroneous self-love. I had to find encouragement outside myself, partly by resolving to make my Lord Derby happy and partly by striving to do all possible good to my fellow man. I inquired about the poor people of the place and sought to bring them relief. It was then that my good Rosina told me of our landlady's two nieces, poor orphaned girls, loathed by the landlord. Although they are the daughters of his wife's sister, he treated her badly, too, because of the little that they consumed. I had them brought to me and searched out their inclinations to see what knowledge they already had or might still wish to acquire. Both wanted to learn Rosina's skills, and so I shared with her the instruction of these good children. I also gave both of them clothes, and the very next day they came to watch me get dressed. Within a fortnight they were attending me by turns. I spoke to them of the duties of the station in which God had placed them and also of those pertaining to mine. Thus I brought them to consider themselves fortunate to be chambermaids rather than ladies, because I spoke

---

[*]But do not her very faults become beneficent through this warning example? Why does she not find consolation in that reflection?—because even the noblest souls are not beneficent at the expense of their self-love [Wieland].

much to them of the great responsibility that has been placed on us because of our advantages and our power over others. Their ideas of happiness and their wishes are in any case limited, and my predictions of each girl's future according to her character amused them very much. They think I can read their thoughts. I pay the landlord for their board and provide everything they need for instruction. I give them lessons in writing and arithmetic, and I am also trying to develop their taste in ladies' fashions. But in particular I teach them to recognize all kinds of human character and to tolerate them patiently. The landlady and her nieces look upon me as their good angel and would every moment kneel before me and thank me if I would let them. Oh, what happy hours I spend with these children! How often I remember the words of a modern philosopher: "If you feel melancholy, if you see nothing to console you anywhere—read the Bible; attempt to conquer your inherent faults or help your fellow man. Thus your sadness will leave you."

A noble and infallible resource! With what great pleasure I walk with my pupils and tell them of our Creator's goodness! My heart is gladdened when I see them moved by my words, see them lift their eyes to heaven with reverence and gratitude and then press my hands and kiss them. Emilia, in such moments I am content to have fled because otherwise I would not have found these children.

Lady Sternheim to Emilia

My girls have become twice as dear to me since my Lord was here, for through the joy in these innocent creatures my mind and heart have been strengthened. My lord is not pleased with the gravity of my disposition; he cherishes only my wit. My shy and gentle tenderness is not the right answer to his impetuous and violent love, and he reacted to my burning his books with a husband's domestic rage. During his three weeks' stay I dared not see my girls because his mood seemed so changeable. Sometimes it was gay and passionate, sometimes cold and gloomy. He often looked at me with a smile but often, too, with an expression of secret discontent. He asked me to tell him the reasons for my earlier aversion to him and for my change of heart. Then he inquired about my feelings toward Lord Seymour, and my blushing at that name caused a look which struck me with indescribable terror. On a much more delicate occasion I had noticed that he was jealous of my Lord Seymour. It appears then that I shall have to suffer constantly because of others. My lord loves splendor and has given me many costly jewels; and though I prefer to shine in modesty rather than in splendor, I shall attempt to enter into his spirit. May God grant that this is the only point in which we differ, but I fear there are more. Oh Emilia, pray for me! My heart has misgivings. I shall spare no compliance, no effort to

please my husband; but I shall often have to give in. If only I do not have
to sacrifice my character and my principles!

I chose him; to him I entrusted my well-being, my honor, and my life.
To him I owe greater submission and gratitude than to a husband under
other circumstances.

Oh, when I am once in my own house in England and my lord is engaged in affairs suitable to his proud mind, then I hope that, in the midst of
his family, his bold blood will flow more gently, that his pride will change
to noble dignity, and his impetuosity to virtuous zeal for praiseworthy actions. I will endeavor to support that ardor; and since I was not fortunate
enough to have been born an ancient Greek, I will try at least to be ranked
among the best of the English ladies.

Lord Derby to His Friend

Curse you and your predictions! Why did you have to interfere in my
love affair? You said my enchantment would not last long. How the devil
could your silly mind see this in Paris, while I was quite deluded here? But
my good fellow, you are not entirely right. You spoke of satiety; I do not
have it and cannot have it because I expected much greater pleasure. And
yet I can no longer bear the sight of her, of my Sophia, my own supposed
lady whom I loved to distraction for five months! But destiny has placed
my pleasures and her inclinations in opposition, and my heart wavered between the two. She has misjudged the force of habit. For her lover's warm
embraces she has returned nothing but the feeble affection of a cold wife.
She whose compassion is so lively, who is so zealously ardent and active
for mere ideas and phantoms, gives me cool kisses interrupted by sighs. I
imagined the sweetness and fascination of loving and possessing her. Proud
of my conquest, I looked upon the prince and his helpers with contempt.
Oh, how eager I was for the moment that would unite me with her! I would
have sacrificed horses, postilions, and servants if I could have speeded my
journey. My heart, my pulse beat with joy when I caught sight of the village where she lived, and in my impatience I almost pistoled the wretch
who could not instantly open the door to my chaise. I bounded up the stairs
in five leaps. There she stood in a white English dress, looking beautiful
and majestic. Overjoyed, I embraced her. She welcomed me, stammering,
blushing, and growing pale by turns. Her dejection would have made me
happy if her face had even once expressed the yearning of love; but all her
features were marked only with anxiety and constraint. I went to change my
clothes; and soon returning, I saw her through a doorway sitting on a bench
with both her arms wrapped around the window curtains, all her muscles
tense, her eyes lifted up, her lovely bosom slowly moving with violent,
deep breaths. In short, she was the picture of silent despair. Judge what an

impression this must have made on me. What was I to think of this? My arrival might indeed fill her with new and unknown sensations; she might well be a little afraid. But if she felt any love for me, was such a violent conflict natural? I was hurt and angry. When I stepped into the room, she started with alarm and then let her arm and head sink down. I threw myself at her feet and grasped her knees with stiff, trembling hands.

"Smile, Lady Sophia," I cried; "smile if you do not want me to lose my mind!"

A flood of tears gushed from her eyes; my anger increased, but she put her arms around my neck and inclined her beautiful forehead on mine.

"Oh my dearest lord, don't be angry at seeing me still sensible of my misfortunes. I hope your goodness will soon make me forget them." Her breath, the motion of her lips which I felt on my cheek while she spoke, and some of her tears which fell on my face extinguished my anger and gave me the sweetest sensation I have felt during the three weeks I was with her. I embraced her, reassured her, and during supper and the rest of the evening she tried hard to smile. Sometimes, when my looks appeared too ardent to her, she covered my eyes with her hand with all the charms of virgin modesty.

Charming creature, why did you not stay this way? Why did you show me your sympathetic inclination toward Seymour?

In the days which followed, she tried to be gay. I had brought her a lute, and she was kind enough to sing for me a pretty Welsh song of her own making in which she asked Venus for a band to detain forever the heart she loved. The thoughts were beautiful and expressed with refinement, the music was touching, and her voice so affecting that I listened to her with the sweetest and strongest passion. But my dream evaporated when I observed that during the tenderest passages which she sang best, she did not look at me but with hanging head fixed her eyes on the floor, uttering sighs that certainly did not have me for their object. When she had finished, I asked her if this was the first time she had ever sung that song. "No," she said, blushing. So I asked when she had first begun to think favorably of me and about her opinion of Seymour. But cursed be the frankness of her answers! With them she broke all the tender bonds that bound me to her. A hundred trifling incidents, and even the effort it cost her to appear affectionate and happy, convinced me that she did not love me. A little admiration for my wit and generosity, the joy at going to England, and cool gratitude that I had delivered her from her relatives and from the prince: this was all she felt for me, all that had brought her to my arms! Yes, she was even careless enough to answer my amorous request to name the attributes that she would most admire in me by painting a picture of none other but Seymour. And always she urged our journey to Florence—a clear sign that she was thinking not of my happiness but the satisfaction of her ambition. She poisoned all the days I was with her by reminding me of this promise, giving it every possible turn, and even assuring me that she could not love me until we got to Florence. I told you she poisoned my happiness and with it, at the same time, my heart, which had sometimes been foolish enough to reproach me for our false marriage and plead her cause against me. In the third week the evil grew worse. I had given her some English books in which lascivious pleasure was painted in the most lively and flaming colors. I had hoped that a few sparks would kindle the passionate side of her imagination, but her obstinate virtue made her burn my books after only leafing through them and condemning them. The loss of my books and all my hopes caused an attack of ill humor on my part which she bore with calm resignation.

Two days later I came upon her at her dressing table, just when her beautiful hair was being combed. Her dress was of white lawn, set off with red taffeta and fitted closely to her body revealing the perfect proportions of the Greek ideal of beauty. How enchanting she looked! I took her locks and wound them under her right arm and around her hips. The picture of Milton's Eve came to mind. I sent her chambermaid away and asked her to undress for a moment, to give me the pleasure of admiring in her the image of nature's first masterpiece.*

A blush of shame suffused her whole face. Furthermore, I received a flat refusal. I pressed her, but she resisted until my impatience and desire caused me to tear off her clothes from the neck down, and against her will also to accomplish my final purpose. You cannot imagine how upset she was at this liberty which, after all, means so little in our circumstances.

"My lord," she cried, "you tear my heart and my love for you! I shall never forgive you for this lack of delicacy. Oh God, how blind I was!" She cried bitter tears and pushed my arms back violently while she uttered these exclamations. I told her dryly that I was sure she would not have shown such insensibility to Lord Seymour's desires. "And I am sure," she said in a high tragic tone, "that my Lord Seymour would have thought me worthy of a nobler and more refined love!"

Did you ever see such a strangely foolish virtue as in this case, where a woman does not want to have her most perfect charms be seen or admired? How silly and obstinate, to make such a distinction between my eyes and my feelings! In the afternoon I wanted her to explain it to me, but although she thought about it, she could not account for it, other than to say that she would feel the same aversion to having the best properties of her

---

*What a request, my Lord Derby! Could you not choose your time better? [Wieland].

soul uncovered. Nevertheless, she admitted that she enjoyed it when people spoke favorably of her wit and her figure. Yet, she would rather forego that pleasure, than to obtain it through her own efforts.*

Do you think that I could live happily with such perverse wrongheadedness? This mixture of wit and folly pervades her whole being and pours languor and indifference into my veins. She is no longer the creature I loved; I am, therefore, no longer obliged to continue to act what to her I once seemed to be. She herself has opened the path by which I shall escape her chains. In any case, my brother's death has raised my thoughts to higher matters. I shall probably have to return to England soon, and then Seymour can try his luck with my "widow"; for I think she will be that soon and will owe it only to her own conduct. Because she thinks herself my legal spouse, was it not her duty to submit to all my wishes? And has she not completely lost sight of that duty? Does she not love another? And is it, therefore, not also just and right that because her ambition betrayed me I should now punish her ambition? I look about me with satisfaction when I think that I was the chosen instrument for punishing her uncle's baseness, the prince's lust, and their agents' folly. After all, it is a well-known dictum that providence makes use of scoundrels to punish the sins of the pious. Thus, I was merely the engine through which Lady Sternheim's flight was to be expiated, and I was endowed with the necessary talents and skills for this task. I have received my reward. Let the others now profit from their chastisements!

By the way, I want you to know that I have really become Seymour's confidant. He was stuck in a lonely village bewailing the loss of the girl's virtue, while I stealthily put her up elsewhere and laughed at him. He wanted me to tell him who might be the husband with whom, according to her letters, she had eloped. He has sent couriers to Florence, but I have found a means of stopping his inquiries. I took the last letter Lady Sternheim wrote to me at D., tore off all those words that might have betrayed me, and threw the remaining piece among the papers of John, the secretary. His absence had been noticed and now, on my advice, his room was searched. When this paper was found suspicion centered on him, and he was declared to be the deliverer whom this delicate lady had chosen. The discovery seemed to show that she was ruled by very bourgeois ideas

---

*Indeed, this answer does not solve the puzzle. Lord Derby, after all, saved her own efforts. Why was she, nevertheless, displeased? Why did she say that he tore her heart, when all he tore was her *deshabille?* Presumably because she did not love him, had not been properly and gradually prepared for such a scene, and, in any case, was in a frame of mind too different from his to condescend to acquiesce to a suggestion that seemed motivated more by wantonness than by affection [Wieland].

and inclinations, providing the text which all the ladies of quality will preach to their daughters against marrying beneath one's rank. Seymour's love has turned into vexation and contempt; he never mentions her name anymore and no longer sends out his couriers; but as for me, I await one from England and then you will hear whether I will come to see you or not.

Rosina to Emilia

Oh my sister, how shall I describe the terrible misfortune that has befallen our beloved lady: Lord Derby! God will punish him, *must* punish him! The wicked man has deserted her and gone alone to England. His servant, who is as impious as his master, performed the ceremony dressed as a cleric. Oh, my hands tremble as I write it. The infamous scoundrel himself brought the letter in which he took his leave, so that seeing his face, we might have no doubt about our misfortune. The lord says my lady did not love him, that she had always carried my Lord Seymour in her heart, that this had extinguished his love, which otherwise would have remained unchanged. The wicked wretch! Oh dear God, I too have helped to bring about the marriage. If only I had gone to Lord Seymour! Oh, we were both blinded. I cannot look at my lady; my heart breaks; she eats nothing. All day long she lies on her knees before a chair on which she rests her head. She is motionless, except that sometimes she stretches her arms toward heaven and calls out in a dying voice, "Oh my God, oh my God!"

She weeps very little and had no tears at all until today. For the first two days I was afraid we would both lose our minds, and it is a miracle that has not happened.

For two weeks we had heard nothing from the Lord. His man went away, and five days later came the letter that made us so unhappy. The cursed scoundrel gave it to her himself. She became pale and motionless. Finally, without saying a word, she violently tore up his letter and another piece of paper, threw the pieces on the floor, pointed to them, and with a pitiable expression of pain, said to him, "Go away, go away!" At the same moment she fell to her knees, folded her hands, and remained lying there, silent and as if half dead for over two hours. I cannot tell you what I suffered; God alone knows it! I knelt down next to her, held her in my arms, and questioned her for so long and with a thousand tears that with a broken, weak voice she told me stammeringly that Derby was leaving her, her marriage had been a deceit, and she had nothing left to wish for but death. She does not want revenge; it is with you, my dear sister, that she wants to conceal herself from all eyes. We shall leave here the day after tomorrow. Oh, may God be merciful to us during our journey! You must receive her.

Your husband will consent to it and advise her. We are taking nothing with us that came from my lord. She has torn up his letter of exchange for six hundred carolines. Three hundred is all the money she has. Of that she will give the two girls fifty and another fifty to the poor. Her jewels and the trunk with clothes are all we will take with us. You will hardly know us— we are so altered by our grief. She no longer speaks to anyone. The two girls' brother will accompany us half the way. We are coming dear sister, to seek consolation from you. She would like to write you herself, but she can hardly move her dear, beneficent hands. I cannot bear to think how good she was to everyone—and now she is so unhappy! But God must and will surely protect her.

Lady Sternheim to Emilia

Oh my dear Emilia, if from this abyss of misery my voice can still reach your heart, stretch forth a loving hand to the friend of your youth, so that she can pour her grief, her life into your bosom. Oh how severely, how cruelly am I punished for my flight! Oh Providence—but I will not arraign my fate! For the first time in my life I had permitted myself to harbor thoughts of revenge, of secret cunning; must I not take it as just punishment that I have fallen into the clutches of malice and deceit? Why did I believe appearances? But, oh God, how is a heart like the one Thou has given me—how is such a heart to know that good, generous actions can proceed from bad principles?

Self-love has made me miserable. It persuaded me to believe that, because of my virtue, Derby could learn to love me. He says that he "only deceived my hand," but that I "deceived his heart." Cruel, cruel man, how you have abused the probity of my heart which so sincerely endeavored to show you the tenderest love and respect! You do no believe that there is such a thing as virtue, otherwise you would have sought and found it in my soul.

It is true, my Emilia, that I had moments when I wished that I owed my deliverance to Lord Seymour, but I tore that wish out of my heart. It was filled with gratitude and esteem for the man whom I took for my husband—fatal name, how could I bear to write it down—but my thoughts and feelings are laid to waste, as is my fortune, my reputation, and my happiness. I have been ground into the dust. I lie prostrate on the earth and pray God to preserve me only until I am with you and have the consolation that you can see my heart's innocence and weep a compassionate tear over me. Then, oh Fate, take it—take this life which is un- soiled by vice but which for the past four days has been made so wretched through your workings that without the hope of a speedy end it would be insufferable.

Derby to His Friend

I am going to England, but first I will visit you. Don't say a word about my latest love. I don't want to think of her anymore. It is bad enough that her disquieting memory forces itself on me against my will. My "almost wife" has left the village where her fantastic character met with an equally fantastic fate. She departed in a state of prideful wrath, tore my letter of exchange into a thousand pieces, and left all my presents behind. Because of that I almost followed her, but if she had found it possible to forgive my pranks, I would have despised her! After all that has passed, it is impossible that she can love me, and I could not have been happy with her anymore. To what purpose then should I have played my role any longer? No matter what, she must always respect my truthfulness and admire my knowledge of the most secret motives of our souls. I left her, uncertain what I should do about her and our contract; but her incessant demands to take her to Florence and her threat to leave without me if necessary, caused me to write her quite bluntly as follows: "I plainly see that you only used my love to escape from your Uncle Loebau and gratify your ambition. You have never considered my love and the happiness of my heart because you never valued any part of my character and respected me only when I have molded myself to your fantasies and adorned my ideas according to your whims. I cannot become like your picture of what you would most love in a husband because I am not Seymour, for whom alone you nourish that tender passion which I had hoped to merit. Your consternation when I mentioned him, the care with which you avoided speaking of him, yes, even the caresses you used to destroy my suspicions—all these are proofs of your continuing inclination for Seymour. You are the first woman who has made me resolve on marriage; yet I remained cautious enough to want to assure myself, beforehand, of your true feelings. I did this by means of disguising one of my men as a clergyman. My love and honor were as firmly bound by this pretended marriage as if it had been performed by the primate of England or the Pope himself. But because the first essential, a union of our minds, is missing, I think it best that we separate without noise and without witnesses, in the same manner in which we came together, because I am not mean-spirited enough to take pleasure in possessing your charming person without also sharing in your heart. Neither am I simple enough to conduct you to England only for the benefit of Lord Seymour. You have no reason to complain about me because it was I who snatched you from the prince's persecution and your uncle's tyranny. I have deceived only your *hand* but you, in assuring me of a love you did not feel, have deceived my *heart*. I, therefore, now give you back your full freedom."

I sent off one of my men with this letter and went to my dancer at B. who is an infallible remedy against all species of uneasy thoughts; and she has, accordingly, restored me to a good part of my former liveliness.

My brother could not have died at a more convenient time. My money had been forthcoming less frequently, and this silly romance has been a little expensive (though she would have deserved all it cost me, if only she had loved me and renounced her enthusiasms). I was silly enough to repent of my letter two days ago and to send someone to inquire about her; but she was gone, and, come to think of it, she did right. We cannot and should not see each other again. I have torn up her letters and her picture, as she did my letter of exchange; but D., where everyone speaks of her and everything reminds me of her, has become unbearable to me. See if you can find me an amusing partner, such as becomes an English heir, so I can make good use of my regained freedom. For my father will throw the yoke over my neck as soon as I come near him. He can give me whomever he wants; I shall feel no love for her. What little remained of my heart has been used up by my German country maid. The place is void; I feel it. Here and there, some stray ghosts are still flitting about; and if I listened to them, I would hear them whisper to me of my wife of forty days whose shadow, they say, still wanders about there, but I pay no attention to their buzzing. Reason and circumstances justify the plan I followed, and in the end it is nothing but habit that recalls her picture here in D., where I used to see her in all the assemblies and always hear her spoken of.

But with all that, I swear to you that never again shall a metaphysician or a moralist become my mistress. Ambition and pleasure alone have votaries daring enough for their service. They shall, therefore, be my only deities in future. The first, because I shall obtain by her means all the respect and power necessary to assemble and promote all kinds of pleasing enjoyment, until my life shall be ended by a drunken bout at a parliamentary election or I break my neck in a horse race. Now do you see how thoroughly all the usual lordly traits have been roused in me? First, through all kinds of artifice, I attracted a fine young girl and tore her away from those who would have made her happy. I indulged in senseless waste, and after being satiated, have assumed the tone of the patriot at horse races and elections and shall let time determine whether, after these various fermentations, anything useful remains at the bottom of the vessel.

Here, my friend, I must take up the tale again myself, to give you a connected history of the events that followed the unhappy change in my beloved lady's fortunes.

My sister's house was now the only place where we could take refuge, under the circumstances. My lady would not hear of either revenge or restoring her rights; and under these circumstances the idea of going to her estates was also unthinkable. Her anguish was so great that she hoped it would kill her. I believe this is what would have happened if we had remained any longer in the house where the disastrous union had been consummated. Several times as we prepared for our departure I opened the door to Lord Derby's sitting room; and when she cast a glance into it, I believed the pain would instantly stifle her. Weighed down with extreme grief, she remained in my room while I packed our effects. I was ordered to give all of Lord Derby's presents, of which there were a great quantity and very beautiful ones, to the landlady. We took nothing but the few things we had brought with us on our flight from D. The landlady, who had been paid a month in advance, wanted to keep us longer; but we left at four o'clock in the morning on the second day, accompanied by her blessings and her imprecations on the villainous lord.

During our journey, my dear lady sat by my side silent and pale as death, with her eyes cast down. No word, no tear relieved her oppressed heart. For two days we traveled through magnificent country without her noticing anything. Sometimes she embraced me with a violent convulsive motion and for a few moments laid her head on my breast. I became more and more anxious and wept noisily, whereupon she looked at me tenderly and, pressing me to her heart, said in her heavenly voice, "Oh my Rosina, your grief shows me the full extent of my misfortune. You used to smile when you saw me, and now seeing me breaks your heart. Oh, that I have made you unhappy too! Be calm, and you will see me composed, too."

I was glad to hear her say at least this much and to see a few tears fall from her deadened eyes. I answered, "I would gladly be calm if you seemed less dejected, and if I saw some of the joy you used to feel at the sight of a beautiful countryside."

She was quiet for a few minutes and looked at the sky and all around her. Then she said with tearful tenderness, "It is true, dear Rosina, I live as if my misfortune had devoured all that is good and pleasing on this earth; yet the cause of my grief lies neither in the creatures nor in their beneficent Creator. Oh, why did I stray from the prescribed path."

Then she recapitulated her life and the most notable circumstances of her fate. I tried to reconcile her with herself and the motives for her actions, especially her secret marriage and flight from D.; and I succeeded to the extent that when she saw the overflowing barns and bustle of harvest activities in the villages through which we passed, she looked animated and pleased at the well-being of the country people. But the sight of young girls, especially those who seemed to be of her age, renewed all her sadness. Then she folded her hands and prayed God to keep every pure and innocent girl from the torment that preyed upon her heart.

Meanwhile, we had safely arrived at Vaels.[13] My brother-in-law's and-sister's welcome gave us all the consolation a virtuous friendship can provide. They tried to calm my dear lady, but on the fifth day she became ill; and for twelve days we thought she would surely die. She wrote a short summary of her misfortunes and even drew up her will. But against her wishes, she recovered. When she could be up again, she sat in my Emilia's nursery and taught her little godchild to read. This occupation and her association with my brother-in-law and sister visibly calmed her, so that on one occasion my brother-in-law ventured to ask her about her decisions and plans for the future. She answered that she had thought of nothing, except that she wanted to spend the rest of her life on her estates. However, until the three years were up, during which her revenues were to go to the Count of Loebau, she did not want to communicate with anyone. We had to accede to her fixed resolve on this point. She even took a new name; in allusion to her unhappy fate she wanted to be known as Mrs. Leidens[14] and to live with us under the guise of a young officer's widow. She sold the fine diamonds set around her parents' miniature portraits and also disposed of the rest of her jewels in order to live on the interest. She still wished to do good and resolved to teach needlework to some poor girls of the neighborhood.

This idea later became the foundation for the remaining part of her life. One of these girls, the goddaughter of one of the richest women in those parts, a Mrs. Hills, visited that lady to show her some of her work. The lady asked who her teacher was, and later requested my brother-in-law to ask Mrs. Leidens to help her found a charity school in her house and live with her there as a companion. At first my dear lady declined, fearing it would make her too public; but my brother-in-law so earnestly argued that it would be losing an opportunity of doing much good, that he finally persuaded her to agree, especially as she feared causing inconvenience in Emilia's house, though she paid for her board there.

She dressed simply in a striped linen gown with a large apron and white handkerchief, for even now the English manner appealed to her. She concealed her beautiful hair and a part of her features under a large bonnet to disguise herself, but her fine eyes, her smile of noble benevolence shining out under an expression of secret sorrow, her fine figure and carriage, and the most graceful walk, drew every eye to her. Mrs. Hills was very proud of having her as a companion. We were sad at her leaving us, because Mrs. Hills's residence was three hours' journey away, but her letters consoled us again. I am sure you, too, will read them with greater pleasure than my scribbles.

Lady Sternheim as Mrs. Leidens to Emilia

I write you on the tenth day of my stay here, my sisterly friend. Until now I was unable to do so. My feelings were too agitated to suffer the slow progress of my pen. But getting used to my new home and the effect of two sunny days, affording me a view over a most beautiful and extensive landscape, have permitted me the calm to look back, without anxiety or dizziness, on how destiny has dashed me from my former elevated state. My fondest tears flowed when I remembered my youth and education; shivers ran over me at the thought of the day that brought me to D.; and with closed eyes I hurried past the scene that followed. I dwelled with fondness only on my arrival at your house, for after fate had robbed me of everything, I was more observant of the refuge I had chosen and the welcome I received there. Tender pity marked my faithful Emilia's face, as did reverence and friendship her husband's. I saw that they believed me innocent and pitied my heart. I could look upon them as witnesses of my innocence and virtue. Oh, how refreshing to my injured soul was that thought! The first night I was with you I shed grateful tears for the consolation God had let me find in my Emilia's faithful friendship. The following morning was made painful through retelling all the particulars of my piteous story. But your husband's reflections and exhortations consoled me, and even more so did my walking through your house—where all the virtues of our sex reside with you, and with your husband all the wisdom and merit of his. I ate with you, observed you with your children, and saw your noble contentment despite your small income. I witnessed your tender maternal care and the excellent way in which your husband cares for his parishioners. All this, my Emilia, poured the first drop of the balm of peace into my soul. I saw you, who have all your life been prudent and virtuous, your most estimable husband, and five children, burdened by a hard fate, with fortune never once smiling on you. You bore it all with the most praiseworthy resignation, and I—should I blame fate because of the misery I have brought on myself? Despite my sincere love of virtue, my obstinacy and imprudence have exposed me to sorrow and contempt. I have lost much and suffered greatly; but should I, for that reason, forget the happiness of my early years and regard with indifference the opportunities to do good that still present themselves, exclusively devoting myself to the sensibilities of my self-love? I knew the value of all I had lost, but my illness and the reflections that followed it showed me that I still had life's true blessings. My heart is innocent and pure, the powers of my intellect are undiminished, the faculties of my soul and my good inclinations remain in full measure, and I stil have the capacity to do good.

My education has taught me that virtue and abilities constitute the only real happiness, and that to do good affords a noble heart its only true felicity. Fate has proved this to me through my own experience.

I moved in the circle of great and brilliant people; now I find myself lowered to medium rank and fortune and am even bordering on that condition where humiliation and poverty join hands. But no matter how much I may have sunk according to the common concepts of happiness, I can do much good in these two circles.

I give friendship and knowledge to the rich Mrs. Hills through my company and my conversation, my poor girls benefit from my careful instruction, and I show them a pleasing prospect of their future days.

Mrs. Hills gave me a pleasant room with two windows overlooking the fields. From there I go to a special hall set aside for the lessons of my thirteen girls. She feeds and clothes them and provides books and work projects. She never misses a lesson and is pleased with my instruction. Sometimes she sheds a tear or presses my hands, and many times nods her head to show me her approbation. Whenever this happens, a ray of joy falls into my heart. It is indeed pleasing to be loved for one's own sake! And now I have a thought, Emilia—but your husband must help me work it out completely.

Mrs. Hills has a certain pride, but is noble and benevolent. She would like to use her great wealth to institute a perpetual foundation, but she says it must be one that is quite new and will bring her honors and blessings. She wants *me* to think of something. Might not my small girls' school be the beginning of a "seminary for domestics," where poor girls could be trained to become good and skilled servants? As a test, I divided my thirteen pupils according to the characters of their minds and hearts:

1. Gentle, goodhearted creatures I would educate to be nursemaids;
2. Those with wit and skilled fingers would become chambermaids;
3. Girls with good sense and diligence would be trained as cooks and housekeepers;
4. The last class, possessed of physical strength, would be fitted for labor in house, kitchen, and garden.

For such a project I would need a suitable house with a garden, a sensible clergyman to teach them to know and love the duties of their station, and, besides that, some worthy and well-meaning poor widows or aged spinsters to take charge of the different branches of instruction.

This idea keeps me occupied enough to divert me from contemplating my painful past and to pour out over my bitter sorrow the sweet consolation that I might do much good in the future. This idea makes me think, by way of a simile, that self-love is like a polyp: one may sever all its branches or arms and even injure its trunk; yet it finds means to spread out anew. How wounded, how humbled was my soul! And now—just read again these pages of my contemplations and note what sturdy props my shaken self-love has found, and how I have gradually risen to the height of a grand project. Oh, if benevolent love of my fellow man had not woven its roots so deeply into my self-love—what would have become of me?

Second Letter from Mrs. Leidens to Emilia

So, my dearest friend, you are better pleased with the tone of my last letter than with what I have written since my departure from D. But let me accuse my Emilia of an injustice because she notes my changed ideas and expressions. I myself am conscious of this difference, but I think it is the natural effect of the great changes in my life. At D., I was respected, surrounded with happy prospects, and satisfied with myself. So I was more apt to make lively observations about objects that were new to me. My wit played freely with little judgments of all that did or did not agree with my ideas. Subsequently, I was snatched from fortune and self-satisfaction. Tears and grief became my portion. How could I engage the unfettered and joyful flights of my imagination, when all the powers of my soul were employed to enable me to bear my fate with patience (a virtue that depresses the mind)? Your husband knew me well; he saw that it was necessary to draw me out of myself, so to speak, and to convince me that it was still in my power to do good. This thought alone could guide me back into an active life.

I thank you, my dear friends, for approving my plan for a school for domestics. It was as if someone stretched out a hand to me and lovingly encouraged me to rise again, now that I have been led from a thorny path where a blinding brilliance had lured me. I have been guided onto a level way from where the eye is afforded the pure charms of unspoiled nature in its moral effects.

I needed this encouragement, my friends, because for a long time I thought I could no longer claim the noble pride a faultless life confers. After all, I owed at least half of my unhappy fate to my own indiscretion, and the fruits of that conviction were resignation and patience. Had I acted prudently and not broken certain laws through my secret union and my flight, I would have found in constancy and magnanimity the support and noble pride on which innocence leans when faced by unexpected misfortune and the malice of others. He can look boldly into the eyes of those who have injured him or turn away with silent contempt. He does not look for pity but rather for witnesses of his admirable conduct. With his mind thus occupied, his soul is invigorated and collects its powers to find new means for honor and happiness. On the other hand, remembering my imprudence,

I had to seek the veil of obscurity before I could again trust myself to be guided by my destiny. But now I see blossoms strewn on my new path by the promise of a successful project, beneficial to many in the future. Peace and contentment smile at me. I hope that Virtue will hear my prayer and be my constant companion. My heart's happiness will be greater and nobler because it contributes to the well-being of so many others, forgets its own favorite habits and wishes, and dedicates its life and talents to the welfare of its fellowman. Further, my new life makes even plainer the wisdom of my education, which showed me everything in its proper moral perspective. My feelings were formed in accordance with this, while my mind was led to make fruitful observations about mistaken ideas and the deep-rooted habits they cause.

How fortunate that I learned that before God only the moral difference between our souls is important! Oh, how I would now suffer were I burdened with the usual prejudices of my class! How estimable, how meritorious is the prudent use my beloved parents made of the self-love inborn in all of us in educating me! For instance, if I had ever set my heart on finery, how painful it would be for me now to dress in striped linen! Cleanliness and the good fit of my clothes leave my female vanity satisfied before the mirror; and what more can my wildest fantasy wish for, when in this humble dress I find myself loved and respected and know that I owe these sentiments only to the expressions of my moral convictions?

I rise early and, looking out at my window, see how faithfully nature fulfills the duties imposed on her by the eternal law of utility, in all kinds of weather and for all seasons of the year. Winter approaches, the flowers have vanished; and even when the sun is shining, the earth no longer sparkles. But even the empty field presents a pleasing picture. I remember the corn that grew there and lift a grateful eye toward heaven. The kitchen garden and orchard are bare, but remembering the stores they yielded mingles a warm feeling of joy with the shivers the north wind begins to bring. The fruit trees have shed their leaves, the meadows are faded, gloomy clouds pour down rain that softens the earth and makes it unfit to go walking. Foolish folk murmur at this, but the thoughtful man regards the malleable surface of our earth with tenderness. The autumn rains change dried leaves and yellowed grass into future fertility. Surely this reflection will make us grateful for our Creator's providential care and give us a preview of the coming spring. In the midst of losing all her pleasing external features—yes, even despite the discontent of her children whom she nourishes and re-creates—our maternal earth begins to labor in her depths for their future well-being. Why, I am moved to ask, why is the moral world not as true to its mission as is the physical one? The acorn never brought forth anything but an oak tree; the grape vine produces only grapes. Why then does a great man produce mean-thinking sons? Why do the scientist and

artist have ignorant, wretched descendants? Why do virtuous parents have
vicious children? In thinking about this incongruity, chance showed me innumerable obstacles in the moral world as well as sometimes in the physical one (such as lack of fair weather) that cause the best grapevine to bear
sour grapes, and excellent parents to raise bad children.

There I stopped and in my imagination asked, "Haven't my bright
days also turned gloomy and the outward luster fallen away from me like
dried leaves?" Perhaps our fate also has its seasons. If so, I shall use the
fruits of my education and experience as moral nourishment during the
gloomy days of my winter; and as the harvest was so plentiful, I shall share
what I can with the poor man whose small unimproved plot has borne little.
In fact, I have put some seed grain into a third hand, to cultivate a piece of
poor, arid soil. I have entrusted its care to gentle friendship, and for a week
I will supervise this project myself. Farewell!

Mrs. Hills to the Reverend Mr. B.

Do not be startled, reverend sir, that you are receiving a letter from me
instead of one from Mrs. Leidens. She is not ill, certainly not, but the dear
young woman has left me for a fortnight. She lives in someone else's house
where she works very hard and, I am sorry to say, is very ill-fed. But listen
how this came about. Oh, I declare—an angel like her has never before
entered the house of a rich person, nor that of a poor one! I cannot say very
well what my thoughts are, and can write them not at all. But listen, your
wife knows what happened to poor Mr. G. and his wife and children after
he lost his position. Well, I always gave them something, but I could not
abide these people. Besides, everyone was always saying that he is proud
and she careless, and that all good deeds were thrown away on them. This
made me angry, and I talked about it with Miss Lena, whom I am also
helping. (But then she works hard!) Mrs. Leidens was also present and
asked Miss Lena about these people, so she told her their whole story,
which she knew well because she had been with them since she was a
child. The next day Mrs. Leidens visited Mrs. G. and came home very
moved. At supper she told me so many affecting things about these people
that I cried, and I felt so much compassion for them that I immediately
promised to take care of the parents and children. However, she would have
none of it. But on the following morning, she brought me the enclosed
paper. You must return it to me; it will be placed with my last will, signed
by me, with something in praise of Mrs. Leidens added by my own hand.
There will also be something else for Mrs. Leidens, but I don't want to talk
of that now. Well, she went to see her girls and left the paper with me.
Never in my life have I seen anything more cleverly contrived! She certainly knows how to kill two birds with one stone and how to go about

making people prudent and skillful. I was astonished and twice cried, for I had to read it twice, to understand it properly. I wrote under it, "approved, everything approved!" and I told her that it should begin tomorrow. I also wrote on the paper (which I will attach to my will) that she must not call me her benefactress. After all, what did I give her? A little food and a small room. But just wait, I shall think of something. She shall not leave my house as she supposes. If only I live to see the construction of my "seminary for domestics," as she calls it. There I shall have her name cut in stone next to mine, and there I shall call her my adopted daughter; and then everyone will be astonished that she did not keep my money for herself and marry another pretty husband. They will praise her and me together, and I certainly will not begrudge her that. She must also stand godmother for poor infants, so that we can have children of her name; and these, as well as my own little Annies, shall have preference in being admitted into the seminary.

My spectacles made me tired. I could not continue to write this morning; and because I got impatient to see Mrs. Leidens, I went straight to Mrs. G.'s house. But I was sorry for it because these people thanked me too much (and perhaps they believed that's why I had come). Yet it was only to see my daughter—for I tell you, when she returns she must call me her mother!

I had my maid open the door a little, and to be sure, the people in the room made it look beautiful, even though there is no beautiful furniture there, just rush-bottomed chairs and a couple of tables. In one of the corners, the father was sitting with the oldest son who was writing and figuring by his side. Halfway across the room stood the other table. Here Mrs. G. sat knitting; Miss Lena sat between the two little girls and taught them how to sew; and Mrs. Leidens had in front of her a bouquet of Italian flowers, which she was copying for chair seats to be sold. The youngest son and the eldest daughter watched her closely, and she talked to them in a sweet and friendly manner. I was moved to tears over her and the children who hold her so dear and thanked me so much. The rough husband turned red when he thanked me, and the woman laughed in a carefree way. But never mind that, I shall help them according to Mrs. Leidens's plan until they are quite independent again; and Miss Lena shall be the first among those supervising the instruction of ladies' maids. I sent out for a light supper and some good fruit. You cannot believe how this delighted the children; but Mrs. Leidens was not pleased. She fears that the children will no longer enjoy the coarse food their meager means provide. She says she does not wish to reward them through their stomachs; so now I shall give nothing else. She herself ate only an apple and a piece of home-baked bread. I asked her about that, and, turning to the daughter, she said, "We can grow such apples in our garden, but bread like this can only be gotten through a Mrs. Hills." There—I had caught it! But I did not get angry; she was right. She does not want them to consider eating common bread a misfortune. Now eight days of her stay with these people have passed. Next week she is coming back to me and then will write you herself. Please pray for the dear child and for me. Oh, I will never forget that you entrusted this dear person to me! All my days I have never been more satisfied with my money than I am now that I have her with me!

Plan of Assistance for the G. Family and Miss Lena

My dear benefactress has charged me with writing down my ideas for assisting the G. family. I would treat these people, who have become destitute through their own fault, as a physician treats a sick person who has wantonly ruined his health: He administers all necessary remedies but at the same time prescribes a diet, explaining why it is necessary by describing future dangers and past sufferings. By means of a slow but protracted regimen he helps him gather new strength, so that at last he can live once more without the physician. Medicines strengthening him too rapidly at the very beginning would serve only to reinforce the body's ills and thus be eventually harmful. It would be the same with the G. family if they were simply given large presents. So we should help them cautiously and try to cure the evil at its root.

In the beginning, Mrs. Hills's bounty will supply the necessary clothes, linen, and household equipment. Of the first, only the most necessary items will be given to them ready-made. For the rest, the cloth should be given to them by the piece, so that the wife and daughters can make it up with their own hands. When they have finished that task, they will receive a store of flax and cotton and by processing these will learn to replace worn linen and cotton clothes. The mother and daughters will be in charge of this.

As for Mr. G., I will try to make him use his talents and pride for restoring his fallen reputation through his exertions in properly bringing up his children. He owes his children their education; he does not have the means to hire masters. How commendable it would be for him to make up for the lack of his squandered fortune with paternal diligence and teach his children writing and arithmetic himself. The sons' Latin instruction will be supplied by two scholarships, endowed by you, Mrs. Hills, and dedicated to poor pupils. Mr. G. himself will supervise the teaching and will conduct their review lessons. Certainly, in time, a man who conducts his paternal duties so faithfully will be entrusted with an office in the service of his country. It may here be objected that Mrs. G.'s alleged indolence might ruin everything again, but I hope to forestall that evil through Miss Lena.

She was Mrs. G.'s childhood friend and has received benefits from her parents. I believe she would like to return those favors to the daughter if she were not so poor herself; but since she is rich in her many skills, she could become her friend's benefactress by supervising the gifts to Mrs. G. and by instructing her daughters.

You, Mrs. Hills, have also helped Miss Lena, and I know that she would like to express her gratitude. She can do it in a very praiseworthy fashion by joining with you to rescue her unfortunate friend from perdition. She will gain the esteem of all good people if, through the goodness of her heart, she helps to build and secure the welfare of three innocent children.

If my dear Mrs. Hills approves these thoughts, I myself will convey them to Mr. and Mrs. G. as well as Miss Lena. Then I would ask you to permit me to stay for two weeks in Mr. G.'s house to show them that these regulations for governing their lives are not hard or unpleasant. For through kind words and respect, I intend to make the husband fond of his home and family. Then for a few days I will take first the mother's and then Miss Lena's places, while at the same time guiding the children's hearts and attempting to find out what their abilities are, so that, in time, these can be cultivated to their utmost potential. But with respect to recreation, food, and furnishings, they will continue to feel some want and through this feeling will be made attentive and reflective, until through frugality, industry, and good principles, they regain the station from which they have fallen through waste and negligence. I will not reproach them; but by mentioning some circumstances of my life, I will demonstrate the inconstancy of fortune to them; and I will tell the children that nothing but my education has been left to me, but that has won me Mrs. Hills's friendship and the opportunity to be of service to them. Then I can tell them that we should take pride in making only the noblest use of both fortune and misfortune. For not only do I want to see their bodies well-nourished and dressed but also to know that their principles have been improved and their minds filled with proper ideas.

Mrs. Leidens to Emilia

I am home again and wanted to tell you about the seed grain which in my last letter I said I had entrusted to a third hand, but Mrs. Hills tells me that she has written you everything. Oh my friend, how beautiful would be the moral part of our earth if all rich people thought as does Mrs. Hills, who rejoices at the opportunity to make good use of her wealth. Let me now tell you why I chose Miss Lena for the office of administrator. You are aware how I came to know this poor family. It was this very person who talked of their circumstances at Mrs. Hills's. I observed in her half compassionate, half accusing tone a kind of envy at the favors bestowed on them and the desire to attract all these benefits to herself. At the same time she repeatedly mentioned how she would act in Mrs. G.'s place. I was annoyed to see such cold and malevolent thoughts as the only remnants of a youthful friendship, and was encouraged to devise a plan to render her half-dead heart useful to a former friend. I did not let her know what I thought and told her only that she should take me to that house. She was moved by the sight of distress and the affection the woman showed her. While she was thus affected I took her to my room, read my plan to her, and vividly sketched the part I had assigned to her, in which she would be pleasing to God and earn the esteem and blessings of all righteous people. I convinced her that she would do more good than Mrs. Hills, who in giving money merely enjoyed the pleasure of distributing, from time to time, a part of her superfluities, whereas her own daily efforts and patience would demonstrate a most noble heart. I won her over more easily because I secured her Mrs. Hills's praise by saying that the scheme was Miss Lena's. My plan was approved and for the firt two weeks I carried it out myself.

To employ someone as an administrator seemed troublesome, but I received permission nevertheless, especially as I promised to live there myself for two weeks.

On the first day I distributed Mrs. Hills's presents to each of them, accompanied by admonitions to be careful of them. I told them that by conserving these benefits, they would show their gratitude as well as the sentiment of a noble heart that does not wish to misuse another's goodness. I told them how I viewed their situation and showed them the plan I had drawn up for their life and employments; but I nevertheless asked each of them what his wishes and objections were.

Before I answered, I gave them a short and useful summary of my own history. I emphasized the condition of respect and wealth in which I had been born and educated. I related my former desires and the present impossibility of gratifying them, and I concluded my account with kind words of advice and encouragement for them. By these means I disposed their hearts to trust me and follow my advice. The best things that a rich and happy person could have told them would have made little impression on them, but the thought that I, like them, was poor and dependent on others made their minds receptive. I asked them what they would have done in my place; they answered that they found my principles good and wished to emulate them. Then I told them what I would have done in their place, and they heartily approved of my answers. Oh, I thought, if only, in doing good, people would always consider the circumstances and inclinations of those they wish to serve and not attempt to suppress by force the self-love that dwells in us all, but rather use it with the same cleverness as the flattering seducer who knows how to use it to gain his ends! Then morality would have long since extended its boundaries and increased the number of its disciples.

Self-love—oh pleasant restraint that the loving hand of our benevolent Creator has put upon our free will to guide us toward our true happiness—how ignorance and rigidity have defaced you and caused man to make unholy misuse of this great boon! But let me get back to my story.

On the second day I played the part of Mrs. G. and in that character spoke to Miss Lena of their old friendship, assuring her in Mrs. G.'s name of how glad I was to see her fill her assigned post, because I believed that her good heart would make the best use of it. As Mrs. G. and I had previously agreed in private, I now told her in that character what I expected of her, recommended the girls to her, and added that in everything we would think and act in concert. For the next two days I acted the part of Miss Lena and in the following three played the parts of the three girls.

While we were at work, I used religion as an aid to show them how the observation of nature pours tranquil pleasure into our hearts, albeit in differing measure. Mrs. Hills provided the books I had selected, and the two boys tooks turns reading passages from them, while I taught the other children to make observations and applications as they listened. The two older girls are very ingenious and sensible. I taught them how to embroider tapestries, and the oldest one how to draw patterns for them. I encouraged their industry by rousing their pride, telling them they might either sell all their work outright to the merchants or barter half of it for new wool and other things they needed. I also promised to teach this kind of work to no one else. Now the two girls and their mother sit at their embroidery during the day because the idea of selling it flatters their vanity.

Miss Lena says that everything is progressing satisfactorily and she is exceedingly happy, because she receives much praise for her supervision and true friendship.

I shed tears when I left the house, and I will go there for two half-days every week. The fortnight I spent there passed in innocence and peace. Every minute of it was filled with the exercise of practical virtue, because I did good and taught what is good. Now, dearest Emilia, pray God to turn these seeds, scattered by my impoverished hand, into a rich harvest for the well-being of this family. Never, no never, have my revenues that allowed me to help the poor given me so much true joy as the thought has that, without gold, through sharing my talents, my principles, and several days of my life, my heart alone has done the most possible for this family.

Through my little drawings, the second son is turning into a painter of miniatures because he is copying them with the greatest exactitude and in extraordinarily fine detail.

The whole family loves and blesses me. Mrs. Hills is already having the stones for the seminary delivered to the site and squared. Don't you think, dearest friend, that at the same time the moral foundation for a new happiness is being laid in my soul?

Mrs. Leidens to Emilia

Emilia, perhaps your husband's metaphysical skills can explain the contradiction between my strongest and most lasting impressions and my ideas, as when I was asked by Mrs. Hills to help her persuade her dearest friend, the beautiful and amiable widow C. to decide in favor of one of her admirers? Why was it that I could speak in favor of the happiness that springs from a man's love, although my continual sufferings through love should have made me support the beautiful widow's cold-heartedness? I cannot believe that the natural spirit of contradiction is the only cause. Or can it be that one corner of my love-torn heart retains a memory of how I used to picture love in the happy days of my youth? Or can it be that my protracted afflictions have made me mature enough to decide upon another person's circumstances without intermingling any sentiments of my own? Please assist me, for you can see I am in doubt about this. Here is my conversation with the widow:

"Four meritorious men are vying for your favor; why is it, dearest madam, that you take so long to choose?"

"I am not choosing; I simply wish to enjoy the freedom I have purchased with much bitterness."

"It is not wrong of you to love your freedom and enjoy it in every possible manner; but would not its best use be to make someone happy of your own free will?"

"Oh, the happiness of which you speak exists most often only momentarily in a burning lover's heated imagination; it vanishes as soon as the dying flame has given his imagination time to cool."

"This, my dear madam, may be true in the case of a young man whose love has entered his soul only through the eyes and burns for a maiden in the flower of youth, whose undeveloped character cannot nourish that fire for long. But you, who are loved because of your mind and your noble heart, can surely render it unquenchable."

"You are saying, then, that my merits have the properties of Persian naphtha. But which of my admirers has the heart to sustain such a permanent fire?"

"Each one of them; for love and happiness are the irreducible matter of which our hearts are made."[*]

"But everyone has his own idea of happiness. Thus, in making my second choice, I might once again pick the heart whose ideas of happiness do not coincide with mine; and we would both lose."

---

[*]The somewhat precious style of this dialogue, which deviates so strongly from our heroine's usual, beautiful simplicity, indicates, it seems to me, that during this conversation with Lady C. she was not quite at ease [Wieland].

"That is an artful excuse, but it is not quite just. The ten years that have elapsed between the first and present choice have given you experience and insight to assess correctly the differences between various persons and their circumstances, and especially to recognize the force with which the latter drew you into your first union."

"How precisely you marshal your arguments! But tell me, dear Mrs. Leidens, which one would you choose if you were in my place?"

"The one I would hope to make happiest."

"And in your eyes that would be—"

"The amiable scholar in whose exalted and enlightened mind not even the least of your merits would remain unrecognized and unloved. In associating with him, the noblest part of your being would enjoy the neverending privilege of being led tenderly through the farthest reaches of his knowledge, where your mind could pleasantly divert and improve itself. How happy the pleasure, the merits, and the love of his esteemed wife would make him; what happiness your sensitive soul would derive from being the cause of this worthy man's happiness! How sweet would be your share in his fame and his friends!"

"Oh Mrs. Leidens, how forcefully you present the fair side of love! Should I not expect that this estimable sensibility will also discern my inherent and accidental faults? Then to which side will the balance incline?"

"To the side toward which your inborn sweetness and complaisance will direct it."

"Dangerous woman! You conceal the chain by covering it with flowers."

"You wrong me! I only show you the flowers whose worth I know and which love invites you to gather into a garland of contentment."

"But you overlook the mass of thorns under these roses."

"If I answered that I would offend your intelligence and judgment."

"Don't be angry, but go on and show me what other beautiful ribbons you intend to tie into snares for me."

"Let us see—perhaps your charming exuberance will be tamed more easily by a noble Prussian warrior than by the gentle hand of the muses. This ribbon is indeed beautiful: an illustrious name, noble soul, true love, and admiration of your character are woven into it. The golden threads of exalted rank, of the new and shining circle into which you would be transported, form the background. As you can see from the letters of the Most Honorable Lady—, his love has already made friends and admirers for you there. Does not the magnanimous sacrifice of all the prerogatives of ancient nobility demand the countersacrifice of your indecision and suspicion?"

"Enchantress! How artfully you mix your colors!"

"Why enchantress, my dear—do you mean you feel the strong attraction of these shining threads?"

"Yes, but heaven be thanked, their brilliance frightens me."

"Charming reticence, if only I could place you into the soul of every sensitive woman who, blinded by the brilliant colors of an artificial fire, succumbs—and suddenly finds herself alone in darkness."

"Dearest lady, what a touching tribute! How strongly you rouse my maternal solicitude for my young daughter!"

I embraced her tenderly for having a truly good heart. "In this moment consecrated to sensibility," I said, "allow me to direct your attention to the less brilliant but firmly grounded happiness which awaits you at Mr. T.'s delightful country seat, where by uniting yourself to him, you can fulfill three of the most sacred duties at once: you will crown the wishes of a meritorious, amiable man who loves you not because of your charms (for these he does not know), but because of your soul. He is a man who, after expressing all his feelings for you, said with the noblest impluse that ever moved a rich man's heart that your daughter should be his also, that she should inherit all his wealth. Would you not, therefore, at the same time fulfill your maternal duty by providing for your child's worldly comfort? Furthermore, surely your obedience to your father's will when you were a child could not have pleased him as much as it would now that you are free. If you followed his advice and tender wishes for this union, you could live close to him and, in his declining years, recompense his paternal heart for all his cares over his children's education. You, whose benevolent and generous heart would gladden everyone around you, should consider well! I will say nothing, madam, of the fourth candidate, waiting in a beautiful provincial capital for a favorable sign. Many good people there will attest to the virtuous heart, the wide knowledge, and the tender affection this handsome and good man entertains for you. In winning you, he hopes to win the best, most worthy mother for his two children, and thus to become the happiest of men. You know that he has a fine fortune, and you know all the social advantages that await you in that town. But my dear Lady C., you must do what you will; I have given you my suggestions. I well know that our perceptions are governed by different viewpoints. But there is one aspect to which we must all pay heed—the happiness of our fellow man, which ought to be as dear to us as our own! We must not prevent or delay it because of trivial motives."

"You embarrass me deeply," she said, shedding some tears; "but my sad experiences make me rebel against the idea of *any* union. I wish worthier wives for these men than I would be, even if I were as they imagine me; but my neck is so bruised from my first yoke that even the lightest silk tie would oppress it."

"I have complied with your friend's request; and since you are firmly resolved, I have nothing further to say, except to wish that you may always be happy!"

She embraced me, and, upon returning home, I asked Mrs. Hills to trouble her friend no more. But once I was in my room, I felt astonished at my zeal in participting in this affair.

Help me light up this dark part of my soul, for it seems to me that I embrace all the wrong causes.

Lord Seymour to Dr. T.

Dearest friend, please give me your advice and pity for the grief into which I have fallen again, and this time certainly forever. You know that I had quite suppressed my passion for Lady Sternheim because her base union with John had destroyed all my esteem for her mind and character. I had even begun to feel a quiet affection for Lady C. as she did for me, when my uncle was unexpectedly ordered by the court to travel to W. This separation grieved the sensitive Lady C., and I was as sad as she. Dissatisfied and grumbling at being bound by my family's ambition and my uncle's regard, I sat silent and gloomy by the side of that amiable man during the journey. Feeling rebellious, I was vexed with his composure, so that I disregarded the patience with which he bore my ill-humor. But my friend, imagine my emotions, if you can, when on the evening of the second day in very foul weather, the postilion lost his way and we stopped in a village where we resolved to lodge for the night. As we drove up to an inn and were just about to alight, we heard the hostess cry out, "What, you are Englishmen? Drive on! I shall not let you into my house. You may sleep in the forest for all I care. No Englishman shall ever cross my threshold again."

While she uttered these last words, she pulled her son, a civil young man who tried to placate her, by the arm toward the front door in order to lock it. The noisy resentment of this woman roused my attention; our men shouted and argued back, and so did the postilions. My lord ordered our people to be quiet and said to me, "Something serious must have happened here, since it was important enough to suppress the customary greed of these people."

He called to the woman in a friendly voice, asking her to tell him the cause of her refusal to put us up.

"The English are people without conscience, and they do not scruple to make the best people miserable. For the rest of my days I shall not shelter one of them ever again. So you may just drive on with your fair words; all of you know how to give fair words!"

She turned away from us and said to her son, who was trying to reason with her (presumably because of the profit they might make), "No, even if they filled my parlor with gold, I shall not break the vow I made to the dear Lady!"

I was boiling with impatience, but my lord, whose parliamentary office had accustomed him to the rabble's outbursts, calmly beckoned to the young man and asked him why his mother despised and reproached us.

"About six months ago," the young man answered, "an Englishman brought his wife, a beautiful benevolent lady, to our house. He went away and came back many weeks later. In the meantime, the young lady, who was always melancholy, gave my cousins clothes, taught them many fine things, and did much good for the poor. Oh, she was as gentle as a lamb! Even my father grew gentle from the time she entered our house. We all loved her. But one day, when the evil lord had been gone for a long time, one of his people came riding up and said that he had letters for the lady. We asked whether his master would return soon. 'No,' he said, 'he will not return. Here is money for the rest of the month.' He said this in a wild, defiant manner, like a vicious dog. Suspecting no good, my mother slipped into a room next to the lady's chamber, to overhear what was in the letter. From there, through a chink, she saw the dear beautiful lady on her knees, all in tears, and heard her chambermaid tell her what was in the letter: her marriage was a counterfeit, the messenger bringing the letter had performed the ceremony in a clergyman's habit, and she might now go where she pleased. So, she set out two days later, but she was so ill and in such low spirits that she probably would have died on the road. For this reason my mother will allow no Englishman to stay at her house."

Looking at me with concern, my uncle asked me, "Charles, what do you say to this story?"

"Oh my lord, it is my Sophia," I cried, "but the rascal will pay for it! I will find him; it is Derby; none other is capable of such cruelty."

"Young friend," my lord said to the hostess' son, "tell your mother that she is right to hate that evil Englishman. He will be punished severely by the king. But hurry now and see that I am admitted."

"Please step out," he said; "I will calm my mother."

He ran into the house and soon the woman approached us herself, saying, "If you will see to it that the evil man gets punished as you say, then you can come in, and I will tell you how it all came about. You are a gentleman advanced in years, my gracious lord; you can understand the wrongdoing of young men. I hope you will make an example of this evil man; otherwise he may yet commit other crimes."

Silently and slowly I followed her and my lord up the stairs. When we arrived upstairs she said, "The dear angel stood here when her lord first came to visit her. Well, he seemed affectionate enough, and she had stretched out her dear hands so daintily toward him that it was a joy to see them together. But she spoke so softly and so little, and he so loudly! His eyes were very big and looked her over busily. He called out for his men quickly and frequently, so we suspected something. My husband is rough, too (though when we were first married he was as friendly as can be, spoke quietly, and used to wink at me), but I suppose every man has his way; and how could anyone think it possible to deceive such a beautiful, virtuous lady!''

We were then in the closet where her maid had slept. Afterwards, she showed us the lady's chamber. She called one of her nieces, Gretchen, who showed us where the lady had sat and how she had taught the girls. Afterwards she took a picture from the wall, saying, "There, you see—my little garden, my beehives, and the little meadow where my cows grazed—she drew them."

As she handed it to my lord, she kissed the picture and said crying, "Dear, dear lady, may God bless you. I don't suppose you are still alive."

A single look convinced me completely that Lady Sternheim had made the picture. I recognized the exactness of the outline and the delicate shadowing. My heart felt heavy and I had to sit down. Tears filled my eyes as I considered the fate of this noble young woman. The woman's rough but sincere affection moved me, too. She was pleased to see me thus and, patting me on the shoulder, said, "You are right to feel sad. Pray God to give you a good heart, so you will never deceive anybody. For you, too, are English and a handsome man. You might well strike someone's eye."

She asked the son, the maid, and all the other people of the house to tell us about the lady's goodness and what she had done, and then she showed us her bed chamber. "She never again entered it after she received the letter," she continued, "but slept in her maid's bed. I think it natural, for who would want to continue sleeping in a villain's bed? Here is the wardrobe where she kept all the gold and jewels. Oh, he brought her many things that she put here and told me to return them. For she took nothing with her. Two days after she left, another letter came, in which he told her he would return soon, but I gave him his packet of things and sent him out the door."

My lord asked her for even more details about everything that had happened, but I heard only half of it. I was beside myself, and since the woman could not tell me where the lady had gone, nothing else meant very much to me. I had heard enough to die with compassion and with renewed tenderness my soul embraced the beloved image of suffering virtue. I took her maid's room for the night because I had noticed in it the spot where she had knelt, where she had felt the unspeakable pain of being betrayed and abandoned. Derby's bed chamber held the same horror for me as it did for her. Fully dressed and half senseless, I threw myself on the bed where Sophia had spent such anguished nights. Hopeless love and bitter pleasure overpowered me with the sensation that here the amiable creature had lain in whose arms I would have found my whole happiness; here her heart groaned under the faithlessness of the infamous wretch! And I—oh Sophia,

I weep at your fate, your loss, and my cursed hesitation in winning your love for myself! Pleasure? Yes—I enjoyed a painful pleasure at the thought that my despairing tears fell on the traces of hers and mingled with them. I arose, knelt at the same spot where her silent heartrending grief had prostrated her, where she reproached herself for succumbing in blind trust to the most cruel man, and where I vowed by her memory to avenge her.

Oh my friend, why could not your wise maxims strengthen my courage? How miserable, how lamentable was my condition as I cursed every hour when she was his possession. All her beauty, all her charms his possession! She loved him; she received him with open arms at the top of the stairs. How was it possible that a heart so noble, so pure and good could love a man so insensible and malicious?

From the landlady's son I bought the little pillow on which her head and mine had tossed in the same agony, which her tears and mine had moistened. Her misfortune links her soul forever to mine. Separated from her, perhaps forever, it was inevitable that in this poor cottage my soul's sympathetic bonds with her became even stronger.

In the morning my lord found me in a fever. His surgeon opened a vein and an hour later we proceeded on our journey. But before we departed I took her little drawing of the garden and gave some guineas to the girls who had been my Sophia's pupils.

That coldness which politics insensibly always imparts to even the warmest heart, causing it to look beyond a particular evil, supplied my lord with a multitude of reasonable arguments to distract and arm me by turning my grief into rage. I was obliged to listen and be silent; but in the night, exhausted and consumed with grief, my pillow consoled me. My grief is calmer now, and I am regaining my resolution to avenge Lady Sternhheim's misfortune on Lord Derby, even if he were the first man of the kingdom. Observe him when you go to London; see if he exhibits signs of disquietude and remorse. I wish I could make him suffer the torments of remorse through all eternity, that hateful man!

I am taking all possible pains to find out the young lady's subsequent fate; but so far all is in vain, just as your efforts will be in vain if you attempt to erase her image from my memory. My grief for her has become my sole joy and diversion.

Count R. to Lord Seymour

You send news of my dear unhappy niece; but, oh God! what news my lord! The noblest, best of girls—the victim of an infernal villain! When you mentioned your uncle's secretary I thought that so low and common a man could never have won her hand. I felt certain that she must have been dazzled and led astray by a hypocrite who knew how to give himself the appearance of being wise and virtuous. I implore Lord G.'s assistance in bringing the villain to justice, even if he were under the protection of the entire nation.

Nothing but the frail health of my wife and only son could prevent my departure, but I have at least done this much for the sake of my amiable niece: I have asked the prince to let one of his counselors administer her estates. In accordance with her wishes, the revenues will be reserved for Count Loebau's children, but their father and mother will not have the use of them. After all, they were the first to tear the dear child's heart and are the only reason that, numbed by anguish, she walked straight into her own ruin.

If only I could come to D. soon and we could shed some light on her whereabouts! But whenever one or the other may happen, the wretch who did not know how to value her will be held accountable for abduction and abandonment.

I pity you, my lord, because your revived love has increased your soul's torments. But how could a man who knew women misjudge this exquisite girl and measure her merits by the common yardstick? Was she not exceptional in everything? Forgive me, my lord; it is unkind to increase your grief in this way, but the warm affection engendered by my closeness to her has heightened my indignation. It makes me resent the sins of commission and omission in this affair equally. Please spare no expense in trying to find the dear child. I fear that we will not see her alive again!

Let Lord Derby beware! And the same goes for you, too, if you do not join hands with me in avenging her! But anything you do to prove your unselfish love, even though it comes too late, will make me your best friend and most devoted servant. I will share all expense with you, just as I share all your cares and pain. Here, I keep everything secret because I do not want to grieve my wife's affectionate heart.

Mrs. Leidens to Emilia

Mrs. C., the amiable widow I spoke of, has a beautiful and tender soul. She noticed the other day that I had concluded my representations rather abruptly. A few days later she came to see me to ask why. I, too, felt that my sudden silence was rather awkward; but since my motives were compelling, and I did not want to hurt her feelings, I saw no alternative but to break off and go home. I felt distinctly vexed with her because she did not pursue the opportunities for benevolence as eagerly as I would have. I am glad to know that my Emilia's husband attributed my zealous intercession on behalf of love to my inclination for doing good, even though he accuses me of being overly enthusiastic in this virtue. (Oh, may this excess in the good passion be the only fault of my remaining years!)

I answered the dear lady frankly that I found it strange for a soul as sensitive as hers to regard the subject of doing good so coldly. She answered, "I understand perfectly that your active mind must be displeased with my irresolution. You did not know that beneficence directed my first choice, but I have learned too well that one can make others happy without being so oneself. I don't have the heart to venture once more onto the uncertain ground where the flowers of pleasure soon fade under the blight of care."

All the features of this charming blonde showed her feeling. Her tone was appealing and reminded me of the sudden ruin of my own tender young hopes. My own sufferings had deepened my compassion, and I now felt her misgivings as strongly as I had once imagined the future happiness of the man she might marry.

"Please forgive me, dear madam," I said. "I recognize that I have been guilty of demanding that you share all my principles, and I was more insistent the more I was convinced of the nobility of my motives. Why did I not put myself in your place sooner? As you see them, some aspects of my proposals have indeed something terrifying in them; and without thinking you wrong, I shall not speak of any of this again."

"I am glad you seem satisfied with me, but you have caused me much unrest and displeasure with myself."

I asked her quickly how, and with regard to what.

"By making me cognizant of all the opportunities I have to make other people happy. I regret my aversion and evasiveness. I would like to do something useful to make up for it. Can you give me employment in your seminary?"

A frank "no" was my answer. "But," I said, smiling and taking her hand, "I would like to use your eagerness to make amends, and, as you no longer wish to marry, ask you to instruct the daughters of your relatives and friends through your association with them. In this way you would create amiable women within your circle of influence; and while Mrs. Hills for her part is training good servants, you would educate good mistresses for them."

She liked this suggestion and immediately asked me to draw up a plan for its execution. "That I shall not do, dear madam, for I cannot suppress my own self enough to fit my plan to your views and inclinations. You have prudence, experience, knowledge of local customs, and a kind heart. Together these things will show you how best to execute this plan."

"I doubt that very much; at least tell me a book where I can find a plan for my lessons."

"To follow the method prescribed in a book would soon tire you and your young friends. The latter have been variously brought up; the circumstances of most parents do not permit educating their children methodically.

Even girls as young as fifteen, like your daughter's companions, can no longer easily get used to it. Besides, you are not to keep a *school*, but to instruct these young girls casually, as occasion permits. For example, if one of them complains about the snow that fell while she was visiting you and the discomfort of the return journey, you might ask her if she would like to know where snow comes from. You might explain briefly and clearly its utility in the wise design of the Creator. You should gently show her the injustice of her complaints and point out that the snow, which seems unpleasant today, will, in a few days, provide means for a sleighride. This will lead your young listeners into talk of fine winter clothes, the best kinds of sleighs, etc. Do not, by any means, interrupt these conversations with some serious or displeased expressions, but show them that you enjoy listening to their various thoughts. Say something about good taste in clothes and jewelry, and how you would arrange and hold a party. Let their imaginations sketch all of this in the most pleasing colors. Admit that your young listeners have the right to enjoy themselves, but add tenderly that they should illuminate the stage of their diversions with the twin torches of virtue and good conduct.

"During this first trial conversation you can sound the hearts and minds of your girls, but I believe they will eagerly come back to hear more of what you have to say."

"I agree, but allow me to mention one doubt: You lead these young girls to the knowledge of the physical aspects of snow and to the moral consideration of God's beneficence, but will not the vision of the sleighride obliterate all the rest, and consequently render your instruction useless?"

"I do not believe that, for we hasten to forget only what is unpleasant. Hence, true wisdom tells us to indulge human weakness by making the path of truth enjoyable. Virtue need not be described in somber colors to be revered; its essence, its every act is dignified. Dignity is an inseparable part of it, even when it appears in the dress of joy and happiness. Indeed, it commands confidence and respect only then. Never raise your hand menacingly, but only in a friendly gesture! For, while we are in this temporal world, our souls act only through our senses. If these are sternly repudiated, the contrast between the formal constraints of lessons and the natural desire for pleasure will have dire consequences in our moral development. The Creator has made us susceptible to joy and has enabled us to appreciate its many variations. Therefore, mix virtue with pleasure, and see whether youth and gaiety will flee it and seek recompense in forbidden joys. Does not divine morality itself attract us to the path of virtue and wisdom with the promise of heavenly bliss?"

As I spoke, Mrs. C.'s beautiful eyes were fixed on me with an expression of surprised pleasure. I asked her forgiveness for having talked so much, but she assured me that she had listened with satisfaction. She wanted to know why I had preferred teaching aspiring servants to becoming the governess of young ladies.

I told her that in comparing the happiness of the various ranks, I found the lower classes had so little that I was glad to add something to it. The first and middle ranks, apart from having all the advantages that arise from fortune and respect, find instruction both in books and in the conversation of learned persons, whereas the inferior, yet useful class, receives the scanty remains of the others' abundance in knowledge and well-being.

"You speak of knowledge; shall I try to make my young women learned?"

"May God preserve you from that intention, for even in the leisure class there is hardly one among a thousand women for whom learning would be suitable. No, my dear Mrs. C., encourage them to practice every domestic virtue; but besides that, let them attain the simple knowledge of the air they breathe, the earth on which they set foot, the plants and animals that nourish and clothe them. Give them also a summary of history, so that they will not sit there silent and bored when men are speaking about these things in their presence, and so that they see that virtue and vice constantly permeate the entire human race. Let them understand at least the terms that define the sciences. For example, tell them what philosophy, what mathematics is; but be sure they know the meaning of the term "noble soul" and learn the practical virtues, partly through description but mainly through examples of persons who excel in this or that virtue."

"Shall I also let them read novels?"

"Yes, especially since you will not be able to prevent it. But as much as you are able, select only those in which people act from noble principles and where scenes from real life are described. If one were to forbid the reading of novels, one would also have to avoid talking before young people of local love affairs. Our fathers, husbands, and brothers could not talk so freely of the gallant adventures and observations their voyages and travels afforded them. Otherwise, the contradiction between prohibition and practice would again create a harmful contrast. I know an excellent man, well acquainted with human nature, who believes that to satisfy their curiosity, the youth of both sexes should be given most travel descriptions, especially those that deal with the natural history and customs of another country, because such books disseminate useful knowledge. I would also like to see someone collect biographical portraits of the moral virtues of all classes, but especially of our sex. In this, French women are more fortunate than we are. Female merit is accorded lasting public respect among the French."

"Perhaps we are more praiseworthy than they because even without reward we endeavor to deserve it."

"True, but only a few transcend the vicissitudes that others overcome only with constant encouragement. Therefore, I would like to see examples drawn from each social class, so that one could say, 'her birth, her circumstances, were like yours; her zeal in the cause of virtue and the good use she has made of her mind have rendered her respectable.' Her reward might be a special seat in the public assembly or a certain piece of clothing—just as the great connoisseurs of the human heart practiced in ancient times. But we are not charged with instituting this arrangement, only with doing as much good as we can. These days I find myself among poor and servile persons, and so I consider myself duty bound to guide them to virtue and happiness through instruction and example. But I will try my best to avoid instilling in them principles commensurate with my former circumstances, because I would fear that this would engender misguided wishes, with all their inherent faults. You are a widow of the first rank at your place of residence. Your condescension, your sensible and pleasing company cause you to be sought out by everyone of your rank. You are educating a daughter. You would, therefore, greatly benefit all the girls of her age if you would allow those whose mothers are too busy for much contact with them to attend your daughter's lessons. Make them think and act as becomes women of their rank, so that they will excel within their class. This will be your only means of compensating society for your decision to remain unmarried."

She smiled at this and at my excuses for having prescribed how she should act, and we parted with every sign of friendship and satisfaction.

Mrs. Leidens to Emilia

Very reluctantly, my Emilia, I am accompanying Mrs. Hills to the spa. It is true, my health is deteriorating and admittedly I need the restorative powers of the water. My silent grief gnaws at my body's strength, and the passionate zeal I have lately applied to my moral life has also increased my weakness, which you, my dear friend, noticed during my stay with you for the past ten happy days. Yesterday your husband overcame my reluctance, but only by promising to stay with us for the first week. He hopes that by then my hatred for great and strange society will lessen. He also claims that in serving others this winter, my heart has so exhausted my mind that nothing but the outdoors and pleasant company can restore it. I am thin and pale; my eyes, which were once considered affecting, are seldom raised, and my dress is so simple that I need not fear solicitations from men. Farewell for two months, dearest friend; tomorrow morning we depart with your husband, a maid, and a manservant.

Mrs. Leidens to Emilia from the Spa

Tell me, my friend, what is the source of your husband's power over me? First he led me to join Mrs. Hill's circle, then he brought me here, and

despite my resistance, introduced me, on our fourth day here to Lady Summers. Now, my dear, because of him I am bound to accompany her to
England. He has told you of our safe journey, and that Mrs. Hill's wealth
has procured four very comfortable rooms for us. It has obtained for us a
measure of respect we did not seek. On the very first evening your husband
went to see the lady, and on the second day he pointed her out to me during
a walk we took. Her figure is noble though frail; the expression of her face
is all affability; her beautiful, large eyes express great sensibility, and all
her movements have dignity and grace. She greeted us silently and looked
at us attentively, even though Mr. B. was trying to call her away from us.
On the following day, she took him from our side to lunch and only said
to me in English, "Tonight you shall be my company." When I bowed
and wanted to say something, she was already far away. But I would only
have stammered; for, Emilia, you cannot imagine my soul's pain when I
heard English once again. With lightning speed I noticed its effect on me,
and just as quickly, sad memories crowded my soul. It was good, Emilia,
that the lady did not require my presence immediately. My embarrassment
was all too noticeable. In the evening, Mrs. Hills and Mr. B. dined with me
at the lady's. She was very kind, but her penetrating eye followed everything I did and said. She praised Mrs. Hills for her endowment of the seminary and added that she would follow her example and create one in
England. Mr. B., who translated all this for Mrs. Hills, pleased the good
woman with this news; and her honest heart smiled through her weeping
eyes as she took my hand impulsively and said to Mr. B. that he should tell
the lady that she had merely contributed superfluous money, whereas I
had invented the plan. I blushed deeply when she said this, and the lady
patted my cheeks and said, "This is good, my girl; true virtue should always be modest."

The care I took to entertain Mrs. Hills and translate even the most
trivial things that the lady or Mr. B. said to me, also pleased her.

"She will certainly be happy, because she endeavors to give happiness
to those of advanced age." This reference to my future moved me deeply,
and I found it impossible to keep dry eyes. The lady saw it and leaned over
toward me with a firm but affectionate look.

"Poor dear young woman," she said, "I know of a hand that will wipe
all your future tears away."

I bowed and looked at Mr. B. who replied only with a cheerful nod.
The lady motioned to him and said, "Nothing more today; tomorrow you
shall arrange everything."

That morning came six days ago, when my heart wavered between various suggestions and finally resolved to spend this year with the lady at her
country seat and return with her next year in time for the waters.

If it had been London, I would not have gone—may God preserve me from any chance of meeting those Englishmen I know already! But none of them will seek out an old lady at her lonely residence, and I can safely satisfy my longing to see that country and inquire after the Watson family. Mr. B. has enjoined Mrs. Hills not to hold me back, since I am to establish a seminary for servants there; and he has quieted most of her concerns by saying that in England people will say it had been established according to her plan and inspired by her noble example.

Oh Emilia, my Lady Summers is a perfect angel. She has long wandered among men in order to pour the sweet balm of friendship into sensitive souls. Mine is quite restored!

Mrs. Leidens from Summerhall

My first letter has already informed you of my happy arrival with the kind lady. I hope my Rosina and Mr. B. have safely returned. I was sorry that Rosina did not want to join me in crossing the sea (which does make one ill, but this is soon over). You have certainly read descriptions of English country houses. Now think of the most beautiful of them in the old style and call it Summerhall. Place it next to a park, a large fine village, and imagine my lady and me as we walk, with arms linked, through the lanes, talk with children or laborers, visit an invalid, and dispense aid to the needy. This is my lady's employment in the afternoon and evening; in the morning I read to her and see to the household. The visits she receives from the few neighboring nobility and her association with the excellent pastor of the village fill out the remainder of our days so that little time remains for my own personal reading. Among the books chosen by my lady, some concern the national spirit and some her due sense of her approaching end. The former subject is applied by English historians and court newspapers, the latter by the best English preachers. In addition, I have taken up the natural history of England, and we speak of that during our walks with the pastor's family because his wife and two daughters are very sensible and because I like to hear and speak about my favorite branch of knowledge. I am well and enjoy a gentle contentment which, however, resembles a calm repose more than true well-being. I am not eager for the activity that once ruled all my thoughts. Perhaps I have been touched by the gentle melancholy that rules the best of the British and casts a subtle haze over their colorful characters. I am once again singing and playing the lute. Both are invaluable to me, especially when I see my lady throw me a kiss while I am singing or fold her hands while I play an adagio. But judge for yourself how strong my love for England is, as, despite my cruel memories of one of their native sons, I nevertheless breathe the air of the park with considerable joy and view the land as that of my fathers. I have quite assumed the English style of dress and tone of language, and I only wish I had also acquired the pursuits and manners of the English ladies. But my lady says that all my endeavors will not drive out the amiable foreign genius that pervades my every movement. The fact that I have gained her people's trust, the extraordinary attention and deference they show her—both of which she sees as the result of my influence on their minds— these she seems to value above all the things I do for her, and for these she feels most grateful. Rarely have I gone to bed without feeling completely happy, as the kind old lady blessed me in my bed, and her domestics wished me an affectionate good night. In the morning, when the sun rises, I feel the sweetest emotion as I stroll through the park. The shepherd and his son are astonished to see me and call out, "Good morning, dear miss!" As I see the Creator's bounty spread out before me on field and meadow, their greeting seems to testify that I, too, enjoy freely fulfilling my duty to do good. Then, with tearful eyes, I thank our Creator that he has left this power in my heart. You know that a piece of moss, the smallest kind of flower, can afford me hours of carefree pleasure, and so you can imagine me seeking out these old friends of my best and earliest time and looking upon them nostalgically. The memories of the past and the sensations of the present are always united in me. A friendly piece of moss and some shoots sprung from the root of a fallen tree made me say, "Aren't I like the young tree that has lost its crown and trunk while in full bloom, through the blows of an unhappy fate?" For a long time the stump stood sad and dry, but finally new shoots sprouted from the roots, growing strong and high under the protection of nature, to spread shade in due time. My reputation, my fortunate condition, my position in the great world— all these I have lost. For a long time, pain numbed my soul. With time, the roots of my life gathered new strength, and the good principles of my education grew into fresh, albeit small, shoots of beneficence and usefulness for my fellow men. Just as the shoots of my emblem the tree grew among low-growing moss and small blades of grass, these moral "shoots" have sprung up among the lowly class of my neighbors. But it pleases me to have observed this class at close quarters. I have seen many beautiful flowers among them that, unknown to the majestic crown of the tall and straight tree, bloom and wither in its shade. And for my sweetest consolation, I remind myself that in the "shade" of my association and my care, the generosity of the seminary's loving benefactress has cultivated many useful creatures. And now my beloved Lady Summer's noble heart takes respite, undisturbed by all life's great and small cares and protected by all my efforts from the hard path we must walk in our later years, where every step takes us farther from our fleeting joys and closer to our approaching infirmities.

Mrs. Leidens to Emilia

My dear Emilia, aren't there wealthy people who feel a kind of want which they try to supply by heaping up all manner of enjoyments without being able to do so? No one has told them that our minds and hearts also have their needs and that for their satisfaction not all the gold of India nor all the beautiful and luxurious treasures of France can suffice, because the only remedy is found in the instructive and diverting association with a sensitive friend. How few of the rich know these advantages! I truly have many of life's blessings. I fully appreciate these gifts of providence but I need a friend to whom I can unburden my heart. I am generally well liked; the principles I now and then espouse with the proper modesty have earned me the respect of others. My appreciation of the beauties of Shakespeare, Thomson, Addison, and Pope has given my mind a new and living kind of nourishment in talking to our pastor and a very philosophical nobleman in our neighborhood. The pastor's oldest daughter is gentle, sensitive, and, besides that, endowed with genuine good sense. She is very dear to me, but in midst of a tender embrace I feel she cannot fill my Emilia's place. Do not call me ungrateful because I say this; I know I still have your friendship and, at the same time, that of the amiable Emma. I write you only of that part of my soul which I cannot show here, and with Emma I talk only about what pertains to my English circle. But I cannot help thinking about the great distance that my poor letters must travel to reach you; and I cannot help feeling that this distance is a disadvantage to my favorite pastime—to talk with you! Perhaps, my dear Emilia, I am destined to pass through the whole gamut of moral sensations, and thereby to become well fitted to distinguish their many bitter or sweet gradations and nuances. I shall gladly submit to this part of my fate if I can keep the same degree of sensibility toward my neighbor's weal and woe and continue relieving his sufferings as much as I can.

Lady Summers wanted to satisfy her honor as well as my supposed pride when she introduced me as a person of very noble birth, who, having lost her parents, married with only a small dowry and soon after lost her husband. My hands, my elegant linens and laces, my bracelets with the portraits of my parents so beautifully painted in enamel, and my social conduct have done more to confirm that idea than sense could have. But it is a beautiful monument to Lady Summer's virtue that she believes in the purity of mine, and because she loves me, no one else doubts it. Our clergyman says that the air the lady breathes is so moral that the vicious do not dare to approach her. Don't you agree that this is the epitome of true fame? Oh, what a connoisseur of mankind, of that which is good and noble, your husband is. He was the one who assured me that in that revered lady's house I would find my virtue strengthened and my mind improved. Lord Rich, the philosophical nobleman of whom I spoke at the beginning of this letter, lives a mere mile from here. His house is very simple but exquisitely tasteful. The best decorations of its interior consist of several beautiful collections of natural curiosities, a complete assemblage of all mathematical instruments, and a great collection of books among which are twenty folio volumes in which he has, with his own hands, dried almost all the noteworthy plants of our earth. His well-designed garden, where he himself works, and his park, which adjoins ours, first tempted me to go over there. But the simple, clear way in which he showed us all his treasures and named them, his descriptions of the great Asiatic travels he has undertaken, and his wide-ranging knowledge of the fine arts make his company so charming that the lady has herself decided to visit him more often. She says it is very enjoyable to be given, so near the end of her life, such delightful views of the wonder of creation. Lord Rich, who lived quite alone until now and used to see no one but the pastor, is very pleased with our acquaintance and comes to see us often. Everything he does or does not do appears to be characterized by the perfect tranquillity of plants that grow insensibly but incessantly. But it also seems to me that he now examines the moral part of creation as closely as he once did the physical world. My Emma and Lady Summers will gain much from this; but as for me, I feel afraid! The other day, when I asked his opinion of my thoughts, he said, "I would gladly talk about the roots of your refined sentiments, but we see them only in the mist that always clouds their place of origin." I found myself embarrassed by this and, relying on my wit for help, asked him if he meant that my mind was beclouded. He looked at me penetratingly yet tenderly. "Certainly not in the way you imply," he said, "but does not this tear I see in your eye prove that I was right? Else, why does even your soul's slightest emotion condense the mist I mentioned into rain? Dear Mrs. Leidens, I shall not speak of this again; but don't you ask me either what judgment my heart forms of yours."

You see, my Emilia, how much I miss you. I would show you all those sentiments that are crowding together within me. Then my heart would be relieved and no longer obscured by that mist. I was glad to regain my composure enough to answer him in the same physical idiom, that I wished he would believe that these clouds were caused by my circumstances and not by my nature. "I am convinced of it," he said, "but be at ease; it took all my powers of observation to see this delicate cover. Others are not as attentive or experienced as I am." Our conversation was interrupted by Miss Emma and since then my Lord Rich takes care not to observe me too closely.

Mrs. Leidens to Emilia

Tell me, my Emilia, why even the best men stubbornly insist on following their prejudices? Why may a high-minded, virtuous girl not say, "I love this worthy man!'' Why is she not forgiven when she tries to please him and earn his esteem in every way?*

These questions occurred to me because of Lord Rich. He seems to have thrown off all the fetters of delusion and intends to follow only true wisdom and virtue. He seems to have an aversion for Miss Emma's tender inclination toward him, although previously he always spoke of her with the highest esteem, praised her mind and her heart, and gave all her actions his approval, enjoying hers in return. But lately he counters the gentle passion his merits have kindled in her heart with severe coldness. Probably because of the same caprice he is beginning to show me a constant affectionate attentiveness that makes me uneasy, because I am quite indifferent toward him, apart from my respect for his wide knowledge. I often keep silent merely to avoid his praise and not wishing knowingly to add even one spark to the nascent fire. For, as I am not inclined to accept his love, why should I increase it merely to please my female vanity? This afternoon we are to visit him to see a new experiment (the attempt to sow a piece of land by means of a machine). My dear lady enjoys being present whenever the ground is cultivated or planted. She says, "Every day brings me closer to the union with our mother earth, and I think that this thought makes me love it the more."

Dearest Emilia, I would have had a happy day yesterday if chance had not worked against me and my good Lord Rich. I was seated next to the clergyman when Lord Rich spoke to us of the tillage, the different kinds of soil, and consequently the different ways to cultivate it. His language was noble, clear, and simple. He told us of the many different inventions to which this or that nation had resorted because of the low yield of the fields and how the country people had been rewarded for their efforts. When he finished speaking, I could not help saying in a low voice to the parson that I wished the moralists, too, would inform themselves of the different kinds of human inclinations and then devise means for cultivating each and mak-ing all of them good and useful in their own way.

He said, "They have been doing that for a long time already, but there is much moral soil incapable of being improved and where the best seed and cultivation would be wasted."

"I would be sorry to think," I answered, "that in the moral world, too, there are sandy parts where nothing grows—tracts of heath that yield nothing but small, dry shrubs, and swamps, where the general moral im-provement is as far off as improvement in the physical world, where many generations must pass before trees and hedges grow in the sand, at least

---

*This question is not at all hard to answer. A high-minded, virtuous girl may not do so because we cannot make special rules of moral conduct for her [Wieland].

preventing the wind from blowing it onto good land and spoiling that, too. It takes a long time for heath to become cultivated and swamps to be drained, making both useful. Nevertheless, all our experiments show that all ground is fertile, if only we clear away the obstacles. The basic stuff of the moral world also contains, I am sure, the potential of virtue; but its cultivation is often neglected, often attempted badly, thus preventing blossoms and fruit from developing. History proves this, I think. Barbaric peoples become noble and virtuous; others who previously were so, revert to savagery because of neglect, just as a field that once yielded enough wheat to nourish a whole family begins to bear thorn bushes and weeds through neglect.''

The parson listened to me quietly and patiently, but Lord Rich, who had seated himself behind us, suddenly stood up and, leaning over my chair and taking hold of both my arms, said with some emotion, "Dear madam, whatever did you do in the great world with a heart like yours? You cannot have been happy there!''

"Nevertheless, my lord," I answered, "there one learns to distinguish truly between mind and heart and comes to see that the former can be cultivated like a beautiful garden."

He answered enthusiastically, "Your soul has been nobly cultivated; you have grown up in fruitful soil, and sweet humanity has nurtured you."

My heart was moved and I kissed the portraits of my parents which I always wear in my bracelet. My tears fell upon them and I arose and went to the window. Lord Rich followed me; and when I looked at him after a few minutes, I saw sympathetic sadness in his face. His eyes were fixed on the portraits, and he said softly, "Are these your parents, madam? Are they still alive?"

"Oh no, my lord, otherwise I would not be here and my eyes would cry only tears of joy."

"Has a storm brought you to England then?"

"No, my lord, for friendship and free choice cannot be called a storm," I countered, trying to smile.

Lord Rich said in a lively manner, "Thank you for your partial confidence, for it lets me know that you are free to choose. The noblest inclination that ever a man nurtured will build its hope on that ground."

"That cannot be, my lord, for I tell you that the owner of that ground is forever divorced from all hope."

Lady Summers was next to us when I said that, and at my last words she stretched out her hand as if to put it over my mouth. "You must not say that," she said; "why will you arbitrarily confound your future with your past? Providence will not forget you, my dear, but do not make stubborn demands of it."

This reproach wounded my sensitivity and I blushed. I kissed the hand that had wanted to silence me and asked her tenderly, "Dearest lady, when have you found me stubborn in my demands?"

"In your constant sadness over the past, and in your demands that your loved ones return from the dead," was her answer.

"Oh my beloved, worthy Lady Summers, why—oh why!"

This exclamation escaped me because, moved by her kindness, I deeply regretted that we had deceived her with a false tale; but she took it differently and, interrupting me, said, "My dear girl, do not say 'Why, oh why?' anymore. Direct your heart's sensibilities toward objects of contentment that are within your reach, and be assured of my maternal affection for as long as you want it."

I pressed her hand to my breast and looked at her with filial love. Her heart felt it, and she rewarded me with a mother's embrace.

Lord Rich had watched us with emotion, and at that moment I saw Emma's fine eyes rest on him in languid love. I said to him in Italian that there alone he could find the unmixed emotions capable of filling the days of a high-minded man like himself with exquisite happiness. He answered in the same language, "No, madam, that kind of sensibility is not adapted to make a solitary person happy."

What did he mean by that? I shook my head, only half pleased, and said, "Oh my lord, of what kind then are your sentiments?"

"Of the most durable—for they have sprung from practical virtue."

I made no answer, but, bowing to him, took Emma's arm; and she walked back with me to Summerhall, wrapped in silence. I have just heard that she will be leaving us.

Mrs. Leidens to Emilia

My dear Emilia, if we divest superfluity of its power to do good it does not confer happiness. Instead it impedes the proper use of wealth and, in those who are irresponsible, breaks down the barriers to the gratification of desire, weakens the enjoyment of pleasure, and (as I myself am finding out) causes a kind of unpleasant embarrassment in a frugal heart that harbors only modest wishes. You are probably at a loss, my friend, where to look for the cause of this sally into a subject so far removed from my previous one. However, knowing that things often strike me in an unusual way, you will not be surprised when I tell you that Lord Rich's sentiments are the real cause of my indignant observations on overabundance. He persecutes me with his love, admiration, his proposals, and—sadly—with the conviction that I can make him happy. Oh, if I had thought that the conformity of our tastes would have led him to believe I, too, feel sympathetic love, I would not have let him see even half the effect that the beauty of creation has on my soul and I would never have talked with him. I felt the more easy in this respect, because I knew that he had brought back with him from the isle of Scios a very accomplished Greek beauty, named Assy, whom he kept with him in his house. For a long time, I attributed this eagerness for my company and for knowing my thoughts only to the pleasure he found in conversing on his favorite subject. Without the least interruption, with unwavering attention, I tirelessly listened to the history of a country, the description of a plant, of a Greek ruin, a metal, or a stone. Thus I afforded him the pleasure of showing me his knowledge and of realizing that I appreciated and approved of the noble use of his life and wealth. Because of his knowledge and conversation, his company was of great value to me. After ten years of travel through the most remote areas of the world, his decision to spend his remaining days cultivating the earth rendered him exceedingly agreeable. All this made me glad, but his love for me is the superfluity that bothers and embarrasses me. He has made inquiries of Lady Summers about me; and though her answer has not increased his zeal, it has made it more insistent, and one word from me to the lady made him decide to marry off his Greek and send her to London with her husband. You cannot believe how heavily this supposed sacrifice weighs on my heart. After all, he has robbed himself of the cheerful effect which the charming girl would have had on his life because of the empty hope of future happiness in a union with me. He says that his secretary has loved the girl for a long time already and that she has returned that love. They have thanked him on their knees for allowing their union. But he feels the emptiness that her departure has left in his heart, for since then he is in the park every morning at sunrise and robs me of the morning air because I want to avoid meeting him, as he seems to feel I should compensate him for his loss. Never again will I call on subterfuge to free me from a perplexity.

When Lady Summers teased me one day about my lord's growing passion, I contradicted her for a long time in the same tone and claimed that it was nothing but self-love because he saw that I liked listening to him. She rebuked me quite seriously for this accusation, "Lord Rich admires your noble thirst for knowledge; he seeks to satisfy it by transmitting his learning to you. Should his reward be your biting raillery?"

I was touched, because I cannot abide even the appearance of injustice and had now committed one myself; but my lady continued quite kindly to give me many proofs of his tender esteem and noble inclinations. I also admitted that they deserve a return on my part; but as she answered everything I said about my friendship for him by shaking her head and demanding more for my lord, I assured her that it was unthinkable that Lord Rich could wish for more from me, because he could find in his beautiful Greek everything that love could contribute to make him happy. My lady kindly remained silent without letting me know that she had now discovered the only obstacle to my union with Lord Rich. He too was silent for a few days on the subject of his love, but he appeared very lively, especially when in a calm and relaxed manner he told us of Assy's marriage and departure. I was taken aback and feared that he would offer me his heart now that Assay had returned it. He said nothing to me, but the lady spoke for him. I was moved to ask her, "Why, dearest lady, do you want to remove your adopted daughter from your side? Have I become disagreeable to you?"

She gave me her hand and said, "No my dear child, you are infinitely dear to me, and I shall certainly feel the absence of her who takes such tender care of my declining years. But I have sufficient fruits to provide for the autumn of my life and need not rob you of the fairest flowers of your spring. You are young, charming, and a stranger here; what will you do when I am gone?"

"If I live to survive that misfortune, I shall return to my Emilia."

"My dear young lady, consider well; a woman of your birth and amiability must either live with close relatives or be under the protection of a worthy man. Lord Rich enjoys your complete esteem; indeed, the noble man deserves it. You know that you can make him happy. His friendship, his association is pleasing to you. Your will and your person are free, and the noblest motives guide you toward this union. Then give me the joy of seeing united in you and Lord Rich the most perfect models of male and female virtue."

Thus the dear lady pressed me. I reclined my head on her hand, which I kissed and bathed with tears of tenderness. My soul seemed to have heard an echo of my beloved mother's tender voice. Such virtues had indeed been the bonds of her union! How differently had I chosen! My Lord Rich's merits were indeed equal to my father's excellent attributes; my happiness would have been equal to that of my mother. But my involvement, my unholy involvement! Oh Emilia, write me very soon what you think. I feel I can no longer love, cannot give myself again. Even the tender esteem itself in which I hold my Lord Rich rebels against that thought. Through a perfidious hand my fate has cast me into the dust. Human kindness took me in, and to that gift alone I feel entitled. My gullibility has robbed me of all others, and I do not want to claim a happiness to which I am a stranger and of which I am unworthy.

Mrs. Leidens to Emilia

Oh my friend, a new and unexpected evil is rushing in upon me. I doubt whether all my constancy will be sufficient to bear it, especially because, as it is, I must have recourse to dissimulation, my most odious enemy. But because in my present circumstances candor cannot help me and would harm others, I will lock up in my bosom the gnawing grief that consumes it. I will even use the remaining powers of my imagination for the amusement of him who caused that grief. Read this, my Emilia, and see how misfortune has returned to persecute the friend of your youth.

A few days ago I was obliged to hear the whole history of Lord Rich's heart, its last part being an avowal of his love for me. "This," he said, "is the passion of a man of forty-five years of age. Reason implanted it in my heart; all my experiences and knowledge of mankind have strengthened it."

"My dear Lord Rich, you deceive yourself. Reason has never pleaded in favor of love against friendship. My heart offers you the highest degree of that noble inclination but let—"

"Not another word, madam, before you have heard me. My reason has made me your friend and a *man* of equal merit would have inspired me with an equal degree of esteem." Then he enumerated virtues and accomplishments of which I was compelled to say that they did not depict me. This remark caused him, so he said, to enlarge on the compliment his fair countrywomen had received from a stranger, on account of their modesty. "In your case," he said, "your mind's excellencies are as unknown to you as their physical charms were to them." Then he described my own "femininities," as he called them, as "the fruits of fiery genius and gentle, sensitive grace." From all this he drew the conclusion that my head and heart were precisely such as would agree completely with his own, creating the most perfect harmony in a moral union.

He then painted the picture of his resulting happiness in such affecting colors that I was convinced he knew all the springs of my soul and also where the idea of doing good might lead me. With all possible delicacy he drew a quick sketch of it. Oh my Emilia, it was a faithful copy of my former wishes and aspirations for my married life. Deeply touched and astonished, I could not keep back my tears. He rose from the green bank on which we were seated and took both my hands pressing them to his bosom. There was a contemplative, manly tenderness in his face as he looked at me.

"Dear madam," he said, "what an expression of deep unhappiness has spread over your face! Either death has robbed you of all the joys of life and youth, or there is in your situation a hidden source of the bitterest grief. Tell me, my dearest friend, will you not, can you not, unburden yourself to your faithful, your adoring friend?"

I let my head sink upon his hands, which were still holding mine. My heart was more oppressed than ever before in my life. The thought of my misfortune, the merits of this noble-minded man, the heavy chains of my union, even though it was feigned, the loss of my contentment forevermore—all this oppressed my soul at once. I could not speak, but was unable to suppress my sobs and sighs. For a moment he was profoundly silent, and then, with trembling hands and bending his head gently toward mine, he said in the saddest but gentlest voice, "Oh, your grief sheds a sad new light: your husband is not dead. An accident brought about by the laws of nature could not rend a soul like yours but only sadden it. But the man is unworthy of you and the remembrance of these bonds wounds your soul. Am I right, oh tell me, am I right?" His words made me shiver, and I was even less able to speak than before. He was kind enough to say to me, "No more today! Calm yourself; let me earn your trust."

I lifted up my eyes and from an involuntary emotion squeezed his hands. "Oh my Lord Rich!" was all I was able to say.

"Oh best of hearts, who was the inhuman wretch who failed to see your worth and made you miserable?"

"My dear lord, you shall know all, all. You deserve my trust."

I had hardly said this, when one of Lady Summers' servants came to tell me that she wished to speak to me because important letters from London had arrived. I strove to compose myself and hastened to the lady who immediately told me that her only niece had just married my Lord N., and that she eagerly anticipated their visit a fortnight hence. "We must think of a pleasant country celebration," she said, "so these young people enjoy their stay with their old aunt." Then, in leaving the room to dismiss the messenger, she gave me the letter to read that the young couple had written to her. Oh Emilia, what horror seized me when I recognized the handwriting of Lord Derby who was now the real husband of young Lady Alton! With trembling feet I hurried into my chamber to conceal my bewilderment from Lady Summers. I could not weep, but I felt almost stifled. How sensible I was now of my imprudence in coming to England. I now would lose my refuge; it was impossible to remain at Summerhall. I did not begrudge the villain his happiness, but why must I once again be its victim? I went to the window to breathe more freely and lifted my eyes toward heaven. "Oh God, my God, ruler of all, sustain me in this affliction! What shall I do?" Oh my Emilia, pray for me. It was a miracle, yes a miracle, that I managed to compose myself.

I resolved to dissemble, to assist my lady with all preparations for their reception and then to pretend an illness and exhaustion as long as the guests should be here and stay in my room with closed draperies, as if the daylight were hurting my head and my eyes. That was the only solution I could think of in this extremity. So I suppressed my tears and went to see my lady, whom from my window I had heard calling out to the departing messenger. My lady then told me of the great wealth and reputation of Lord N., who had become sole heir after his brother's death. Now she said her own brother would be at last contented because ambition was his only fault. She now shared his joy.

Oh Gratitude and Friendship, you did indeed succor me at this time! For where else would my reason, my tortured soul, have found the strength for me to feign a smile? But the part I took in the joy of my benefactress strengthened me. All the evil had already happened. If I had spoken out, I would have interrupted only the course of good and not of evil.

The first hour was the most painful one my heart had ever felt, but I would have been cruel indeed if I had burdened the heart of my dear lady with my revelations. She loves me; she is just and virtuous. She would be filled with the most violent revulsion against that evil man who was now her nephew, the beloved husband of her niece! Perhaps he is even now on the path to improvement, I thought; and certainly he himself would be very perplexed if he knew that I was here. He never knew me, never thought that fate would one day give me the power to do him great harm. But I will not use this power. He will enjoy undisturbed the happiness that providence has apportioned to him, and that same providence will not have offered my heart a test of virtue in vain—the opportunity of doing good to my enemy. "Oh Providence," I cried, "let me keep this attribute of a truly great soul!" After this supplication, many soothing tears streamed on my pillow. I was rewarded with the most blessed tranquility for the benevolence I had vowed to exercise toward my greatest enemy. My heart felt the true enno-bling value of virtue. Now my hands were joined in pure gratitude, whereas only a few hours earlier they had been clasped in pain and despair. Gently I fell asleep, tranquilly I awoke. With equal tranquillity I have already planned a rural party for my lady to give. But observe, my Emilia, how easily evil insinuates itself into what is good. For a few moments I enter-tained the thought of recreating a more modest version of Count F.'s party at his country seat to confuse Lord Derby. But this, too, I rejected as being merely revenge in disguise that tried to creep into my imagination, when it was banned from my heart.

I believe, Emilia, that Lord Rich can almost read my thoughts. He re-turned on only the fourth day after my conversation with him. My lady told him at lunch why we were all so busy and in the afternoon showed him the prepared rooms. I was invited to accompany them and also to read to them the list of preparations for the tenants' festival. Lord Rich seemed very attentive, praised everything (though only briefly), and followed all my movements with an uneasy and curious eye. Lady Summers left us alone for a few moments, and he came to the table where I was sorting and tying bunches of Italian flowers. With a solicitous, tender expression he took one of my hands and said, "You are not well, my friend. Your hands tremble while you work. There is a certain haste in all your movements that, de-spite yourself, shows through your assumed gaiety. Your smile does not come from the heart. What is the meaning of all this?"

"Lord Rich, your penetration frightens me," I answered.

"Then I perceive correctly, after all."

"Ask me no more questions, my lord. My soul has suffered the most violent conflict, but at present I will sacrifice all consideration of what concerns me to the pleasure of Lady Summers."

"I fear only that you are sacrificing yourself as well," said the lord.

"Fear nothing," I answered; "fate has destined me to suffer, and it will preserve me for that purpose."

I thought I said this calmly and with a smile, but Lord Rich looked at me with dismay. "Do you know, madam, that what you have just said indicates the highest degree of despair and throws me into fatal disquietude? Please speak to Lady Summers! You will find her a maternal heart."

"I know, my dear lord. But at present that cannot be. Please banish your cares on my account. My trembling is nothing but the last agitation of the storm that will soon be followed by calm."

"Oh God," he cried out, "how much longer will you torture me thus with thoughts of your grief?" Here my lady returned, saving me from becoming too much softened. Lord Rich left us with an air of defiant discontent that we both noticed.

Lady Summers said to me with a smile, "How can you be so good hearted and yet torment such a good person? If I could only hope that one of these flowers will adorn you on your way to the altar as Lord Rich's bride! My brother would take the place of your father, just as I would stand for the mother."

"Dearest lady," I answered with the deepest emotion, "my resistance becomes every day more painful to me, but so far it has been impossible for me to make a decision. Kindly let me stay as I am for a little while longer." A torrent of tears that I could not hold back made her ladyship also weep, but she promised not to importune me further.

Excerpt from a Letter of Lord Derby, now Lord N., to Lord B., His Friend in Paris

You know that I am married to the rich and dainty Lady Alton and that she is quite proud of having caught me in the bonds of Hymen. The simpleton gives herself airs when, to get the measure of her silly mind, I ask her with a complaisant face how I might oblige her. I wanted to amuse myself with this for a while in order to complete my register of female fools. As it turns out, I have rendered myself an essential service by this means. After all that wretched display was over with which newlyweds seem to lead each other about in triumph, I asked my lady whether she would not like to go to the country for some time. She suggested a visit with her Aunt Summers, a tiresome woman; but she is rich and her estate will be pleasant to inherit. We wrote to her, and I dispatched John with our letter announcing the visit. The old lady received him very kindly; and while she was busy writing a reply, John walked up and down in an ante-chamber with the steward. Upon reading the letter, my lady had immediately asked for a Mrs. Leidens; and a quarter hour later a refined young woman, dressed in the English manner, stepped nimbly into the room and with downcast eyes passed them and entered the lady's chamber. John, as if thunderstruck, recognized Lady Sternheim in her but instantly recovered himself and asked who this lady was. The steward told him that she had come from Germany with Lady Summers, who loved her exceedingly. He said she was an angel of goodness and wisdom and that Lord Rich, whose estates adjoined those of Lady Summers, would marry her. That poor devil John trembled from fear of being called before Lady Summers and tried to hasten his dismissal. The old lady came in, but alone. John got himself dismissed as soon as possible and galloped back.

Judge for yourself how surprised I was at this news. I never felt more uneasy over any of my pranks than I did now for the tricks I had played this enthusiast. Where did she find the audacity to show her face in England? But is it not always thus? The most fearful creature becomes courageous in the arms of a man. I must have communicated to her some of my impudence, which she might well return to me in Lady Summers' house. I could not afford exposing myself to it, since my plans unavoidably demanded the observance of good conduct. I felt indeed lucky to have kept John in my service, for the cunning dog found a way out sooner than I did. He suggested that I have her abducted! This had to be done soon, and the place of her new sojourn had to be far removed from Summerhall. I settled on the same place in the Scottish highlands, on Hopton's estates, where a few years earlier I had detained Nancy. Because that young lady, whose father was a lawyer, could not be found, who then would look there for a foreigner? I confess I think it a cursed fate for one of the finest girls to be taken so many hundreds of miles from her home to eat oat bread in the hut of a poor wretch working in a Scottish lead mine. But why the deuce did she have to cross my path in England? It is mere justice that I reward her thus for her impudence.

By now she has already arrived safely at her destination, and I have left orders to treat her well.

John made all the arrangements; and since he knew from Lady Summers's steward that Lord Rich and the parson's wife and daughters often talked with my heroine in the park, he had her informed that Miss Emma wished to see her there for a moment. She came; he seized her and carried her off. He says it was with much trouble that he conveyed her to Scotland alive. All the way she would take nothing but a few glasses of water; and except for exclaiming about me under the name of Derby, she sat in the chaise like an image of death. Had you been here, mad fool though you are,

I would have put her under your care. If the wild genius that used to rule you had hovered about her, you certainly could have changed her and would have had in her a greater treasure than all your gold could have bought for you in the fancy shops of Paris. She is certainly one of the finest among all the flowers that have withered at your friend's fiery bosom.

As soon as I had news that she had been missing for two days, I went with my lady and her father to Summerhall, where the old lady was keeping to her bed and lamenting the loss of her foster daughter. All the people of the house and village, the parson's family, and especially Lord Rich, an old bachelor who plays the philosopher, bewailed the loss of Mrs. Leidens. Lady Summers implored my assistance; and I pretended to take all possible pains to help find her. On this occasion, I found out how she had come to England. Everyone praised her charms, her talents, and her kind heart. Those fools made me quite angry and tired with their rantings, especially Rich—wise Rich, who made me the confidant of his passions and is so wise that he imagines she has fled from him because he brought her to the point of telling him her story. He thinks that her experiences must be very singular, because everything in the young woman's conduct shows all the marks of the most excellent education, the most perfect virtue, and the most refined womanly sensibility. He believes that some villain had taken advantage of the goodness of her heart and thus prepared for that distress with which he has seen her incessantly struggling. Wasn't it a strange affair, to listen to all this and feign ignorance? He showed me her picture, an exact likeness. She is represented sitting at a table with a rack of mounted butterflies on it. These were to serve for I don't know what use in an entertainment to be given in my honor, for which she herself had invented a plan. But this was not a happy idea; she knows little about hunting butterflies; otherwise she would not have let my wings get free. I must tell you, her picture made a stronger impression on me than all the attributes of her character. Upon my life, I pity her! I would like to know what sin she, who so deeply reveres providence, has committed in the eyes of that power to be thus, in the flower of her youth, snatched from her home, ruined, and cast into the most dismal corner of the earth. And why did providence choose me to execute that judgment? Oh, I swear, if ever I raise a daughter, she will know all the snares with which our sex encircles the innocence of hers! But that does not help you now, poor Sternheim!

Come back soon, friend; we shall visit her in the springtime. This winter she must endure her exile, even though I feel sorry for her.

Interpolation of the Copyist

Here, my friend, I find myself obliged once more to resume my pen, to fill a void in the letters I am summarizing for you.

In keeping with the impious lord's scheme, my dear mistress was
called into the garden to meet the parson's daughters, just as she was fin-
ishing her last letter to my Emilia. She took the entire roll of paper with
her, to prevent anyone from finding anything disadvantageous to Lord
Derby. She set out in the direction of the park; and when she had walked
some twenty paces along the side of the garden facing the village and had
seen no one, she turned back. But suddenly a woman appeared in the park
and waved to her. She hastened toward her, and that person also advanced
toward my lady and took her by the hand. At the same moment, two
masked persons came on the scene, threw a round heavy hood over her
head, and carried her off by force. Her violent resistance, her attempts to
cry out, were in vain. They forced her into a light carriage and set off
instantly, traveling all night at high speed. In the middle of a forest, they
offered her food and drink; but she would not and could not take anything
but a glass of water, and they quickly resumed the wild journey. Exhausted
and dejected beyond expression, she sat next to a person in woman's
clothes who kept a tight hold on her. Once she slipped down on her knees
to ask for pity but received no answer; and at length she found herself in the
hut of a Scottish lead miner, where they laid her on a wretched bed. This
was all that she could say about her release from her abductors, for she was
almost mad. Her journal will show how a violent affliction of the soul can

distract a noble heart; but it proves at the same time that no sooner had she
recovered her strength, than the excellent principles of her education regained their full efficacy.

You can better imagine than I can describe the grief Lady Summers
experienced through this event and the lamentations of my Emilia and the
rest of my family over the news of Sophia's disappearance, especially as
everything we did to find her was of no avail. All winter long, unavoidable
obligations kept my brother-in-law from coming to England himself to tell
Lady Summers his suspicions about Lord Derby. This winter was indeed the
longest and saddest that our small family, grieved by the misfortunes of a
most beloved friend, ever experienced.

The Journal of Mrs. Leidens in the Scottish Highlands

Emilia! Dear and precious name! Once you were the consolation and
support of my life, but now you serve only to increase my suffering. The
plaintive voice, the letters of your unfortunate friend can no longer reach
you. All has been snatched from me, and feeling the anguish of my friends
adds even more to my heart's bitter grief. Worthy Lady Summers! Dearest
Emilia! Why should your loving hearts share the torture that providence has
made my lot? Oh God, how severely You punish me for the single step I
took from the path of convention! Can my secret marriage have offended

You? Poor thoughts, where are you wandering? No one hears you; no one will read you. These pages will die and decay with me. No one but my persecutor will learn of my death, and he will be glad to know that this testimony to his inhumanity is buried with me. Oh Providence, you see my submission, you see that I ask nothing of you. Slowly you want to crush me. Do it—but preserve the hearts of my virtuous friends from the grief that oppresses them on my account!

In the Third Month of My Exile

I have lived through another month and have recovered my senses, but only to understand the full extent of my misfortunes. Where now are the blessed days when at the first light of dawn I lifted my hands toward heaven in gratitude, full of joy at my preservation? Now, at my awakening, new tears fill my eyes, and I mark my first waking hours by wringing my hands. Oh my Creator, is it possible that You look with more pleasure on the bitter tears of distress than on the sweet ones of filial gratitude?

Destitute of all hope, robbed of any chance of assistance, I struggle with myself. I reproach myself for my sadness as for a crime and follow my inclination to write.

Just now a hopeful whisper of happier days to come rises up in my soul, but did it not sound even louder in those fateful days gone by, and did it not deceive me then, too? Oh Fate, did I abuse my happy state? Was my heart too fond of the splendor that surrounded me? Or was pride in the soul I received from you my crime? Oh poor creature that I am, with whom do I presume to dispute? I am nothing but an animated handful of dust, yet I rise up against the power that tests me—and still preserves me. Will you, oh my soul, through grumbling and impatience, pour the worst evil into the cup of my sufferings? Oh God, forgive me, and let me acknowledge the benefits with which even here You have surrounded my sensible heart!

Oh faithful remembrance of my Emilia, come and bear witness that her friend's heart renews its vows to virtue! Witness, too, that she reenters the path of duty, renounces her heart's stubborn sensitivity, and no longer closes her eyes to the evidence of an eternally benevolent providence. It has now been almost three months since my abduction by a most cruel man who made me travel day and night to bring me here: Derby—no one but you was capable of such barbarous conduct! Just when I was laboring for your amusement, you were weaving a new web of grief for me. You must indeed be a stranger to honor and magnanimity, because you could not

imagine that they would oblige me to keep silent and out of your sight.
How can you play at tormenting a heart whose sensibility you know so
well? Oh Providence, why did you decree that all the malicious schemes of
this evil man must meet with success, while all my benevolent plans are
exiled with me in these dismal mountains?

How self-love renders the progress of our virtue wavering and uncertain! Two days ago, my heart full of noble resolve, I intended to accept my
unhappy fate; and then self-love appeared and added those memories which
diverted my attention from the present and future to the unchangeable past.
Are the lessons of virtue, knowledge, and experience then all lost on me?
Shall a vile enemy have the twofold power of not only, like a robber, strip-
ping me of my outward fortune and respect, but also of destroying my principles, the will to do my duty, and the very love of virtue in my soul
as well?

Oh happy hour of my life, in which I rediscovered my whole heart, in
which the blissful conviction returned that even here the paternal hand of
my Creator provides for my soul's true benefits! He has saved my mind
from the madness that almost overpowered me in the first few weeks. He
inspired my ignorant hosts with kindness and compassion for me. My soul's
pure and moral impulses are slowly rising above the gloom of my grief.
Though I cannot look at it without sighing, the serene sky encircling this
desert gives me as much hope and peace as the sky over Sternheim; the
towering mountains proclaim to me the omnipotence of the hand that made
them. The earth is everywhere filled with the testimony of His wisdom and
goodness, and I am everywhere His creature. Here He intends to bury my
vanity, and the last few hours of my trial are to pass without any witness
but His eye and the protestations of my heart. Perhaps it will not take long.
Should I not seek to fill my last hours with the virtuous actions that I still
am able to perform? How comforting is the thought of death when accompanied by the assurance that our soul is immortal! How it awakens in us the
lively sense of our duty, and how eager it makes our will to do good! I
thank it for overcoming my grief and for the renewed strength of my soul's
virtue! It animated me with the resolve to fill my last days with noble
thoughts and to try to find some good to do even here.

Yes I can, I shall yet do good! Oh Patience, virtue of those who suffer,
not of the fortunate person to whom all wishes are granted, dwell with me
and guide me into calm obedience to the decrees of providence! Labori-

ously, one by one, we gather the roots and herbs that cure our bodily ills; we ought to gather the remedies for our moral afflictions with equal care. Like the former, they can often be found in our very path. But we are accustomed to seek good things at a distance and to disregard that which lies close at hand. This was my case: my wishes and lamentations carried my thoughts far from the objects around me. I have only recently reflected on the comfort of having brought with me a whole roll of paper for collecting and writing down my thoughts. Further, was it not the goodness of providence that preserved me from all offense during my troublesome journey to this place and that allowed me to keep everything that I could use during this time of enforced idleness?

Emilia—sacred friendship, beloved memory! Your image rises smiling above the ashes of my happiness. Many tears you have cost me! But come, these pages will be dedicated to you! From my early youth, my most private feelings have been poured into your faithful, tender heart. It is possible that chance may preserve these papers; they may yet reach you, and you will read that my heart never forgot the virtue and goodness of yours. Perhaps then tears of friendship and love will fall on these reminders of your unfortunate Sophia. You will not be able to weep at my tomb, for I will be put in an unmarked grave—the victim of Derby's malice. Because the thought of death and eternity has now replaced all my complaints and wishes, I will use this period of calm to describe the sudden turn of fate that takes me to an early grave. I could not do so before because I was too deeply affected whenever I thought of it.

I arrived here almost lifeless and remained for three weeks in a state of mind that I cannot describe. What my condition was in the second and third month of my stay here is evident from the pieces I wrote during my hours of calm. Judge for yourself, Emilia, how disordered my soul must have been, as I could not pray. Neither did I call on Death to relieve me; but realizing fully the extent of my misfortune, I would not have stepped aside to avoid the lightning bolt threatening me. For days on end I was on my knees, not from submission, not to implore Heaven's mercy—outraged pride had filled me with the thought of undeserved misery. But, oh Emilia, that thought aggravated my calamity and hardened my heart against practicing those virtues still within my reach, even though their performance alone could pour the balm of consolation into my soul's wounds. I was conscious of this for the first time when I felt myself affected as the poor five-year-old girl who had been ordered to watch me was trying to raise my dejected head with her little hands. I did not understand her language, but the tone of her voice and the expression in her face were natural, tender, and innocent. I clasped her in my arms and shed a flood of tears. Those were the first tears of consolation I had wept. My gratitude for this little creature's love was mingled with the realization that God had given this poor child the power to let me taste the sweetness of compassion. From that day I compute my soul's cure.

I now began to gather the crumbs of happiness that were lying next to me in the dust. My physical exhaustion and the pain of eating the oaten bread made me think my death was near. No one who had witnessed my former life remained near me, but I resolved to return to my Creator a heart filled with resignation and love of Him. This thought restored all the former force of virtue in my soul. I kept my small benefactress with me in the miserable corner that had been partitioned off for me in the hut. I shared my bed with her and received from her my first lessons in the simple idiom that is spoken here. I went with her into my hosts' room. The husband has worked in a lead mine for many years and is now disabled by illness. With his wife and children he cultivates the small field which Lord Hopton has granted him near an old, ruined castle. Here they grow oats and hemp. They grind the oats between stones for food, while the hemp provides their clothing. They are poor, good-natured people whose whole wealth consists of the few guineas they receive for keeping me. They were pleased to see that I was calmer and had come to sit with them. Each was eager to instruct me in their language, and within a fortnight I learned enough of it to be able to formulate short questions and answers. They have been told exactly how far from the house they may let me go, and on one of the last days of autumn the husband guided me somewhat beyond that point. Oh, how poor is nature here! One can plainly see that her bowels are of lead. With tears in my eyes I beheld the rough, barren piece of field where my oaten bread is grown and the weeping skies above me. Remembrance made me sigh, but a glance at my emaciated guide reminded me that I had enjoyed an abundance of blessings in my youth and that this good man and his family had been in misery and want all their lives. They are creatures of the same divine Creator; their bodies lack no sinew, no muscle they need for enjoying the satisfaction of physical needs. In this there is no difference between them and me. But in their souls—how many faculties sleep and remain inactive! How deeply concealed, how incomprehensible are the causes that render our corporeal faculties common to us all, while at the same time leaving millions of men disadvantaged in their development as intelligent and moral beings! Even here and now I feel fortunate because my mind and feelings have been cultivated, so that I know what I owe God and man! Therein lies true happiness; those are the only riches we can collect on earth and take with us. Impatience will not make me abandon them; I will endeavor to reward my poor hosts' goodness of heart with loving-kindness.

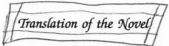

I said these things to myself as I continued eagerly learning their language. Upon inquiring about their occasional harshness toward the little girl, I learned that she was not their child but Lord Derby's, that the mother had died with them, and that his lordship contributed nothing to the child's support. On hearing this, I retreated to my corner. I was again painfully sensible of my entire misfortune. The poor mother! Undoubtedly, she had been beautiful like her child, and young, and good—my grave will be next to hers. Oh Emilia, how can I endure this trial? The little girl came and took my hand, which was hanging over the bed while my face was turned to the wall. I heard her approach; her touch, her voice made me shudder, and involuntarily I snatched my hand away. Derby's daughter was hateful to me! In tears, the poor little girl went to the foot of my bed, bewailing her fate. Then I felt the injustice of making this unfortunate, innocent child suffer. I vowed to suppress my aversion and to love the child of my murderer. Joyfully I arose and called her. I took her in my arms, and, leaning my head against her little chest, I resolved henceforth to be kind to her. I will not break my vow; I have bought it too dearly!

Oh Derby, how full is the measure of your harshness against me! Today a messenger came and brought a large package of supplies for making tapestries. With base mockery Derby wrote that he feared that without tapestry work, time might grow long for me here as it had at court. He said he was sending me this work for the winter, and he would have it sent for in spring. The pieces are intended for a closet; the drawings are included. I will begin this work. He will receive the pieces after my death. He will view these reminders of his barbarity toward me and remember how happy I was when first he saw me doing needlework. Then he will have to reflect on the abyss of misery into which he threw me and where he let me perish.

Never again, oh Fate, will I yield to grumbling self-love! How falsely it makes us judge! I complained about what has become my joy. My work brightens the dark winter days, my hosts observe me with rude delight, and I am instructing their daughter in this skill. The girl looked around at us with joyful pride when she completed the first little leaf.

Misfortune and want often make people resourceful, and so it has been with me. I know that Lord Hopton, who owns the lead mine, has a house a few miles from here, and that on occasion he goes there for a few days. On his last journey he brought a sister with him whom he loves dearly and who, being a widow, is often with him. On her I base my hopes, which are stirring anew as my life continues. I have suggested to my hosts that their daughter Mary might be placed in that lady's service. I promised to teach her everything she would need for that position. I am already teaching her to speak and write English. She now knows how to do embroidery; and because I had to crochet two caps of the lace of my neck handkerchief, I have taught her that art as well. As to the rest, I teach her as we work. The girl shows such aptitude for learning and discriminating that I am often astonished. She will clear my way to my freedom, for through her I hope to become acquainted with Lady Douglas. Oh Fate, do no deprive me of this hope!

Here, My Emilia, I want to tell you of another instance where ingenuity lightened my burden. You know how clean I always kept my linens. Yet here I was not able to change my clothes for I don't know how long. Finally as my thoughts became ordered, I resented not being able to change clothes, and upon further thought I was glad that when I was abducted I was wearing a white linen dress. I now took it off and was glad that the fashionable abundance of pleats enabled me to cut three chemises out of it and still have a short dress left over. I made neck handkerchiefs out of my apron, and in turn used one of my petticoats to make aprons. In this way, I can keep my clothes clean with a light sudsing and can change them. I iron them with a warm stone. I have taught little Liddy how to sew as well, and she makes very nice stitches in the background of my tapestry. To please me, my hosts clean their home every day, and the boiled oat bread begins to agree with me. The needs of nature are small, my Emilia. I arise satisfied from the meager table, and my hosts are astonished to hear me talk of other parts of the world. I still have my parents' pictures. I showed them to the good people and told them as much about my education and former way of life as they could comprehend and was useful to them. Tears of unfeigned compassion fell from their eyes as I told them of my former happiness and my new-found patience. I speak very little of you, my dear, for I am not strong enough to think often of losing you or your grief on my account. If, by my sufferings, I could alleviate those which you and my dear lady feel for me, I believe I would be able to say that I no longer suffer. But fate knew what would torture me most! It knew that in suffering my innocence and my principles would console and calm me; it knew that I would learn to bear poverty and want. It gave me, therefore, the sensation of my friends' pain—and that wound cannot be cured because it would be a crime to wish it so! How happy this gift of empathy once made me when my wealth enabled me to gratify my friends' every wish and relieve their every pain. Two years have now passed since I stepped into the brilliant circle and saw before me prospects of happiness, saw myself loved and could choose or reject. Oh my heart, why have you so long avoided one memory? Never again have you dared to think the name "Seymour"; yet now you ask, what would he say to this? And you cry at being forgotten!

Oh Fate, take this part away; let him never again enter my memory! His heart never knew what mine felt for him, and now it is too late!

Oh Emilia, my paper is almost used up; I cannot write much more. The winter is long, and I will keep the rest of my supply for telling you what comes of my still uncertain hopes. Oh my dear, some sheets of paper constituted my happiness here, and now that too is gone! I shall save some of the canvas and sew letters into it.

In April

Oh beneficent Time, how much good I owe you! By degrees you have taken away the deep impressions of my sorrow and lost happiness and have placed them in a misty distance, while shedding a cheerful serenity on the objects that surround me. Experience, which you hold by the hand, taught me to practice wisdom and patience. The more familiar I grew with them, the more the bitterness of my grief was diminished. You, oh Time, who heal all the soul's wounds, will also pour the balm of quietude into the hearts of my few friends and allow them to enjoy the bright prospects of their future lives without being embittered by their grief for me. You have helped me recall the consoling goodness of my Creator which shelters even a weak worm under some grains of sand; you have let me find that goodness even in these rough mountains, have helped me to exercise my skills, and awakened and activated the virtues that slumbered in the bosom of ease and prosperity. Here, where the physical world distributes its few gifts grudgingly among the dejected inhabitants, I have distributed the moral riches of virtue and knowledge in the cottage of my keepers, and together we taste and enjoy their sweetness. Stripped of everything that bears the name of fortune, esteem, and power, with my life entrusted to these strangers, I nevertheless became their moral benefactor by increasing their love for God, enlightening their minds, and calming their hearts, while providing recreation for them. I did this by telling them stories of other parts of the world and the history of their inhabitants. By my love, care, and instruction, I have given happiness to an innocent orphan, doubly unfortunate. Thus deprived of what men call "well-being," I enjoy the true gifts of Heaven: serenity of soul and the pleasure of doing good—both fruits of true humanity and tested virtue. Pure joys, real treasures, you will accompany me into eternity, and the happiness of having known you will be the first subject of my soul's immortal songs of gratitude.

At the End of June

Emilia, did you ever put yourself in the place of a man exposed in a light boat to the stormy sea? He is acutely sensible of being alive and, trembling, looks here and there for a hopeful sign. After the waves have tossed him about for a long time, he grows desperate. Then, finally, he perceives an island which he hopes to reach; and with folded hands he cries out, "Oh my God, I see land!" I, my dear, feel all this—I see land! Lord Hopton has returned to his house in the mountains, and his sister, Lady Douglas, has taken my landlady's daughter into her service. Mary took some of her embroidery work and, accompanied by her brother, went to the lady to offer her services. Surprised by her way of speaking and the quality of her work, the lady asked who had taught her; and the girl's gratitude made her tell everything she knew about me and what I had done for her. That kind lady was moved to tears and immediately promised the girl to take her in. She ordered the two young people to be fed and sent the son back home to his parents alone with two guineas and the promise that, before her departure, she would herself come to see them. She sent me her special respects and blessed me for the trouble I had taken with the girl. I have asked her for paper, pens, and ink, and I will take this opportunity to write to my Lady Summers. But I will give the letter to Lady Douglas unsealed, to convince her of my candor. I should be culpable indeed if I did not use every opportunity to achieve my freedom, especially as these are honest means. I will also ask Lord Hopton to extend his favor to my poor hosts. The good people are beside themselves with joy at seeing their daughter so well provided for and at the money they have received. They caress and bless me by turns. I will not leave my little orphan behind. Now that she is used to kind treatment, its loss would make her doubly unhappy; and all my days would be disquieted by remembering her if I returned to a happy life and left her here, the prey of certain misery.

Oh my friend, the simile on my last page, of the boat lost in a tempestuous sea, was prophetic. I am destined to feel the keenest agony of soul and then die at the very moment hope appears. The unspeakable wickedness of my persecutor sweeps me along as a foaming wave sweeps boat and men into the abyss. This power has been left him, and every means of aid has been taken away from me. Soon a solitary grave will end my complaints and show my soul the final purpose of the cruel fate I had to suffer. I am calm. I am content. My last day will be the happiest I have spent in two years. Lady Summers will send my packet of papers to you, my dear friend whom I have tenderly loved until my last moment. You will be consoled by the thought that all my sufferings have disappeared in an eternity of bliss. My last strength is dedicated to you. You were the witness of my happiness; as my strength permits, you will also witness the end of my desolate days.

I was full of hope and surrounded by bright prospects when Derby's closest agent arrived here. Speaking for his master, he proposed that I go and stay with his lordship at London, because he no longer loved his wife, had been ill for some time, and felt that my company would be agreeable to him at his country house in Windsor, where he usually resides. He himself wrote to me that if I would come of my own free will and would give proof of my love, he intended to divorce Lady Alton and to reaffirm our marriage, as the law required and my merits deserved. However, if, true to my former imaginary principles, I refused to consent to this proposal, I must resign myself to my fate as he saw fit to order it. This is what I was forced to hear, for I would not read the letter; but the worst part of this insufferable insult was that I was forced to look at the unholy wretch who had performed my false marriage. Dejected and embittered in the highest degree, I refused all these unworthy offers; and the barbarian resolved to avenge his master. After I had twice formally refused, he grasped me around the middle, dragged me out of the house toward the old tower, and, wild with rage and screaming curses, he pushed me through a door, saying that I would there perish, so that his master and he would be rid of me once and for all. My resistance and my terrible fear that I might be taken to London by force exhausted me and rendered me half unconscious. I collapsed full-length on the rubbish and mire filling the chamber, injuring my left hand and half of my face on the sharp stones, so that I bled profusely from my nose and mouth. I do not know how long I lay there unconscious. When I recovered my senses, I was very weak and in great pain. In a short time, the foul damp air I breathed oppressed my breast so much that I thought I had come to my life's last moment. I could see nothing; but I felt with one hand that the ground was steeply sloping, and so I feared that the slightest movement would propel me into a cellar where I would give up my life in utmost despair. My misery and the sensations accompanying it are indescribable. There I lay all night, while it rained so hard that the water streamed in under the door and drenched me, so that I became stiff with cold. Utterly cast down by my misfortune, I wished for death. I then seemed to become inwardly convulsed.

That much I remember, but when I regained my senses I was on my bed, surrounded by my poor fearful hosts lamenting my condition. My little orphan was holding my hand, uttering anxious moans. I felt very ill and implored them to fetch Lord Hopton's chaplain, since I felt myself dying. The son set out, and the parents told me that they had been prevented from helping me until Sir John (as they called him) had departed. How deplorable an effect of poverty it is that the oppressed seldom have the heart to oppose the violence done them by the vicious rich! The villain had been delayed by the rain, but they said that, before leaving, he had gone to the door of the tower, opened it, and listened. He had shaken his head in vexation, and, without closing the door or saying another word to them, had left. For fear of him they had waited another hour and then came to look for me with a light and, thinking me dead, carried me out. The clergyman

came and Lady Douglas with him. Both looked at me attentively and full of
pity. I held out my hand to the lady and she kindly took it. "Noble lady,"
I said with tears in my eyes, "God will reward your soul for this humane
effort on my behalf. Please believe that I am worthy of it." I noticed that
her eyes were fixed on my hand and the picture of my mother. Then I said
to her, "That is my mother, a granddaughter of Sir David Watson—and
here," lifting my other hand, "is my father, a worthy nobleman of Germany. Both have long since gone to heaven, and I hope I shall be with them
soon," I added with folded hands. The lady cried and asked the clergyman
to feel my pulse. He did so and assured her that I was in a bad way. With
loving solicitude she looked about her and asked if I could not be taken
away from there. "Not without mortal danger," said the divine. "Oh, I am
sorry to hear that," said the dear lady, pressing my hand. She went outside
and the clergyman began to talk to me. I told him briefly that I came from
a noble family and had been removed from my native country through the
despicable fraud of a false marriage. I said that my Lady Summers, under
whose protection I had been, would gladly vouch for me. I asked him to
take the papers that I had written for her and hidden behind a board. Without his asking, I added an avowal of my principles and asked him to write
to your husband. Her ladyship was knocking at the door and entered with
Mary, my hosts' daughter, who approached my bed, carrying a box. In it
she had all kinds of cordials and medicines, which they made me take.
Little Lydia came in, too, and knelt down by my bed. The lady looked at
the girl and me with increasing sadness. Finally she took her leave, leaving
Mary with me. The minister promised to come again in the morning. But
he did not come all day, although twice I heard a person inquiring after my
health. This morning I felt better than yesterday and, therefore, wrote this
down for you.

Now it is almost six o'clock in the evening, and I am getting visibly
worse. My shaky, uneven handwriting is a sign of it. Who knows what will
befall me this night? I thank God that I am mortal and that my heart was
permitted to commune with yours before the end. I am quite calm and near
the moment when earthly happiness and misery are no longer significant.

At Nine O'Clock in the Evening

For the last time, my Emilia, I have feebly stretched my weakened
arms toward the country where you dwell. May God bless you and reward
your virtue and the friendship you had for me! You will receive a paper that
your husband must deliver to my uncle, Count R. It concerns my estates.

Everything that came to me from the P. family will be given to Count
Loebau's sons. Your brother-in-law, the steward, has an exact account of it.

Half of what I have inherited from my beloved father will be dedicated to the education of poor children. Part of the other half I give to your children and to my friend Rosina. Of the other part my poor hosts will receive a thousand talers, and the unfortunate Lydia will be given an equal amount. From the remainder a simple headstone will be erected at the foot of my parents' tomb, with this inscription:

"In memory of their daughter Sophia von Sternheim

Who was not unworthy of them."

I want to be buried here, at the foot of the tree where I have often knelt this spring and asked God for patience. Here, where my mind was tormented, my body ought to be dissolved. Here, too, the same maternal earth shall cover me until, transfigured, I enter into the company of the virtuous, where I shall once more see you, my Emilia! Meantime, oh my friend, save my memory from the calumny of apparent vice! Let it be known that, faithful to virtue, though unhappy and plunged into bitterest grief, full of filial trust in God and love toward my fellow beings, my soul has been returned to its Creator. Say that I have tenderly blessed my friends and sincerely forgiven my enemies.

In your garden, near a rock, plant a cypress, my dear, and let it be entwined by a solitary rose tree. Dedicate that place to my memory. Go there sometimes, and, perhaps, I will be permitted to hover about you and to observe the tender tears you shed as you watch the rose petals fall. You have seen me blossom and wither, too; fate has denied your witnessing only the last bowing of my head and my soul's last sigh. That is good, my Emilia! You would suffer too much if you could see me now. My soul is filled with peace; I shall fall asleep gently, for my destiny has made me tired, very tired.

Farewell, best of friends! Let your tears for me be soothing ones, like those now flowing from these dim eyes for you!

Lord Seymour to Dr. T.

Why, in the name of God, are you prevented by illness from seeing me for even two days! I am close to madness and almost frantic with rage; and despite his stoicism, my brother Rich (whom you knew in the house of my mother's first husband) has been struck down by the same blow. Two days from now we will travel to the Scottish highlands and—oh fatal thought!—search there for the murdered Lady Sternheim's grave and remove her body to Dumfries, where it is to be buried with great pomp. Oh eternal

Providence, how could you deliver the best gift you ever bestowed on this earthto the most odious villain? My people are preparing for our journey; I can do nothing! I wring my hands like a madman and beat them a thousand times against my breast and forehead. Derby, that wretch, has the impudence to say that on my account, from jealousy of me, he had deceived, made miserable, and caused the death of the most noble and amiable creature. He now howls with remorse; the rabid cur howls! His wickedness has brought him to the brink of an early grave which he fears but which he knows will protect him from my just revenge. Listen, my friend; listen to the most dreadful fate that virtue ever met and to the worst deeds that malice ever perpetrated.

You know that four months ago I returned sick to England in the company of my Lord G., and immediately went to see my mother at Seymour House to ponder the evils that had befallen my body and soul. Eventually I also inquired about Derby, now Lord N., and they told me that he lay ill at his country seat at Windsor. I resolved to wait for his and my recovery before seeing him, but some days after I had inquired about him, he sent for me. I was not well and declined. A few days later I went to see my brother Rich, who received me in a mood much like mine: friendly but enveloped in gloom. The difference of fifteen years between our ages hindered our fraternal confidence anyway, and his dull silence did not encourage me to seek relief by talking to him.

Thus we passed a fortnight without speaking of anything but our travels, and that only intermittently, until the arrival of a messenger from Lord N., when we simply opened our hearts to each other in an instant. The messenger brought me a letter in which Derby asked me to visit him with Lord Rich on a matter that concerned Lady Sternheim. I was to tell Lord Rich only that she was the lady he had seen at Lady Summer's and who had been abducted from there. I started as from a frightful dream and merely shouted to the servant that I would come. I seized my brother by the arm and asked him hastily about the young lady he had seen at Summerhall. In turn, he asked me with great emotion if I was acquainted with her and what I knew of her. I showed him the letter and briefly told him everything that concerned the dear and beloved young lady. In as few words and as brokenly, he told me how he had seen her and come to love her. He left to bring me her picture and could not say enough of her mind, her noble sentiments, and the sadness that has oppressed her, especially when Derby's marriage to Lady Alton had been announced.

We quickly decided to set off and arrived at Windsor with Lord Rich thoughtful but kind and me restless and full of resolve. A fevered rage made me shiver and burn as I entered Derby's house. My hate for him was so aroused that I paid no attention to his wretched appearance and the visible weakness that forced him to stay in bed. I glared at him in silent enmity, and he fixed his dimming eyes on me in a supplicating look, stretching his emaciated, fever-reddened hand toward me. "Seymour," he said, "I know you. I know that you hate me, but you don't know how many violent conflicts you have caused in my breast."

I had not given him my hand, and now I said with repugnance in my voice and shaking my head disdainfully, "I know of no cause, except the difference in our principles."

Derby replied, "Seymour, you would not use this tone if I were well, and the pride with which you speak of your principles is as great a sin as the misuse I made of my talents."

Lord Rich interjected that all this was now unimportant and that all we wanted of Lord Derby was news of the abducted lady.

"Yes, Lord Rich, you shall have it," he said; "there is more humanity in your coldness than in Seymour's outraged sensibility. I leave him to tell you what happened when we first became acquainted with Lady Sternheim. We both loved her to distraction; but I first noticed her special inclination toward him and used every means to destroy it. By dissimulation and artifice, and availing myself of the prince's pursuit of her and Seymour's silly scruples, I succeeded in getting her into my power through a false marriage. But my pleasure was of short duration; her overly serious character bored me, and her secret inclination for Seymour stirred whenever my thoughts ran counter to hers in the least degree. My jealousy made me want revenge, and my changed circumstances, brought about by my brother's death, gave me the opportunity to indulge that desire. I left her, only to regret it a few days later, sending a man to the village where she had stayed—but she had gone! For a long time I heard nothing of her, until I found her again in England at the house of my wife's aunt, where I could not leave her, and had her abducted. Even then I was sorry for her, but I saw no other way.

"My disillusionment with Lady Alton made me remember Lady Sternheim. I thought, 'she is mine, and to leave the wretched life in the mountains she will hurry into my arms.' I was the more sure of this as I had heard how tenderly she cared for and educated my daughter by Nancy Hatton, left behind there after the latter's death. I attributed Sophia's kindness to her inclination toward me and sent her my confidential servant with pleasant proposals. But she refused all of them with the utmost pride and bitterness." Here he stopped, overcome by emotion, and looked now at me, now at Lord Rich, until I stamped my foot and shouted at him to continue his story.

"Seymour—Rich!" he said in a low, sad voice, wringing his hands and stammering, "Oh, wretch that I am, if only I had gone myself and begged for her forgiveness and love. My servant, the cur, tried to *force* her to return to me. He knew how happy her presence would have made me. He locked her into an old, crumbling vault, where she lay for twelve hours and finally died of grief."

"She died!" I screamed, "Devil, monster! And you are still alive after this murder? You are still alive?"

Lord Rich says that I looked and sounded like a madman. He held my arms and pulled me away into another room, where it took a long time to calm me and make me promise to say no more. He said, "Derby is tortured by remorse and the remembrance of his life's irretrievable, ill-used days. Would you lift your hand against an object of Divine Justice? Believe me, my brother, all our pain is sweet, compared to the pain of his soul! My heart grieves over Lady Sternheim's unhappy fate, but virtue and nature are wreaking vengeance on her pursuer. I beg you to let me ask him what he wants from us. Control yourself, be magnanimous, pity even unfortunate vice."

I promised, but insisted on being present during the conversation.

The wretched creature wept when we returned to him and asked us to go to Scotland to exhume the angel's body and take it in a pewter coffin to Dumfries for burial. He wants to spend two thousand guineas on her tomb, where the description of her virtues and sufferings is to be engraved beside the evidence of his eternal repentance. He asked us to send an account of all this to the court of D., gave us all the letters he had written about her to his friend B., and begged us to leave at once, so that before his end he might have the consolation of knowing that public honors were paid to the memory of the noblest of women. In a few pathetic words Lord Rich then gave him some reassurance, and I managed to overcome my grief and resentment. We then immediately took our leave.

In the morning we leave for Dumfries. What a journey it will be! Oh God, what a journey!

Lord Rich to Dr. T. from the Highlands

I fear you won't remember me, but the best side of my nature resembles yours, and Seymour is my brother. I am to write you of him and the object of his grief. We arrived here tonight; our journey was sad, and as the distance grew less, our hearts' oppression increased. On the whole surface of the earth there cannot be a corner so rough, so wretched as the environs of this cottage. Here, even nature seems to concur with fate's cruelty in promoting the torture of the most sensitive soul by the most vicious of humans. When I recall her gratitude to the Creator for the beauties of nature, I sense the full extent of the grief she must have suffered at the sight of these barren rocks, the hut where she stayed for so long, and her poor bed where she gave up the noblest ghost that ever animated a female bosom. Oh doctor, even your theological mind, like my philosophical courage, could not have stopped your tears if you had seen this sandy hill that covers the remains of the most amiable woman, here at the foot of a lonely, meager tree. Poor Lord Seymour sank down on it and wanted to cry his soul out and be buried next to her. Assisted by two of our people, I was forced to pull him away. In the hut he wanted to lie down on her death bed, but I had it carried away and conducted him to the place where the people told us she had sat most often. There he has been lying prostrate for two hours, immovable, his head on his arms, seeing and hearing nothing.

These people don't seem very honest to me. I suspect they aided her imprisonment. They look frightened; several times they talked together in private outside the hut; their answers to my questions about the lady were short and confused, and they seemed taken aback when I said that the grave would have to be opened tomorrow. I myself tremble at the thought; I fear we will find evidence of a violent death. Then what would become of my brother? I do not mention myself. I hide my grief so as not to increase Seymour's; but believe me, neither the fear of perishing in a storm nor the torment of burning thirst in the sandy wastes of Asia ever affected my soul so violently as the thought of this angel's sufferings!

My brother has fallen asleep from exhaustion; he is lying on the garments these people have spread on the floor for him. Every now and again he starts, uttering sighs and groans. But the surgeon reassures me regarding his health. I cannot sleep; the coming day tortures me in advance. I try to marshal my courage so I can support Seymour, but I am myself like a reed; and I am afraid of collapsing with him at the sight of the body. It is true, I did not love her with my brother's youthful, violent passion; my love was a sympathetic attachment for righteousness, wisdom, and humanity. I have never seen good sense and sensibility so fully expressed as they were in her; I have never seen great matters treated with such just and true dignity, nor small ones with such charming lightness. Her company would have constituted the happiness of an entire circle of persons of learning and virtue.

Yet it is here, amid these towering rocks and among men as insensible as they, under the most cruel torment, that she had to resign her beautiful soul! Oh Providence, you see the question which arises in my soul, but you also know the reverence for your incomprehensible decrees which restrains me from giving it expression!

Continuation on the Next Day

Dear doctor, friend of humanity! Share with us in our joy! The angelic Lady Sternheim is still alive! She has been preserved by divine intervention. Seymour weeps tears of joy and continually embraces the poor inhabitants of the cottage. One hour ago we dragged ourselves, pale, sad, and mournfully silent to the little garden where they had pointed out her grave to us yesterday. The man and his son accompanied us with visible reluctance. When we came to the sandy hill and I curtly ordered the men to dig it up, my brother, put his arms around me, and calling out "Oh Rich!" he buried his head on my shoulder. His cry, just when one of my people took the first shovel of sand from the grave, pierced my soul. I clasped my arms around him and lifted my eyes toward heaven, pleading for strength for him and me. At the same instant, the man, his wife, and son, fell to their knees before us and begged us for protection. I was seized with the utmost dismay, because I was afraid of discovering that the lady had been murdered.

"What do you want, good people, why are you asking for protection?"

"We have deceived our lord," they cried; "the lady did not die; she has gone."

"Where is she my friends, where?" I called out, "Are you not deceiving us?"

"No, my good lord, she is with Count Hopton's sister. That lady has taken her in and told us tell my Lord N. that the young gentlewomen was dead. We had grown to love the lady and let her go, but if my lord finds out he will punish us."

Seymour embraced the man with shouts of joy and cried, "Oh my friend, you shall come with me. I shall protect you and reward you. Where is Lord Hopton? How did this come about? Rich, dear brother Rich, we must leave immediately."

I assured him I was as eager as he to see the lady again. I told him to arrange for our journey and that I would, meantime, speak to these people. I calmed them with the assurance that Lord N. would himself reward them for their love of the lady because he was displeased that John had treated her so badly. Saying this, I gave them a handful of guineas and asked them about her life with them. Oh doctor, how much radiance did these people's simple and brief tale of my friend's virtue shed on her! Yesterday I lamented her hard fate, and now I feel like thanking providence for the noble example it has provided for the rest of mankind through the trials of this great soul. Oh, the attributes of her character are deeply, indelibly, engraved upon my heart!

We are going to set out now. At the foot of the mountain I sent off one of my people to Lord Derby with news that will surely console him. For as he approaches the moment when one would like to make up for all the neglected good one might have done and erase all one's bad deeds, it must be a comfort to him to see the evils he has caused diminished by such a great crime.

Mrs. Leidens to Emilia, from Tweedale, Seat of Lord Douglas-March

I write you on my knees to express my childlike, humble gratitude to God for the sweet feeling of freedom, life, and friendship. Oh my beloved, my very dear friend! Through what pain I have passed, and how happy I am to be able to end your grief and my Lady Summers's worry on my behalf! Tomorrow Lady Douglas is sending a courier to my lady. He will then immediately leave for Harwich with a package for your husband, in order not to prolong your uneasiness by even a moment. The penciled extracts of my journal will show you how hard and thorny was the path that I was forced to tread in the past year. But how pleasant is the destination to which the hand of gracious virtue has conducted me! Doesn't this show that I was worthy of the care of providence, because it sent one of the noblest souls to my aid? When I wrote the final page of my journal, I thought I had reached the last night of my life; and I also thought that I would die abandoned by Lady Douglas. But at eleven o'clock the clergyman came with a surgeon, and the next morning a litter carried by two horses arrived, accompanied by Lady Douglas herself, who tenderly offered me her house, her care, and her friendship. The excess of my joy proved almost harmful to me, for when I pressed the lady's hand to my bosom and wanted to speak of my gratitude and joy, I sank back unconscious. When I awoke, they asked me to remain calm and said they had prevailed on my hosts to make a hill like a grave in the garden and to inform Lord Derby that I was dead. My lady told me the people agreed and she now wanted to take me to Lord Hopton's house. In the afternoon, about four o'clock, I felt strong enough to get up, and Mary dressed me in her ladyship's presence. I took the five guineas I had on me and gave them to my hosts. At the very moment when I was about to speak to my lady on behalf of my little orphan, poor little Lydia crawled into the room on her knees, sobbing, her little hands upraised, begging me to take her with me. Deeply moved, I looked at her and the lady, who, after a moment's reflection, held out her hands to the little girl and said in a voice full of pity, "Yes my little one, you shall come too."

"God bless you, dearest lady," I said, "for your magnanimous humanity. I wanted to ask you for permission to save this innocent victim, too."

"Gladly," she answered, "very gladly! I am glad you care for her so tenderly."

I embraced my weeping hosts with tears in my eyes; then, sighing, I looked once more at the desolation about me and set off with my lady. My Lord Hopton received me with much civility, but his glances suggested that he was unsure whether I was more deserving of the addresses of a lover or the pity of a virtuous lady. When, after looking at little Lydia, he fixed his eyes on me, I found myself blushing, which made him smile. I suppose that he thought me her mother, and I perceived how that conviction must diminish the favorable opinion he had formed of me. Lady Douglas led me into a pretty room and asked me to go to bed. Mary was present and asked the lady where little Liddy could sleep. "Here" said Lady Douglas, addressing me, "for I am sure you want the little one with you, and I am very pleased that even in misfortune you have remained faithful to the duties of nature."

"Dearest lady," I interrupted, "you—"

"Don't be uneasy, my dear," she said with a lively but tender voice; "lie down. I will return later, but we will not speak about any of your past calamities."

With that, she went away. I threw myself on the bed with the melancholy reflection that I was paying for my first moments of freedom by being subjected to an injurious judgment. I did not wish Lady Douglas to be confirmed in her opinion and asked for paper and writing utensils. Next morning I wrote to the lady, clearing up all her doubts about little Lydia and showing her why I was caring for the child. I also asked her to let me send news as soon as possible to Lady Summers, who would convince her that everything I had told her was the truth and that she did not have any cause to regret her past kindness to me. She could hardly have read the three pages, when she came to see me and, upon entering my room, asked me to forgive her for having disquieted me, but she had found it impossible to believe a stranger could have such tenderness and concern for the child of her enemy. She assured me that she had loved me because of my supposed maternal fidelity but that she loved and admired me even more because of my magnanimous love for the offspring of my unworthy persecutor.

For two hours she talked to me of many things, tenderly and with great delicacy. The dear lady possesses an attribute that is rare among the great: She interests herself in the sufferings of the soul, and with the noblest and most delicate perceptiveness seeks to find words of consolation and relief. During my former association with the great and fortunate of the world, I often noticed that their compassion was moved only by outward evil, illness, poverty, etc.; the soul's grief and pain, of which people spoke to them or which they themselves had caused, made little impression on them and only rarely stirred their interest. Further, they are seldom trained to think of the inner worth or the true condition of things; they blind and are blinded by outward luster. Wit takes the place of good sense; a cold, forced embrace is called friendship; splendor and display are mistaken for happiness. Oh my dear, if I should ever again move in these circles, I will take great care to avoid whatever I found hurtful in the great and fortunate during the days of my misfortune.

The countess herself will care for little Lydia. She says I have done enough for the child, that no one should have occasion to think that the exercise of the highest virtue results from moral weakness. She says that, least of all, should Derby be allowed to suppose that my pity for the orphan was caused in any way by an attachment for him. I saw the nobility of her motives and thanked her tenderly not only for protecting me from future false judgments but also for preserving me from the oppressive praises that people might give me for my so-called magnanimity. The countess read the letters I had written to Lady Summers, although at first she did not want to, to convince me of her trust. I briefly told her the contents of my letters to you; but because they are entirely in German, a complete translation would have taken too much time. As I was eager to send you news, I summarized each page for her; and I gladly omitted the passages telling of the good I did because I thought the pleasure of hearing myself praised would, to some extent, diminish my inner satisfaction. If only I could soon have news of Lady Summers and go to her, and then throw myself into my Emilia's arms!

My enthusiasm for England is extinguished. This is not, as I had thought, the native country of my soul. I wish to return to my estates; there I will live in solitude and do good. My mind and heart are too exhausted for society, and I can be of no further use than to teach some of the unhappy how to bear their misfortunes. Indeed, one of my first wishes since the aspect of my future has become newly pleasant is that of cultivating in each young heart, those seeds of my education, whose refreshing fruits ripened at the time of my most severe sufferings, quieted my earlier complaints, and gave me the strength to practice all the virtues of the unfortunate.

It is impossible for me to describe the full strength of my revived feelings for the beauties of our physical world. They are great and manifold, like the beautiful views of this noble seat, where, across a steep hillside next to the River Tweed, one sees the most fertile hills in all of Scotland teeming with flocks of sheep. My eyes' power to see seems to be multiplied, refined—just as in the highlands it seemed diminished and blunted.

Is it not possible, my Emilia, that *all* the powers of my soul can be revived like the perception of the beneficent wonders of our creation, and, in particular, how the sweet hope of clasping my heart's friend in my arms again soon has been revived?

Lord Rich to Dr. T. from Tweedale

If it is just that the stronger should bear not only his own burden but also that of the weak, then I am fulfilling my duty. I not only groan under the burden of my own sentiments but must also summarize my brother's overflowing feelings. My letters to you are the support that relieves my soul. Even now, Seymour is sitting at the feet of the object of my desires. I left them. Her eyes said she wanted me to stay, but I saw my brother holding her hand. He sensed that it pressed his gently, perhaps unconsciously; I felt it, too, and that feeling told me to go.

It has been two days since we arrived here. Our six horses caused quite a stir in the courtyard, and the servants gathered around us. My brother flung himself off his horse and called out, "Are Countess Douglas and the lady from the highlands at home?" The answer being affirmative, he pulled me by the arm, saying eagerly, "Come, brother, come!"

"Whom shall I announce?" a footman called out.

"Lords Rich and Seymour," my brother called hastily and hurried after the man, who hardly had time to knock before we appeared in the doorway. Countess Douglas was sitting facing the door; Lady Sternheim sat with her back toward us. She was reading something to the countess. Seymour's entrance and the servant's hurried question, asking who we were, made the countess start and my angelic friend turn her head. She jumped with fright, calling out, "Oh my God!" and letting the book fall to the floor as Seymour threw himself down at her feet. "Oh those honest people—she is alive! Oh my divine, my adored Lady Sternheim!" he exclaimed with outstretched arms.

Almost beside herself, she looked at him and me, but in the same instant turned her head and let it sink on her trembling arm. The countess looked from one to the other with astonishment. I had to speak; but first I pointed to Lady Sternheim, saying, "Dearest countess, support the angel who is here with you. I am Lord Rich and this is Lord Seymour."

The countess quickly approached my friend who put both arms around her and for some minutes hid her face in the countess' bosom. Seymour could not bear her turning her face away and called out in anguish, "Oh my uncle, why did you make me hide my love? All my heart's agony and tenderness cannot save me now from the disdain which my thoughtlessness drew down on me! Oh Sophia, what shall become of me, now that at the very height of my joy at having found you again, I see your displeasure directed at me? Oh, vouchsafe me but one kind look!"

Lady Sternheim raised her head with angelic grace and the dignity that accompanies true virtue. Blushing, she gave my brother her hand and said softly, "Arise, Lord Seymour. I assure you that I am not in the least displeased with you; and," she added, sighing, "where would I get the right?"

With passionate tenderness he kissed her hand; my eyes were cast down, but she approached me with friendly looks, took my hand and said, "Dearest lord, what a true friend you are! How did you ever find me? Did Lady Summers tell you? How is she, my loving mother?"

I, too, kissed the hand she gave me and said, "Lady Summers is well and will be overjoyed to see you again. But it was not she who led me here; remorse and the desire for justice roused my brother and me to action."

Blushing, she asked me, "Is Lord Seymour then your brother?"

"Yes, and the son of the noblest mother who ever lived."

She answered only with a significant smile and turned to Countess Douglas saying, "My magnanimous deliverer, here we see two unimpeachable witnesses to the truth of what I told you about my origins and life. I thank God that He let me live to see the moment when you know that I deserved your kindness."

"No," Seymour interjected, "there never lived a soul more worthy of universal reverence than this young woman whom your ladyship has saved! As long as I draw breath, you, noble countess, shall have this heart's eternal gratitude!" While saying this, he pressed the countess' hand to his breast with tears in his eyes.

Meantime, I had managed to compose myself and now wished to explain our arrival. For a few moments we were all silent. Then I took Lady Sternheim's hand. "Can you," I said, "without harm to your health and tranquillity, hear me speak of your pursuer? He is at the end of his life, and his soul's greatest anguish is to remember your virtue and his injustice toward you. His grief at your supposed death is unutterable. He asked me and Lord Seymour to see him and made us take an oath to travel to the highlands, there to exhume your body and inter it at Dumfries with proper testimonies to your virtue and his remorse. I will not mention how sad the prospect of this office made us. Having searched for you so long, we were now to see you dead! My poor brother and (I could not refrain from adding) your poor friend Rich!"

Tears welled in her eyes as she said, "Lord Derby has been cruel, very cruel to me. May God forgive him! I will gladly do so;—but to see him again would be impossible; his sight would be fatal to me." She said this in a low voice and hung down her head.

Seymour felt the touching embarrassment of this pure soul and, endeavoring to compose himself, went to a window. Lady Sternheim got up and left us. Seymour and I followed her with admiring glances. Though she was dressed only in Scottish linen, she was enchantingly beautiful because of her perfect stature and the refinement of her walk and all her movements. Although she had become thin and pale, her soul's beauty and dignity were fully expressed in her features. Seymour and I told Countess Douglas all that concerned Lady Sternheim, and she in turn told us what she had learned of her since she had taken in the lead miner's daughter. She had thought from the beginning that this lady must have received a noble education and in an unfortunate hour must have been separated from her true destiny. She said she had pitied her, especially when she saw the lady's solicitude for the child. She told us that she had then decided to bring her here when she and her brother left the highlands, but that the lady's illness had hastened the execution of that plan. She told us how happy she was to have followed the inclination of her heart. She then left to see to her guest, and we remained alone.

I was thoughtful. Seymour came and embraced me, weeping. "Rich, dear brother, I am unhappy in midst of my happiness and will remain so. I see your love and your merits; I feel that she is displeased with me. She is right, a thousand times right! She is right, too, to show you more trust and friendship, but knowing that, I feel a fatal grief. My health has been suffering in many ways because of my love. Now that I have seen her, I will die because of her, and that is enough for me!"

With a strange emotion I pressed him to my breast, and I believe I answered him somewhat coldly and roughly, "Yes, Seymour, you are unhappy in happiness—but there is one who is completely so! Why must your rivals always be more clear-sighted than you? Derby is right, she prefers you. Her reserve proves to me everything he said. Be worthy of her, and do not begrudge me her respect and trust!"

"Oh Rich, is this, can this be true? Does not your passion blind you as much as mine did me? Oh God—I must either obtain her or die! Who will speak for me? I cannot say anything—and you?"

"I will do it," I replied, "but not today. We must spare her sensibility and her weakened state of health." He knelt at my feet and embraced me. "Oh best, noblest of brothers!" he cried, "Ask my life, ask all I have, I cannot repay you! You will really speak for me? May God forever bless you, my truest, kindest friend!"

"I want nothing, dear Seymour, but your happiness. Be worthy of it! Oh, you do not know the extent of that happiness as I do, but great as it is, I do not begrudge it. I wish it for you!"

The ladies now came back. We talked of Tweedale, and our friend told us how touched she had been to see God's beautiful earth once again. Then she spoke of her abduction and her first days in the highlands. In the evening, she gave me her papers, and Seymour and I read them through. Oh my friend, what a soul is revealed in them! How immeasurable my happiness would have been! But I shall repress my wishes forever. My brother shall live! His soul cannot bear the loss of his hopes again. My greater years and experience will support me. Seymour must have the full measure of contentment; otherwise he cannot enjoy his happiness; a part I value will suffice for me. As soon as you can, send us Seymour's letters to you; when Lady Sophia reads them they will intercede for him.

Lady Sternheim to Emilia

Oh, what else does providence have in store for me? It has preserved me in the midst of great calamities, during the most severe disruption of my life. I have certainly not been preserved only to end in misfortune but rather to undergo every possible trial. Oh my dear, surrounded only by persuasive friends, I stand quite alone at a parting of the ways. Lord Derby is dead! The enclosed pages of my journal from Tweedale relate the arrival of Seymour and Rich and describe the compensation Derby was willing to make me. God grant that his eternal days are happier than he made my earthly ones.

Lord Seymour pursues my heart. He loves me! Oh my Emilia, he loved me tenderly, purely, from the first day he saw me! His uncle's pride, his dependence upon him, and his excessively delicate perception of virtue and honor demanded that he keep silent until I overcame the prince's enticements. You know what his silence brought on me, but you do not know (as I did not until now) how Lord Seymour suffered because of it. Here, read his letters, together with the ones Lord Derby wrote to his friend, and then send them back to me with all the ones I wrote to you. When you read Derby's letters, you will be shocked at his abuse of good sense, virtue, and love. I would have had to be evil myself to suspect his machinations. Oh, how different is Seymour's heart!

I wish you and I had but one mind, so that I might profit instantly from your advice. Lady Douglas is favorably disposed; Lord Rich—noble, invaluable Lord Rich—begs me to become his sister; the amiable Seymour is daily at my feet! All the scruples dictated by my delicacy are being dispelled; and, my heart's friend, you who have known all its emotions from our childhood days—from you I cannot and will not hide that an inner voice tells me to consent to the union with Seymour as a God-given means to bring my restless wanderings to an end. Was he not the man my heart yearned for? He knows it; shall I now turn back? Lord Rich, I fear, would want to take his place.

For many days Seymour showed me the most ardent, tender love; but Lord Rich, though he had long conversations with him, was cold, quiet. Often he looked at me thoughtfully for a long time, and these looks made me resolve to remain unmarried. But two days after Seymour's letters arrived, Lord Rich came to my room and brought me my journal, together with my last letter to you from Summerhall, which I had kept with it. He seemed moved and approached me with significant looks. He kissed the pages of my journal, pressed them to his bosom, and asked my forgiveness for having made a copy, which he, however, delivered to me with the original. "But permit me," he said, "to keep this faithful picture of your sentiments. Oh my angelic friend, let me have these expressions of your soul, and grant my brother the possession of yourself! His letters must have shown you his heart's inexperienced rectitude. By accepting his suit you will make him the happiest and best of men!"

After a short silence, he put his hand to his breast, looked at me tenderly and respectfully, and continued with much emotion, "You know the infinite reverence this heart will always feel for you; you are aware of the wishes I nurtured. They have not died but I have now suppressed them.

Believe me, as long as I might hope, I would not sacrifice the prospect
of blissful days to come if, in the midst of my soul's adoration and desire,
I were not compelled to admit that Seymour is worthy of you and merits
your respect and your pity." Here he looked at me attentively and ceased
speaking.

With a half-stifled sigh I said, "Oh Lord Rich!"

He continued in a voice of manly tenderness, "It is in your power to
destroy a noble young man with the torture of unrequited love; but won't
you, best of women, use that power to make a whole family happy? You
can preserve my mother, a worthy woman, from the grief of seeing both her
sons unmarried, your sisterly love will make me happy, and you will see all
your virtues appreciated in a large and useful social circle."

"Dearest Lord Rich," I answered feelingly, "how closely you press
me! Don't you see my scruples?" I hid my face in my hands.

He clasped me in his arms and kissed my forehead. "Oh best, dearest
soul—yes, I know the doubts raised by your delicacy. They merit you my
brother's greater adoration; but do not destroy his hopes. I beg you, let me
give him your permission to hope!"

The worthy man looked at me with tears in his eyes, and a tear from
mine fell on his hand. He looked at it, deeply moved; but when his trembling hands set it in motion, he kissed it away, and his eyes were for some
minutes fixed on the floor. I took the originals of my letters and journal and
gave them to him, saying, "Take these, worthiest of men—the true expressions of my soul, as you have called them, as a pledge of the purest and
most tender friendship!"

"My *sister*," he interrupted me.

"No wiles, Lord Rich! I want to become, without artifice, what you so
ardently wish I should be."

He knelt down, blessed me, kissed my hands with eager affection, and
hurried away.

"Say nothing yet, I beg you!" I called after him. Then I was alone and
cried, and I resolved to become Lady Seymour. I reaffirmed my decision at
the end of a prayer to Divine Providence.

Post Script: Now Lord Seymour knows. His ecstasies defy the power of
my pen. My Lady Douglas embraced me maternally; Lord Rich did so as
an affectionate brother. Dear Lord Seymour guards me as if he feared
someone might change my mind. He has dispatched his valet to his mother
who seems to be a second Lady Summers in virtue and wit. Oh bless me,
my friends! My heart beats tranquilly. How happy it is to have made a
resolution sanctioned by wisdom and virtue! I look forward to the journey
to my parents' tomb. I will kneel at the foot of their monument with my
husband and implore their heavenly blessings on our union. I will shed
tears of gratitude on their ashes for the love of virtue and benevolence they

poured into my soul and for carefully instilling in me right ideas about true happiness and true misfortune! I will once more embrace my Emilia, see my dependants! Oh happy prospects!

My dear Lord Seymour seeks to emulate his brother; he consults him in all things. I, too, am grateful for Lord Rich's efforts on behalf of my happiness. He does everything in his power to make Seymour's often changeable and precipitate character more even and gentle. "He is like a fine river," says Lord Rich, "that rushes headlong on its course but holds in its bed many grains of pure gold."

Lord Rich to Dr. T.

I have just returned from the altar where my brother has entered into an eternal union and where I have vowed to remain forever free. I gave him the hand my heart desired for so long but did not pursue because I felt I had more strength to bear this loss than he has. It was Lady Seymour's soul, her principles, that I loved! Written with complete and heartfelt candor, her papers show that she gave me the best that was in her power to give: true esteem for my character, genuine trust, and tender wishes for my happiness. The inexplicably mysterious constancy of a first preference, which had long ago, and perhaps without her consent, seized upon her heart, must forever have prevailed. I am sensible of her soul's value; her friendship is more tender than love's embraces in other women! The autumn of life, which is my season, lets me enjoy the pure, tranquil sweetness of friendship.

I will live with this happy pair. Their second son will be Lord Rich; he will be my heart's son! I will talk with Lady Seymour every day and will possess the beauty of her mind. I will contribute to her happiness! My mother blesses my decision regarding her beloved Seymour, and my happiness is linked to the worthiest and dearest people I know.

Soon, my friend, I will see and speak with them again.

Lady Seymour to Emilia, from Seymour House

The first free hour in my home was justly dedicated to my thanking Divine Providence for ending all my grief in perfect felicity. But the second hour belongs to my faithful friend, who shared all my sufferings, alleviated them through her consolation and love, and whose example and advice made me persevere in virtue and prudence. Oh Emilia, I am completely happy, for I can spend all my days in fulfilling the happiest, most sacred duties of my life. My conjugal tenderness constitutes my husband's happiness; his worthy mother considers my filial reverence and love the reward for her virtues; my sisterly friendship pours contentment into the noble and very sensitive heart of my dear Lord Rich:

Lord Seymour has vast estates; he is wealthy and has given me unlimited powers to do good. Oh my dear, it was well that all my sensibilities have been awakened and tested through my misfortunes. I have become that much more appreciative of every drop of happiness. You know that in the midst of all my distresses I thanked God for enabling me to alleviate them by the use of my talents, thus providing my heart with the comfort of doing good. Now I am fully conscious of how good fortune doubles our obligations. Now my former resignation, humility, and submission have changed to eager gratitude. My knowledge and abilities, which formerly supported my suffering self-love and gave me now and then a moment's happiness, will now be dedicated to serving humanity, to the happiness of those around me, to discovering even the smallest, most secret calamities of my fellow men, and to finding the necessary means, large or small, for rendering them loving aid! My experiences, which took me to the very brink of the grave, have shown me that the mind's abilities and the heart's goodness alone constitute our true temporal happiness. They supported my soul when grief had almost delivered it up to despair. They will become the supporting pillars of my happiness, on which I will lean in the tranquillity of peace. I will then implore Divine Grace to make me worthy, at my noble and magnanimous husband's side, to become a model of rightly used wealth and power!

You see, my friend, how all my scruples had to give way to these sentiments. I saw the happiness of so many tied to mine, that, to assure their contentment, I gladly bestowed my hand.

My lord wants to build a school and a hospital modeled on those at Sternheim. He is trying to expedite the plan, because he wants to have these buildings erected during our travels in Germany. Next week we are going to Summerhall. There we shall await my Uncle R.'s letters, and then Seymour and Rich want us to visit every solemn place where my misfortunes took me.

They will then at last see my Emilia and be convinced that my heart's first and strongest inclination was dedicated to the worthiest member of my sex! Tomorrow, my Lord G. and my grandmother's nephew, Sir Thomas Watson, will come to visit us. But with my other relatives, London, and the large circle of my neighbors I will become acquainted only after our return from Germany.

My Lord Rich to Dr. T.[15]

I am once again at Seymour House because without my brother's family the whole earth seems empty to me. Lady Seymour holds me with a thousand spiritual bonds, and my autumn days were suffused with such summery warmth during our journey that I feared for my peace of mind. I observed her at Summerhall, at Vaels with her Emilia, in her seminary, at court in D., at Sternheim among her dependants, at the tomb of her parents—adorable woman! On all occasions, in all places, wherever her life's course has led her, she has shown herself as the true model of female genius and of the practical virtues of her sex. On our return she became a mother—and what a mother! Oh dear doctor, I would have had to be more than mere man not to have wished a thousand times that she were *my* wife, the mother of *my* children! Ah, how justly is the generous sacrifice of our own happiness placed at the head of all the virtues! How dearly it is bought by even the most magnanimous hearts! Do not, therefore, wonder that it is so rare.

But a test like mine is not often called for. I have gladly exchanged my brother's happiness for my own, and I feel no regrets. I have suffered not through feeling base envy but only through my self-imposed silence about my sentiments, which I will not entrust to the profane, to preclude false judgment of my respectful affection and to avoid placing my sister's pure friendship in a dubious light.

I succumbed to gloomy melancholy and withdrew from Seymour's house for a few months. However, this time the tranquillity of my country seat, where I used to enjoy a respite after my extended travels, did not bring me peace. I tried to overcome my longing, but being accustomed to the sweet company of the most sensible soul, I found that her dear letters were no substitute for her person.

Then my little Lord Rich was born, and I hastened to Seymour House. Oh happy moment, when Lady Seymour put the child in my arms, and with all the charm of her soulful expression and voice said, "Here is your young Rich; with your name may God give him your mind and heart!" An exquisite sensation of pain penetrated my soul. It is buried within me; no one shall ever have a description of it.

Little Rich has his mother's features, and this resemblance constitutes my great happiness. If my life is preserved, this boy will have no other tutor, no other companion on his travels, than me. I will assume all his expenses; his servants will be doubly paid. I sleep next to his room; I am even building a house at the end of the garden, where I will reside with him when he has reached the age of two. Meantime, I am training the people who are to be about him. This child has become the support of my reason and my tranquillity. Every embrace, every tender care he receives from his mother makes him more dear to me. How happily he and his brother are growing up! Their parents' every action is an example of goodness and nobility. Blessings and joy rest on every part of my brother's estates. Thanksgiving and good wishes accompany his every step and those of his spouse. With one hand they support distressed merit and help alleviate others' misery; with the other they beautify the whole domain, though with the most delicate discrimination. Lady Seymour says that, in the country, art must never rule over nature; that one should only see traces of her fleeting presence and, here and there, a small place where she has rested for a while on her journey.

Our evenings and mealtimes are charming. They are ruled by moderation and animated by a lively spirit. We mingle joyfully in the country dances of our tenants, whose joy is doubled by our participation. Lady Seymour's company is sought by all persons of merit, just as vice and folly take flight in her presence. In our house every shade of talent and virtue is represented in turn by the people living within several miles of us. In this connection, the character of my beloved Lady Seymour has assumed a new brilliance because she so deeply feels and appreciates the merits of others of her sex. My brother has become the best of husbands and the worthy master of several hundred subjects. Happiness beams in his face when he sees his son at the bosom of the best of women, drinking in her virtues with his mother's milk. Every passing day takes away some of the impetuous fire that used to dominate all Seymour's feelings. He has learned the difficult art of enjoying his happiness without giving pain to others through loud protestations of his bliss.

The simple, yet refined, aspect of our dress and dwelling allows even the poorest family of our neighborhood to visit us with confidence and joy. From time to time, Lady Seymour takes some of their daughters into her house and instills in them love of virtue and knowledge through her example and loving instruction. In short, her charming enthusiasm for beneficence and her lively sensibility of the good and the noble animate my beloved sister's every breath. Not content to *think* of doing good, all her thoughts become actions! I am certain that a more fervent prayer was never offered to Heaven than the thanksgiving I heard Lady Seymour utter, with tears in her eyes, for her heart's sensibility and the power to do good.

What blessings, what rewards, those deserve who give us proof that it is possible to fulfill all the demands of morality and that the practice of these duties does not disturb the enjoyment of life's pleasures but rather ennobles and confirms them and constitutes our true happiness in all life's vicissitudes!

NOTES ON THE TRANSLATION

1. Wieland's daughter Sophie. Sophie von LaRoche also had a daughter named Sophie.
2. Wieland's publisher.
3. In sentimental allusion to the famous Sidney-Devereux-Rich triangle [see entrance of the character Lord Rich, Sophia's other suitor, on page 315]. When making corrections after renaming Sophia's future husband "Seymour," the author probably overlooked this early and isolated use of "Sidney" in the manuscript. (Sophie von LaRoche delighted in showing off her wide reading in her works.)
4. LaRoche wrote *Rechenschaft* ("accountability") but meant *Rechtschaffenheit* ("righteousness").
5. Although Sophia is writing to Emilia, her letters are meant to be shared with Emilia's and Rosina's father, the pastor at P. who is Sophia's "foster father."
6. LaRoche wrote *zu ihr* ("to her") but meant *zu mir* ("to me").
7. La Roche wrote *Vetter* ("cousin"), but Seymour is G.'s nephew. (In German *Vetter* does not have the added meaning "kinsman.")
8. This letter is LaRoche's tribute to Wieland, her cousin, erstwhile fiancé, lifelong mentor, and editor of her first novel.
9. LaRoche wrote *Vorwort* ("written preface") but meant *Befürwortung* ("recommendation").
10. LaRoche wrote *Ordnung* ("order") but meant *Unordnung* ("disorder").
11. A person costumed as a white bat. Like the domino, the bat costume was particularly popular at masqued balls in the eighteenth and nineteenth centuries. (Cf. *Die Fledermaus*, Johann Strauss's operetta *The Bat*, first performed in Vienna, on April 5, 1874.)
12. The German (fast) waltz was introduced at about the time the novel was written. Its ready acceptance and popularity with the aristocracy and bourgeoisie alike give evidence of the new, romantic ideal of *Leidenschaft* (passion) replacing that of *Gelassenheit* (composure) as the desired state of one's soul.

   Characteristically, LaRoche lets Seymour rail against this "indecent whirling-dance." Goethe, in the ball scene in *Werther*, lets the hero and Lotte joyfully participate in it, although in an aside to his friend Wilhelm, Werther says, "To be honest, I vowed that I would never let a girl I loved, on whom I had a claim, waltz with anyone but me, if it killed me!" [my translation].

13. Here as elsewhere, LaRoche weaves personal reminiscences into her novel. In a footnote to p. 189 of the Brüggeman edition, the editor documents that La-Roche knew Vaels, near Aachen (Aix-la-Chapelle), from the descriptions of friends living there. She later visited Vaels herself and traveled from there to Spaa. (Cf., Emilia's trip to "Spa" with Mrs. Hills.)

14. *Leiden* means "suffering(s)." Joseph Collyer, in his translation of 1776, calls her, ludicrously, "Mrs. Suffering." He also, either from deference to the historic Derby family or wishing to emulate Richardson ("Lovelace" = "love-less"), changes *Derby* to *Loveill* (= "love ill"), and in a fit of whimsey completes *Dr. B.* to read *Dr. Burton.* The other English translator, Edward Harwood, retains all names of the original, including the uncorrected *Lady Sidney* (see note 3).

15. LaRoche intends this letter to have been written about two years after the preceding one.